THE
BOOK OF
PLYMTREE

THE
BOOK OF
PLYMTREE

THE PARISH AND ITS PEOPLE
DURING THE LAST THOUSAND YEARS

COMPILED BY TONY EAMES
WITH MUCH HELP FROM THE PEOPLE OF THE PARISH

HALSGROVE

First published in Great Britain in 1999

British Library Cataloguing-in-Publication Data
A CIP record for this title is available from the British Library

ISBN 1 84114 041 4

HALSGROVE
Publishing, Media and Distribution

Halsgrove House
Lower Moor Way
Tiverton, Devon EX16 6SS
Tel: 01884 243242
Fax: 01884 243325
http://www.halsgrove.com

Printed and bound in Great Britain by Bookcraft Ltd. Midsomer Norton

Contents

Foreword   9
Acknowledgements   10
Introduction   11

1   Plymtree in Domesday   13
2   Communications   15
3   Agriculture   21
4   Industry   27
5   Plymtree Church   29
6   Church House and Charities   47
7   Nonconformists   50
8   Overseers of the Poor   53
9   Schools in Plymtree   59
10 Law and Order   71
11 Times of War   75
12 Fires   83
13 Parish Politics   87
14 High Days and Holidays   89
15 Village Pastimes and Groups   97
16 Plymtree Parish Hall   107
17 Recreation Ground and Pavilion   109
18 Growing up in Plymtree after the War   115
19 Some Plants of Plymtree Parish   118
20 100 years of Change   121

The History of Plymtree's Older Houses and Farms   123
Subscribers   157

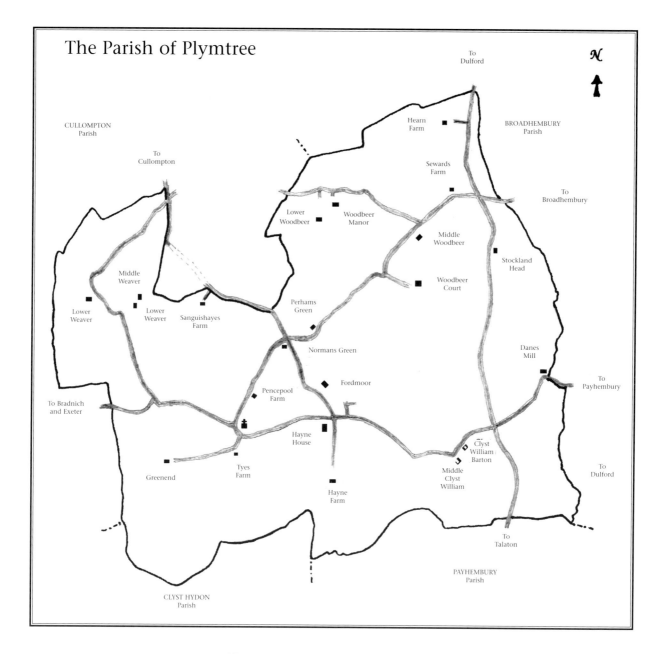

The Parish of Plymtree

To Dulford

N

CULLOMPTON Parish

Hearn Farm

BROADHEMBURY Parish

To Cullompton

Sewards Farm

To Broadhembury

Lower Woodbeer

Woodbeer Manor

Middle Woodbeer

Stockland Head

Middle Weaver

Woodbeer Court

Perhams Green

Lower Weaver

Lower Weaver

Sanguishayes Farm

Danes Mill

Normans Green

To Payhembury

To Bradnich and Exeter

Pencepool Farm

Fordmoor

Hayne House

Clyst William Barton

To Dulford

Greenend

Tyes Farm

Middle Clyst William

Hayne Farm

To Talaton

PAYHEMBURY Parish

CLYST HYDON Parish

Above: A map of Plymtree as it is today.
Opposite, top: Greenwood's 1827 map of Plymtree.
Opposite, below: Detail from Greenwood's 1827 map of the 'County of Devon'.

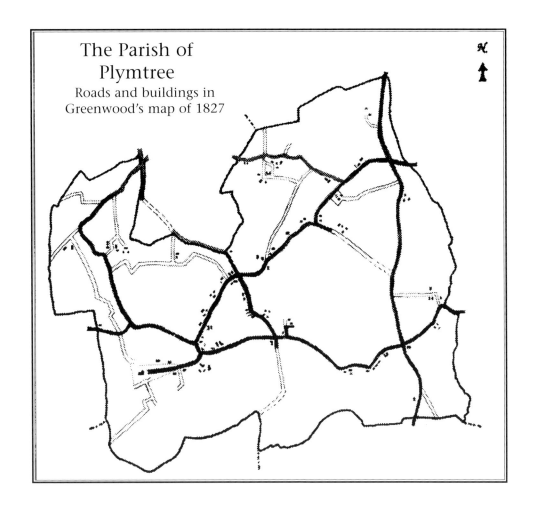

The Parish of
Plymtree
Roads and buildings in
Greenwood's map of 1827

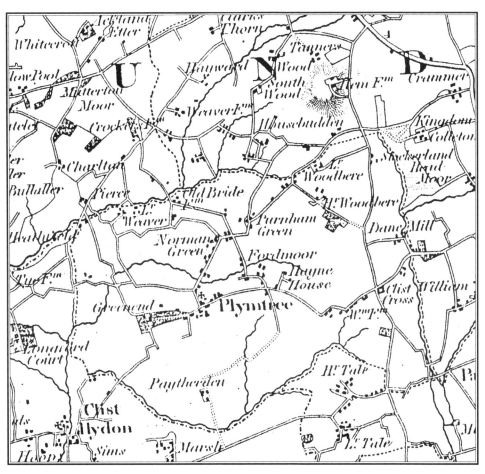

Three friends at Redgate, c.1938. Left to right: Ted Robinson, head gardener at Hayne House, McCahey, head groom at Hayne Farm, and Francis Farnell, village postman.

The family of Mr Bird with the Austin 7 van he used to make deliveries to Plymtree and other villages just before the Second World War.

Foreword

History is boring! How often did I express that feeling when I was at school, having to learn the names and dates of numerous kings and battles? I couldn't see how they had anything to do with me, or that they would ever be of any use – and I dropped the subject as soon as I could.

However, some history stuck, and when I began to research my family's origins I found it important to look at the lives of long-dead ancestors in the context of their own era. It slowly dawned on me that, in simple terms, history is how we (a person or a place or a nation) got to where we are now.

Plymtree was inhabited long before William the Conqueror arrived to claim the throne of England from King Harold – although at that time it was made up of three manors, each held by a Saxon lord. The name of the village derives from the Saxon 'Plum-trei', meaning 'place of springs', which aptly describes the area. It is fascinating to realise that at least three of the buildings in the village rest on the foundations of ones which were standing then. There was certainly a church on the site of the present one; and Woodbeer Court and Clyst William Barton are the direct successors of Saxon manor houses on their sites.

At the Devon Record Office I discovered the list of contents of the Plymtree parish chest, deposited there for safe keeping by the parish officers. To me this was a 'treasure chest' and (with the consent of the rector and churchwardens) I spent nearly five years transcribing every ancient document in the collection. Many aspects of life in Plymtree over the past three centuries came to life as I did so, and I hope you will enjoy reading about some of them. I find them fascinating in their own right, and they most certainly prove the truth of the old adage, 'the past is another country.'

Tony Eames
Tyes Farmhouse
Plymtree
June 1999

Acknowledgements

Until now the only publication on the history of Plymtree has been Jon Carden's work, which he researched and produced in 1981 as a history project while at Blundell's School, Tiverton: copies are still to be found on many bookshelves in Plymtree. I am grateful to him for allowing the use of the photographs he then took of village buildings.

Many other people have helped create the present book, including (in alphabetical order): Reg Baker, Alan Barnett, Glyn Benfield, Bill and Marjorie Broom, Brian Chattey, Ron Cleal, Dennis Cooper-Jones, Ann Crew, Gilbert Daniels and his late brother, the loveable 'Ike', Robin Hussey, John Hussey, George Knight, Bill Lovering, Mrs Maggie Palfrey, Francis Martin, Chris Pratt, Bill Vellacott, Ted Widgery, and Margaret Willmington, but I am grateful to all who helped in any way. Special thanks are due to Mrs Barbara Batten, who was born in the village and loves it dearly, and who provided the vast majority of the older photographs. (Sadly, since the book was completed, the village has lost two of those who helped – Ted Widgery and Bill Broom. There was standing room only at their funerals, showing how much they were valued by fellow villagers.).

In assembling the text I drew freely on the work of others, and hereby express my gratitude for their help. The Ven. Edgar Hay, rector of the parish from 1897 to 1929, and then Archdeacon of Barnstaple, was a tireless researcher; he not only published the Parish Registers from 1538 to 1837, but he also ensured that most of the contents of the parish chest were preserved. It is those records which provided the basis of the 'house histories' included.

The works of the late Prof. W.G. Hoskins and of Robin Stanes (from our neighbouring village of Payhembury) were invaluable in helping me to understand the Devon background to national events, and the staff of the Devon County Record Office and the West Country Studies Library have assisted much of my more detailed research.

Introduction

Plymtree began as a Saxon manor which, with two other manors, Clyst (William) and Woodbeer, eventually grew into the present parish of Plymtree. Its basis has always been farming.

Plymtree is not on a road to anywhere else; if someone comes here, it is because they mean to – or because they are lost.

It is not a 'chocolate-box' village; it straggles, it has some interesting old houses (many of them farms or former farmhouses), a simple but beautiful old Parish Church and a United Reformed Church, plus a primary school, pub and shop (each of which has been under threat of closure during the 1980s and '90s), a parish hall and a recreation ground. It is surrounded by lush countryside, and abounds in springs, streams and small rivers. It is still very much a farming village.

So what makes it so wonderful? The answer is the people who live here. Possibly a third were born in or near the parish, the others having chosen Plymtree as their home. Accommodating and friendly, Plymtree people welcome incomers who are prepared to take their part in keeping the village alive without trying to impose their will on others.

The parish as a whole is supportive of anyone in difficulty, is generous towards charities far beyond its size, and constantly demonstrates the traditional co-operative nature of English village life at its best.

The oldest known photograph of Plymtree, taken in the 1880s before the Poor Houses (on the left) were demolished to enlarge the churchyard and to widen the road. The edge of the great western chimney of the Church House can be seen to the right.

Chapter 1: Plymtree in Domesday

With the coming of the Normans, a feudal structure was imposed on the country. Whereas under English law there had been many 'free-men', who owned their own land, henceforth all land belonged to the King, who could give it, in return for service of one kind or another, to his supporters; thus 'free-men' became tenants of Norman lords. But at first little changed for the average villein or bordar apart from the language of his lord; by the time of Domesday, in 1086, only 130 estates in Devon were held by English lords, the others having been given to new Norman owners by the King. Thus Plymtree, (one of three manors within the present parish), formerly held by Bristric, was given to Odo fitz Gamelin.

It is not surprising that Bristric lost out; he was Earl of Gloucester under the English kings and he had the misfortune, while ambassador at the court of Baldwin, Earl of Flanders, to receive proposals of marriage from Baldwin's daughter Matilda, and to have refused her. That would have mattered little had Matilda not gone on to marry William, Duke of Normandy, later the Conqueror of England. She clearly still felt slighted, for Bristric was relieved of all his many manors in Devon and thrown into prison where he died, with only Torra (Torbryan) and Dodebroca (Dodbrooke) passing in dower to his widow Godiva. Later, Matilda regretted her actions and had a church built at Avening in Gloucestershire (another of Bristric's former manors) where she had masses said for the repose of his soul.

Everyone knows of the Domesday Book, that great work upon which William and his Exchequer based their tax-raising plans for England. What is not so well-known is the Exon (or Exeter) Domesday, which is something of a rag-bag, containing the final summary of the Domesday returns for Cornwall, Somerset, most of Devon, and parts of Wiltshire and Dorset (the rest having apparently been lost), plus records of the Saxon Dane-geld reassessment for the South West carried out in AD1084-86. There are detailed manorial records, including the names of sub-tenants and livestock details, which were left out of Great Domesday. These are the entries for the manors of Plymtree, Woodbeer and Clyst (William):

'The Land of Odo, son of Gamelin, in Devonshire'

PLUMTREI

Odo has a manor called Plumtrei, which Bristric held on the same day on which King Edward was alive and dead, and it rendered geld for two hides and one virgate. These can be ploughed by five ploughs. Of these Odo has in his demesne one hide and two ploughs, and the villeins have one hide and one virgate, and three ploughs. There Odo has fifteen villeins and four bordars, and four serfs, and one pack-horse, and thirteen head of cattle, and twenty sheep, and twenty acres of wood, and twenty acres of meadow; and it is worth by the year twenty shillings, and it was worth as much when he received it.

WIDEBERE

Godfrey holds Widebere from Goscelin; Winemar held it TRE [in the reign of Edward]. It rendered geld for 1 hide; land for 4 ploughs. In demesne 2 ploughs; 3 serfs; $1\frac{1}{2}$ virgates.   6 villagers and 3 bordars with $1\frac{1}{2}$ ploughs and $2\frac{1}{2}$ virgates. Meadow 2 acres; pasture 50 acres; woodland 10 acres. 6 cattle; 2 pigs; 58 sheep; 30 goats. It was formerly worth by the year 10 shillings, but is now worth 25 shillings.

CLIST

Edwinus hold Clist. Alwin held it TRE. It rendered geld for $1/2$ hide.   Land for $1/2$ plough. 1 villager and 2 serfs; meadow 3 acres; pasture 2 acres. Value 6 shillings.

These are the original entries, as translated from the abbreviated Latin. But in order fully to understand what they mean, a few notes are required.

'Hides' and 'virgates' were probably units of physical measurement at one time, but by Domesday had become purely fiscal units, being the basis of the taxable value of the land, hence the term 'it rendered geld' in the entries. The tenant of the manor would have paid his 'geld' to the King. A 'virgate' was one quarter of a 'hide', and the latter originally seems to have varied in size between 120 acres in a fertile area, and 250 acres on less productive land. Since east Devon has very fertile soils, a hide hereabouts was probably the former. The 'acre' also varied according to local custom and land type, being as much land as a team of oxen could plough in a day.

The entries then go on to state how much plough-land there was on the manor. A plough was pulled by oxen, and 'land for one plough' indicated the area which one team could cope with in a year – probably about 55 acres. Land, etc., 'in demesne' indicated the property (including serfs) owned by the named tenant, the remainder being held by his villager, villein or bordar tenants. 'Villagers' and 'Villeins' were the higher-ranking, dependent peasants, and included former free-men, while 'bordars' cultivated small parcels of land (on the borders of the manor) and often followed trades such as blacksmithing, pig-keeping or shoemaking to earn a living. The 'serfs' mentioned appear to include only those attached to the lord's household, since it would have required two or three serfs to operate each plough team, and more 'ploughs' appear in the record than serfs to work them.

'Meadow' described land used to grow grass for hay, and was very valuable, whereas 'pasture' was land on which the various types of livestock could graze.

In modern English, therefore, the entries for the three manors read:

PLYMTREE

Odo is tenant-in-chief of the manor of Plymtree, held by Bristic in 1066 (when Edward the Confessor died), and paid tax on (about 270 acres of) land, which needs 5 teams of oxen to plough it. Odo's own land comprises 120 acres, and he has two plough teams. The 15 under-tenants and 4 small tenants farm 150 acres with 3 plough teams; there are 4 slaves. The manor also has 20 acres of meadow, 20 acres of woodland, 13 cattle, 20 sheep, and a pack-horse. It is worth 20 shillings a year to him in rent or produce, which has remained the same since 1066.

WOODBERE

Godfrey is the tenant of Goscelin at Woodbeer; Winemar held it before 1066. It paid tax for 120 acres, and has 220 acres of ploughland. The lord directly controls 110 acres, and he has 3 slaves. 6 villagers and 3 minor tenants farm 160 acres. In addition there are 2 acres of meadow, 50 acres of pasture, and 10 acres of woodland. There are 6 cattle, 2 pigs, 58 sheep and 30 goats. In 1066 the manor was worth 10 shillings per year to him in rent or produce, but it is now worth 25 shillings.

CLYST WILLIAM

Edwin [probably the English lord, Edwin of Butterleigh] is the chief tenant of Clyst, held in 1066 by Alwin. It paid tax for 60 acres, 28 acres of plough-land, 1 villager and 2 slaves. Meadow, 3 acres; pasture, 2 acres. It produces 6 shillings per year.

If the size of hides, ploughs, etc. suggested by academics (and used here) is correct, the total area of the three manors probably amounted to just over 700 (customary) acres. The modern parish encompasses 2185 (statute) acres. Even if the customary acre hereabouts was similar in size to the modern acre, this does not mean that Plymtree included other unrecorded manors in 1086, since the lands of manors were not necessarily co-terminus. There were almost certainly many farmsteads outside the control of a manor, and too small or too remote for the lord to bother with. There would also have been large 'waste' areas – marshland, uncleared forest, etc. where bordars and serfs could gather wood or keep livestock.

The population of the three manors was probably less than 150 (not including farming families outside the manors). For the first 34 years of Norman rule there was little movement of people and the major change in the pattern of life was the increasing oppression of their Saxon subjects by the landowners who, through their manorial courts, had total control over their lives and could levy taxes at will.

Because of the need to raise more crops or livestock to pay increasing taxes, or possibly by Baronial direction, new land was cleared for farming and the population grew. The manor of Plymtree incorporated that of Clyst William shortly after Domesday, the latter probably being too small to be viable on its own – or perhaps because the Norman lord disliked the idea of a Saxon owning property nearby.

The manorial system, under which the lords or their 'senechals' (bailiffs) controlled the transfer of land within the manors, lasted until the 1700s, but it seems to have died out due to pressure on land caused by the need to produce food during the Napoleonic wars. The manorial records of Plymtree and Woodbeer have completely disappeared, though a few single entries from the 15th and 17th centuries have survived.

Chapter 2: Communications

Today, many villages in this country are campaigning for by-passes, but not Plymtree – it has always been by-passed. Village people joke about their isolation – Plymtree is 'five miles from anywhere', has 'five roads in, none out' and is 'not on the road to anywhere': there are no mile-posts, because 'no roads pass through it'. It was surely always thus.

The major Roman road to Exeter from the east was a branch of the Fosse Way from the Roman city of Ilminster, its junction with the road from Dorchester being where Honiton was later built. They garrisoned Hembury Fort as well as Exeter, built forts at Cullompton and Tiverton (where there was also a 'marching camp'), and possibly another at Killerton, no doubt creating roads of a sort in the process, perhaps even on the routes of the present A373 and B3181 (the pre-motorway A38). In any case, they certainly came no closer than a mile from the parish boundary. After the departure of the Romans in AD410, their roads were neglected and became trackways like the rest of the 'road' network.

Travel for our pre-Conquest forebears would have been a rarity, unless under the orders of their lord; when undertaken it would have been on foot. Only muddy trackways existed – the standard Saxon track was 6 feet wide, with the topsoil removed and thrown up either side to make banks to keep back the forest or mud from the fields – broad enough for the lord or his steward on his horse, for oxen to pass to and from the ploughlands and for produce and other large or heavy loads to be transported using pack-animals. Heavy timber was dragged to where it was needed, and when stone began to be used for building, a device (known in the 18th century as a 'trucka-muck') was employed, whereby the tops of two young trees were fastened to an ox or horse and dragged by the roots. When they wanted to move a really heavy weight, they used four trees lashed together.

But for the following 1300 years, most people travelled everywhere by foot, only occasionally being able to hitch a lift on a cart or, if a long journey was essential, hiring a horse, regular travel by horse being largely the domain of the rich and those serving them, such as letter-carriers. Plymtree must have been on a route of some sort for pilgrims or travelling priests in early times, or

its church would not have been deemed so important as to become the head of a deanery. Throughout the ages travellers of all types have had to traverse rivers, and the county sheriff demanded cash from all parishes to fund the building or repair of bridges. Thus in 1681 the overseers paid 7s. 'unto the Constable for a bridge reate', and the year following 13s.-10$\frac{1}{2}$d. 'towards the reparacion of Honitone Clist & Bishops Clist Bridge'.

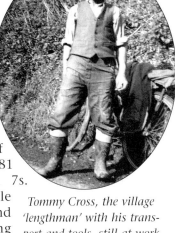

Tommy Cross, the village 'lengthman' with his transport and tools, still at work in the early sixties.

The 18th century saw the creation of public coaches, and of turnpikes for them to drive on. Plymtree remained connected, internally and externally, by tracks – more numerous than the roads we have today. We have a record showing that one or more surveyors of the highways was appointed in 1702, since 1s. was paid for a warrant for the office, but sadly no surveyors' accounts have survived. By law, every parishioner could be called on by the surveyors to provide three days labour each year, or the equivalent value in stones or other material, or the provision of transport for the repair of roads in the parish.

Nonetheless, throughout the 18th century wheeled carts were virtually unknown in east Devon, horses being kept for riding, to pull sledges, or as pack-animals: ploughing and other field work was done by 'oxen' (i.e. bullocks or cows). Horse-packs were specially designed for carrying different loads – stones, dung, marl, hay, turnips, apples, wood, thatching-reed or whatever (the capacity being described as a 'seam') – and a string of six or more pack-horses, led by a boy, could carry as much as a horse-drawn cart could elsewhere.

That the state of the roads and trackways was far from perfect, however, was graphically illustrated by young Samuel Taylor Coleridge. On 18th August 1791, 19-year-old Samuel left the mail coach at Cullompton, and began to walk to Ottery St Mary. He had been brought up in that village, where his father was both vicar and school master, and he had many friends in Devon. It is clear that he tried to follow the 'direct' route, using roads, trackways and footpaths, via Plymtree, Talaton and Escot: it was not a happy experience, and he expressed his feelings in a poem he wrote (*see right*):

It should be noted that it was in August, and not mid-winter, that Samuel travelled through Plymtree. Although the roads did not improve, bridge-building continued, and in 1793 Polwhele noted, 'At Danes Mill, over the River Tale or Tale-water, is a new bridge of two arches, built very lately of stone; the repairing of which, in future, will fall to the parish.'

Greenwood's map of Devon, published in 1827 (*see page 7*), shows a number of roads in the parish which no longer exist. Among others, one ran south from Greenend to Clyst Hydon, and another north towards Langford; beside Old Forge Cottage, a road went behind Sanguishayes to join up with Weaver Lane; another ran through the garden of Perhams Green Farm north to Motts Lane; while the lane to Woodbeare Court continued on to Danes Mill. It is not, of course, clear exactly what Greenwood considered to be a 'road', but he did differentiate paths, using parallel dotted lines instead of solid ones for roads. By 1842,

Devonshire Roads

The indignant Bard composed this furious ode
As tired he dragg'd his way thro' Plimtree road.
Crusted with filth and stuck in mire
Dull sounds the Bard's bemudded lyre;
Nathless Revenge and Ire the Poet goad
To pour his imprecations on the road.
Curst road! whose execrable way
Was darkly shadow'd out in Milton's lay.
Where the sad fiends thro' Hell's sulphureous roads
Took the first survey of their new abodes;
Or when the fall'n Archangel fierce
Thro' all Confusion's quagmires floundering went.
Nor cheering pipe, nor Bird's shrill note
Around thy dreary paths shall float;
Their boding songs shall scritch owls pour
To fright the guilty shepards sore.
Led by the wandering fires astray
Dar'd through the realms of Night to pierce.
What time the Bloodhound lur'd by human scent
Thro' the dank horrors of the way!
While they their mud-lost sandles hunt
May all the curses, which they grunt
In raging moan like goaded hog,
Alight upon thee, damned bog!

when the great Tithe Apportionment map was drawn, most of these additional roads on Greenwood's map had either shrunk or vanished: the Apportionment list reported $34^3/_4$ acres of parish roads and $10^1/_4$ acres of private roads in the parish.

The great ambition of Rev. Dornford, rector from 1832, was to drive a good pair of horses from the Rectory to Exeter Cathedral in an hour, which would have been quite a feat, given the quite atrocious state of local roads. His record was 62 minutes – but the speed and recklessness of his driving apparently caused a number of accidents, including the permanent maiming of his own gardener.

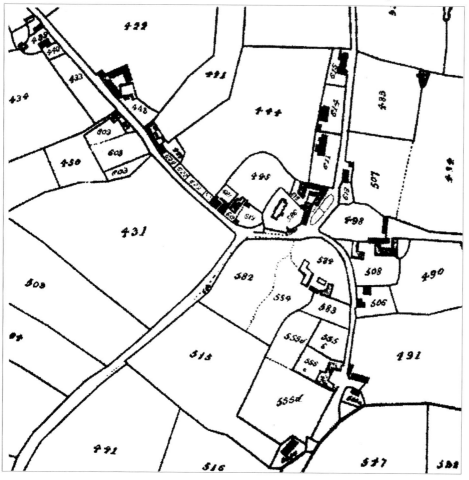

The village centre in the Tithe Apportionment map of 1842.

Until the 'Penny Post' began on 10th January 1840, letters were paid for by the recipient, not the sender. The Post Office had been established in the 18th century, and it appointed postmasters in every town in the land, as well as licensing stage-coach owners to carry the Royal Mail between towns and cities.

Cullompton was the nearest 'post-town' to Plymtree, and the overseers' accounts show that the postmaster there charged one penny, in addition to the postage to his/her office, to deliver letters to the village. Thus in 1833, the account included 'Paid the Post Woman for a letter from the House of Commons – 1d.', though Parliamentary letters were delivered free of postage (as they are today). The charges appearing in the accounts include 2d. for a letter from Tiverton, 5d. from Exeter and 6d. from Wellington, while those from less-easily-reached places cost much more, e.g. from Colyton 10d. and from Exmouth 1s. A letter from London to Cullompton was charged at a standard 10d.

Long-distance travel, and communications generally, took a great leap forward on 1st May 1844, when the Bristol and Exeter Railway was opened. As well as having a station at Cullompton, it was possible to catch a fast train from Exeter to London, the journey taking a mere 5$^{1}/_{2}$ hours, as opposed to 20 or more by stage-coach. The cost of travel came down, and mail was delivered much more speedily. In 1868, The choice of travel to London was doubled, when the London and South Western Railway Company completed its line from Waterloo to Exeter, and Plymtree people could catch trains at Whimple or Feniton.

At about the same time, Mrs Sanders became post-mistress (above) for the village at her shop at Normans Green. In 1897 it was reported to the parish that 'The Post Office has granted Telegraph Office status for the village P.O.: the poles and wires bringing the line are awaited', and the following year Mrs Sanders was authorised to act as an agent for the P.O. Savings Bank, and to issue money orders, thus saving journeys to Cullompton to transact such business.

From its beginning in 1894, the Parish Council spent rate money to maintain the many footpaths in the parish and the foot-bridges over the numerous streams and rivers which would otherwise block those paths. Paths tended to be

Mr John Sanders, blacksmith, ironmonger and postmaster, with his wife Sarah, in the garden of what is now Old Forge Cottage, c.1900.

straighter and more direct than the roads, and people used them to visit the doctor at Clyst Hydon, to walk to church from the outer parts of the parish, or to take cheese and other produce to market at Cullompton.

Another form of 'communication' appeared in 1894, in the shape of the *Parish Magazine* which, apart from an enforced gap during the Second World War, has continued to be produced ever since.

Nothing much changed as far as roads were concerned until 1911, when steamrollers began the work of 'metalling' the roads to the village by compacting small stones to provide a comparatively smooth surface. No doubt this encouraged the use of carts and wagons, since the old sledges (which worked well on mud or grass) would have quickly worn out on the new hard road surfaces.

It appears that the first motorcar in Plymtree was owned by Arthur and George Sanders at Middle Woodbeer just before the First World War, although the occupants of Hayne House also had motors; but local doctors did not rush to acquire the 'horseless carriages'.

Outings by charabanc became popular with village organisations in the 1920s, and visits to such exotic places as Torquay became commonplace. Since the early vehicles had solid tyres, the experience cannot have been too comfortable, despite the improved roads.

In 1930, when the Devon General Bus Company began to extend their services to rural areas, one bus operated on Fridays between Cullompton and Exeter, stopping at Kentisbeare, Broadhembury, Plymtree and Clyst Hydon, returning the same way in the afternoon. In those days, when cars were rarities, the service was very well used and highly appreciated, and some time later the bus company added a Tuesday service, altering the route slightly to include Talaton.

The members of the W.I. petitioned for and obtained a bus service to and from Exeter on Saturdays, to enable the men to attend football matches there, but it was also useful for shopping or a visit to the cinema, since the bus did not return until quite late.

In 1933 the roads into the village began to be surfaced with tarmac, making them both smoother and more hard-wearing. Horse-drawn carts dropped rocks wherever possible beside the roads, and local men spent months sitting on sandbags beside the road breaking them into small stones with hammers. The stones were spread evenly over the road surface, compacted by a steam roller (the driver slept in a caravan pulled by the roller), and tar was then sprayed over the surface to seal it. The first road to be so treated was that from Clyst William Cross, and the one from Langford followed in 1934.

Almost every young man owned a bicycle in the inter-war period, and the newly-smoothed roads helped them attend dances in neighbouring villages. Some even had motor bicycles, allowing them to roam further afield.

The Plymtree 'lengthmen', Tommy Cross and Tom Cross, c.1936. They kept the verges, hedges and ditches clear, as well as repairing holes in the road.

The telephone also came (to Danes Mill) in about 1933. A man cycled from Exeter to work out where the posts should go to bring the line from Broadhembury. He had to negotiate with the farmers, and it is remembered that he got so drunk on their cider that he slept in the hedge.

The roads, and the important drainage ditches beside them, were maintained by Tom and Tommy Cross, the parish 'lengthmen', who could be seen out and about at any time – especially in bad weather – their working tools strapped to the cross-bars of their bicycles, or in hand and in action. They kept the foliage on the roadside banks back from the roads, but were careful not to destroy the plants which grew in them, so that all manner of flowers decorated them, and wild strawberries could be picked in season.

Deliveries of all kinds began to be made to the village by motor. There were at least three bakers competing for custom in Plymtree, and mobile shops; the accumulator man (who recharged the batteries for radios), and others called on householders. Local papers were delivered weekly by a man who caught an Exeter bus and then walked from Poundapit – his delivery day did not, unfortunately for him, coincide with the bus timetable.

When King George VI was crowned in 1937, the Parish Council commemorated the occasion by erecting a bus shelter opposite the church. A seat was also placed at the top of the hill by the Rectory, to be used by passengers waiting there for the bus; later this seat was re-sited beside the church lych gate, where it remains.

In July 1951, the Postmaster-General negotiated with Brigadier Peter Acland, then owner of Tyes Farm, for the plot of land opposite the Church House. Thereafter Plymtree's own, fully automatic (mechanical) telephone exchange was built on the site: it was changed to an electronic exchange in 1996, when Plymtree ceased to have its own STD code, becoming part of Cullompton/Tiverton.

In 1970 there was a bus to Cullompton (and on to Exeter) every Wednesday, and a new service to Honiton was started. Buses were laid on to take pupils to the Secondary School at Cullompton and to the King's School at Ottery. A doctor's surgery began to be held weekly in the village, saving the sick – especially the elderly – from having to travel to Cullompton.

Later in the decade Plymtree Community Care was begun by Maggie Palfrey and other concerned parishioners. A booklet was produced by Frank Sanders giving useful

In 1978 the village was cut off by snow for four days. Above is the 'road' to Talaton at Clyst William Cross, while right is the view in the opposite direction, showing where the road to Dulford should be.

information for everyone, and volunteers with cars were organised in rotas by Maggie to take sick and elderly villagers to Cullompton and elsewhere for treatment or recreational purposes, or to collect medicines from the nearest chemist – a service which is still maintained.

Despite all the improvements to roads, Plymtree still gets cut-off from the outside world from time to time by the weather. Usually, only some of the roads serving the village are impassable, due to flood water rushing over the ford at Old Bridge and standing water blocking the roads to Langford and to Dulford north from Norman's Green: one can nearly always take the Clyst William Cross road to get to the A373.

But, despite the normally mild East Devon climate, Plymtree does get some snow, and in 1978 a very large amount of it fell on the village,

completely isolating it for four days. No matter how high the banks on either side of the roads, they were filled level with their tops. The electricity supply failed, of course, which caused even more problems for the residents. Electricity failed again in 1987, this time due to storms, but people were able to get around, and many were grateful to Robin Rolfe at the Blacksmiths Arms for supplying the food and heat they needed for the duration.

Nowadays, Plymtree has become for many a 'commuter village'. Even for those still working in or near the village, most have access to a car, and a deep-freezer and refrigerator make a weekly shop at supermarkets in the city no problem. This has altered the pattern of life, and among other changes, old country dishes and old country amusements are giving way to more exotic fare.

Getting in the hay in the 1930s.

Above: Reed combing – the hard bit!
John Perry, the machine owner, feeds
the loose straw into the comber.

Below: Old tractors are still loved and get the
odd airing to take part in ploughing matches.

Above: Mowing a hay field in the 1930s.

Below: Cider-making at Middle Clyst William. Derek
Rugg, master cider-maker, begins making the 'cheese'.

Chapter 3: Agriculture

In ancient times, much of England was covered by forest. It is believed that early man tended to travel either by river or along hill ridges, and his settlements were built near these features. There is no evidence of either Stone-age or Bronze-age activity in Plymtree, the nearest Iron-age settlements being at Hembury and Dolbury (Killerton).

Since Plymtree has neither navigable river nor high ground, it is unlikely that the major Celtic tribe which occupied Devon, the Dumnonii, began forest clearance here much before the Second Augusta Legion of the Roman army pressed into Devon in about AD47. It seems the Dumnonii co-existed with the Romans, probably because they were too thinly spread across the county to resist them. They continued to farm their own lands and, at least east of the River Exe, produced metalwork and pottery.

The Romans left Britain in AD410, and the Dumnonii were left to their own devices. There were apparently a number of plagues – a particularly bad one in about AD540 – which reduced the population considerably; there was also much emigration to that part of France which became known as 'Brittany' as a result, and much of previously-cultivated Devonshire reverted to wasteland.

The Anglo-Saxons began to move in. At first they made sporadic attacks from the sea, but then the Saxon land-based forces gradually fought and colonised their way westwards, arriving in Devon via the Culm Valley and the old Roman road from Ilminster in about AD660-70. What farmers won, they held, cleared and farmed. They also founded most of the villages in Devon; locally, only Aunk and Whimple have Celtic names, while almost every other settlement has a name of

Aerial view, late 1920s, with Hayne House in the centre, Fordmore to the right and Bowling Green Cottages between them and the camera.

Saxon origin, including Plymtree and Woodbeer.

Plymtree must have suited the Saxon soldier-farmers very well, with its ready supply of clean water, and its gentle contours helping to ease the burdens of ploughing; the maximum height difference between hill and low-land in Plymtree is a mere 75 metres, the highest point in the parish – farmland between Clyst William Barton and Woodbeer Court – being 125 metres above mean sea level, while the lowest is 50 metres a.m.s.l. at Weaver. The favoured Saxon weapon was the axe, and when not being used for fighting it was very useful for clearing woodland to make room for more fields – and when the Dumnonii and other Celtic tribes were finally defeated in Devon in AD710 there was even more time for creating farms.

Villages owned by a single lord, like Broadhembury and Bradninch, tended to cultivate the land through 'open field' systems, where each villager held strips of land in large, shared fields. Villages like Plymtree, with several lords, its mix of little settlements and lone farmsteads, used smaller, single-owner fields, separated and protected by hedges or banks. At least one hedge at Woodbeer dates from well before the Conquest and no doubt many more are of similar age.

From AD988 Devon was regularly attacked by the Danes, but from 1003 the burning and killing moved to other parts of England, and the Saxon English could return to farming – until William of Normandy caused them to leave their fields and take up arms again. A measure of their success at cultivation is the fact that during their 400 years of almost sole occupation the English had cleared so much forest that, by 1086, 80 per cent of the land being cultivated in 1914 was already under the plough.

By the time the Normans came, there were probably about 80,000 people living in Devon, scattered across some 3000 towns, villages, hamlets and farmsteads. Much land formed part of about 1000 estates ('manors'), owned by the King, his thegns, or the Church. There were some free-men, who owned their own land, but the majority of the people were villagers or villeins (49 per cent) who worked largish parcels of land in return for 'service' to their lord, e.g.: working the Lord's land instead of paying rent; cottagers or bordars (32 per cent) worked less land for less 'service' and probably had other occupations as well; 19 per cent were serfs, men (and women) who were tied to their lord's land, often being considered as 'slaves'.

Nationally and locally, the next 200 years saw a great expansion of small farms and the creation of new hamlets, villages and towns as more and more peasants became free men.

In medieval times, sheep became the mainstay of agriculture and, indeed, of the economy of England. But man cannot live by sheep alone – they were kept not for their meat but for their wool – so various food and fodder crops continued to be grown. Cattle were kept to provide milk, cheese and meat as well as being used as plough animals, and a pig and chickens were kept by every cottager. The land in Devon was exceptionally well cultivated: a system called 'beat-burning' was widely followed, but must have been very hard hand-work as it involved cutting and turning the turf covering a field, letting it dry, and then burning it before ploughing. Marl (a coarse sand) was also used to lighten the soil, and there are still many old marl-pits around. It was also during this period that the land in Plymtree was found to be

Edwin Widgery and Reuben Saunders demolishing a cob building at Weaver, c.1930.

peculiarly suited to growing apples for cider.

Being well-served by streams, much of the land around Weaver, in the west of the parish, was water meadow which provided rich ground for arable and grain crops as well as hay. Eastwards at Clyst William, the land was more hilly and natural flooding of the meadows was not pursued. There is evidence of an early (possibly medieval) irrigation system in some of the fields there, the ditches, crossing points and sluices which controlled the flow of water from the river still being visible.

The earliest rate list we have dates from 1618, and shows that there were then 62 separate tenements in the parish. Such lists cannot tell us about people other than landowners or their tenants, but other records clearly show that between the 14th and 18th centuries a large proportion of villagers were employed in raising sheep, or treating or weaving their wool. Rev. George Ridding was convinced that the River Weaver and the area named after it was so called because of the large number of tucking millers and cottage-weavers who settled there: there are numerous small streams in the area which could have powered such small-scale industry.

France and England were either at war or preparing for it from 1744 until 1815, when the defeat of Napoleon brought peace at last. During that long period the supply of all sorts of crops, livestock, cider and wool was increased to meet the demands of the army and navy, and farmers grew rich. So did the rector, through the tithes he could demand: in addition to claiming a tenth of the value of crops grown by the farmers, the incumbent could claim his due on almost everything else including (according to a contemporary list from Awliscombe) 'for every cow giving milk 4d; for the foal of every mare 1d; for every hogshead of cider 4d; for every herb garden 1d; for every fleece of wool 2d; for every pig 2d; for a hearth 1d; honey and geese in kind. Also an Easter offering of 2d. from each person over 16.'

The larger farmers used their profits to buy more land, so that by 1741 the number of separate tenements had fallen to 39, and by 1781 to only 33.

Little changed, however, for day-labourers on the farms. If they could get work they were paid 1s. for a day lasting from 6am to 6pm during the summer or from 7am to 5pm in the three winter months; if they were provided with food the daily wage went down to 6d. in summer and 5d. in winter, although food was provided free during the corn harvest when they were expected to work from dawn to dusk.

A labourer's diet consisted mainly of bacon and bread. The bacon would come from his own pig, fed on scraps until it was very fat, and then killed, home salted and often smoked in the chimney of his cottage. His bread was made from rye until the beginning of the century, when oats, and then barley became more usual. Rye was still grown in Plymtree in 1750 – probably on the moory ground in the east of the parish – but to provide the best reed for thatching rather than to eat. Wheat was too expensive for a labourer's bread; tea was also a commodity for the rich, so the labourer and his family drank cider.

At some time between 1762 and 1784 the Rev. Jeremiah Milles, Dean of Exeter Cathedral, conducted a survey of all the parishes in the diocese, by sending to the incumbents a printed questionnaire. He was very interested in history and archaeology, but he also asked about agriculture. The respondent from Plymtree noted that there was no common land in the parish, and that wheat and barley were grown, as well as rye for thatching. Over 1700 hogsheads of cider were produced each year, 'of a quality equal to any made in the County.' [A hogshead contained 65 gallons, and good cider fetched 2d. to 3d. a gallon in 1750]. The local cattle were described as 'neat'; and he gave the value of land as £1-10s.-0d. per acre. 'The men are employed in Husbandry, and the women in spinning for ye Serge manufacturers of Exeter and Cullumbton.'

Rev. Richard Polwhele in his *History of Devonshire*, written shortly before 1793, described Plymtree as it was when he visited the parish:

The village is straggling; the farm houses scattered; and the farms not very large. The buildings are all of cob and thatched with reed; to which belong orchards. A very rich deep red marley soil runs through this parish; the whole of which is in high cultivation. The number of paupers are generally about twelve, and the day-labourers about forty, or perhaps more. There are several freeholders in the parish, and the other farmers are rack [lease] holders. The population is healthy and they live to a great age.

Greenend is surrounded by orchards which, in a plentifull year, produce several hundred hogsheads of excellent cider.

Greenend was then owned by the Blake family, whose land-holdings in the parish were considerable; and as they grew, so the number of small tenements decreased. Even so, by 1817 life in Plymtree must have been virtually the same as in the reign of Queen Elizabeth. The population numbered about 370, and agriculture was its life-blood, with probably half of the men working on the land and others in trades connected with the land. There were some 20-25 'farmers', either landowners or tenants, some clergy, and a number of tradesmen such as butchers, blacksmiths, carters, tailors, thatchers, woolcombers and cordwainers (shoemakers): but the remainder were agricultural labourers.

Most poor children had no schooling but, from the age of eight were 'apprenticed' to farmers, living-in and doing light work; as their strength grew, so did the tasks they were given; and all worked at least 12 hours each day – longer in the summer – for six days a week. They were sustained by large quantities of cider to wash down their bread. Girls worked as house-servants on the farms, but were expected to help out in the fields with the harvest, milking, butter- and cheese-making and other less strenuous tasks.

Clockwise from above: Cider making at Middle Clyst William – Derek Rugg inspects the full 'cheese' prior to pressing; a two-horse waggon loaded with cider apples from Pencepool Farm arrives at Whiteways at Hele, c.1930; on the other side of the wall from the Clyst William press, the cider flows through a square hole into a half barrel.

The apprenticeships lasted until the girls were aged 21, the men 24.

When the Bristol and Exeter Railway was opened in 1844, cider was probably one of the first 'exports'. There had been a 'dairyman' tenant at Clyst William (Cross) Farm for ten years, supplying Cullompton and Exeter with milk and butter, but now he could sell to a wider market, and others at Fordmoor, Greenend, Tyes and Higher Weaver started up.

The importance of cider making in the parish is shown by the area covered by orchards in 1842: no less than 181 acres was dedicated to growing cider apples, plus another 44 used as nurseries for young trees (a total of more than 10 per cent of the land).

The other tree which grows abundantly in Plymtree is the oak and, in the days when all ships and most buildings made use of its timber, it was a valuable export from the parish. In the 1851 census, Thomas and Edward Brice were 'timber dealers' at Pencepool Farm, while their brother John farmed the land: no doubt they all pitched in to make the cider.

There was a long drought in 1864 between February and the end of November, with rain on only two days – on 15th September and 21st October. The dew-ponds for watering cattle, then seen in almost every field, dried up completely, and farmers had to rely on what was left in the rivers and streams: field crops were very hard hit, and the cider-apple crop very small.

Throughout the first half of the 20th century cider continued to be made and drunk by all the farmers and shared with their workers; it was not uncommon for a man to take a quart bottle into the fields for the morning's refreshment and, after a lunch washed down with cider, to take another quart to help the afternoon's work. However, the orchards of the parish produced far more cider apples than could be used, and much of the crop was sold to Whiteways Cider Works at Hele.

'Ike' (Cyril) and Gilbert Daniel enjoy a glass of Clyst William cider.

When the Baxter family's 'Plymtree Estate' (based on Greenend) was sold in 1917, the number of owner-occupier farms increased dramatically; those sold included Tyes, Greenend, Pencepool, Hayne Dairy, Little Clyst William, Middle Clyst William, Middle Woodbeer and Chown's Pool, many of which were purchased by their former tenants.

Danes Mill, which had served the village since the 1580s, ceased working by 1930, and its water-wheels were removed in the 1940s. Cottagers used to take their grain there (or to Weaver Mill until it was pulled down in 1759) to be ground in exchange for cider, and some of the flour could then be exchanged for bread at the baker's.

Between the wars the Daniel family used to make a lot of cider at Clyst William, and young 'Ike 'Daniel would sell it to pubs as far away as Ottery St Mary; he used to claim he balanced 54-gallon barrels on his bicycle! Ten days before his 21st birthday (in 1942) he set aside two of these barrels (i.e. 108 gallons), selecting the best cider for the celebration: unfortunately, it had all been drunk before the day arrived!

Pencepool Farm's apples produced excellent cider, much of which was sent to a bar at Waterloo Station in London: John White Hussey won 2nd prize for his brew at the National Fruit and Cider Institute Show in 1928, and later his tenant there, Francis Martin, took the 2nd prize with his product at the 1952 Royal Agricultural Show. But in the 1960s the government wanted to increase

Above and left: David Gibbins and William Cleal getting in the hay at Green End Farm, c.1965; Mr Mason watches his wife at work, cutting hay at Woodbeer Court, c.1956.

Reed-combing

Above: Michael Tidball reaping wheat. The freshly cut crop is 'stooked' for primary drying.

Left: Michael at work on the ancient binding machine.

Right: Bill Vellacott (by tractor) and Harold Moon working the reed-combing machine at Great Down Field, Middle Woodbeer, 1996.

Below: Gilbert Daniel separating the stooks ready for feeding into the machine.

Right: Michael Tidball 'banging the reed on the door' (to level the ends) before throwing the bundle on the trailer.

agricultural production, and it paid farmers to grub out their orchards and turn their land over to cattle or arable farming, which drastically changed the landscape of Plymtree.

In 1998 the ancient cider press at Pencepool Farm was sold to the monks of Buckfast Abbey, where it will once again be used. The press at Middle Clyst William Farm is still used by Michael Tidball to produce excellent cider from his own crop of apples.

Another old art – that of combing wheat reed for thatching – is still practised by Michael Tidball and by Bill Vellacott at Middle Woodbeer Farm. The wheat is cut, stooked and allowed to dry off a little before the combing machine is hired: they last made such machines in the 1920s, so there are not many of them around. The string tying the sheaves is cut and the wheat fed into one end of the combing machine, which first threshes the wheat and throws out the chaff. The stalks are then combed to remove the remnants of leaves, at the same time discarding short and unusable straw (which is passed to a baling machine so that it can be kept as cattle fodder). The combed reed is then tied automatically, but before it is stacked for transportation each bundle is thumped on a hard surface (usually an old door) to ensure the cut ends are level. Despite competition from such countries as Turkey and South Africa, English reed is highly-prized by thatchers: in 1996, Bill Vellacott produced 40 tons of reed from the 20 acres of wheat he had sown.

Today dairy and poultry farming tend to predominate, with many fields being sown for fodder,

but some land is used for specialised crops, and there is some pig and sheep farming.

The major farmers in the parish are Herbert Persey at Fordmore, David Gibbins at Greenend, Bill Vellacott at Middle Woodbeer, Alan Lock at Sanguishayes, Chris and Richard Pratt at Woodbeer Court and Lower Woodbeare, respectively, and Michael Tidball and Roger Clarke at different parts of Clyst William.

Top: Roger Clarke combining at Clyst William in the 1980s (George French driving the second harvester).

Centre: Rob Hussey turning hay on Rectory Meadow, c.1980.

Right: George Knight and Walter Lovering with the heavy horses at Tyes Farm, c.1930.

Chapter 4: Industry

The biggest industry in Plymtree has always been agriculture, so it is no surprise that the earliest industry in the parish had to do with the spinning, weaving and tucking of wool. It seems clear from the few existing records that, with the many streams in the parish (especially the tributaries of the River Weaver) to power the various machines, this cottage industry was widespread locally from the 14th to the 18th century. This industry then gradually fell into decline as other materials came into the market, and the processing of wool became more industrialised.

There being no other industry available to the cottagers to replace wool manufacturing, many who could not find work on the land must have drifted away to the towns. Some, however, would have taken up other trades; in 1850 there were a number of artisans who served the residents of the parish, including two blacksmiths, a carpenter and wheelwright, three shoemakers, two tailors, a miller and a baker.

Towards the end of the 19th century the main village industry was that of making and mending agricultural machinery. At their forge at Normans

Normans Green c.1978. The former M.S.T. site has been taken over by Ken Edwards, who's house, Fairlawns, is being built at the bottom of the picture.

Green the Sanders family had produced all manner of tools and implements for many years. They then turned their attention to owning, hiring and repairing steam engines, as these replaced horse-power on the farms. There being insufficient room for such huge machines at the forge, they expanded into land they owned on the other side of the road, and there they gradually built up a large engineering business.

It is clear from bronze hub-caps and other items which have been found that they manufactured trailers and ploughs there, as well as selling and repairing larger items of equipment.

In 1945/6 George Sanders' firm was taken over by the Lowman Group, becoming Sanders (Plymtree) Ltd, which in the 1960s was merged with other companies to become Medland, Sanders & Twose (M.S.T.), Normans Green being one of their main sites. By the time that site was closed in 1976, much of it resembled a junk yard, with the remains of old tractors and other machinery scattered around, while the company stores contained spare parts for many machines which had long since gone out of production. (Some of this venerable machinery was bought by enthusiasts like George French, who purchased a rusty Fordson Standard tractor with spiked, iron wheels, which he was able to restore to its former glory.).

The land was purchased by Ken Edwards, trading as Car & Commercial Services, and he set up repair facilities for heavy goods vehicles as well as

George French driving a saw-bench at Bill Broom's yard, Danes Mill.

cars and agricultural machinery. He built an office beside Normans Green Cottage, and had his house, Fairlawns, built at the back of the site. He continued to trade there until more convenient premises became available in Cullompton, and the Sandersfield estate was built on the land.

In 1989, John Hussey – who had worked for M.S.T. – saw the need for industrial units to encourage small businesses in the village, and he built four self-contained units beside his house on Farthings Meadow. Since then the occupants have included an antiques restorer, a specialist doll-maker, a beer-engine repairer and a refurbisher of computer-peripherals. Perhaps his most successful tenants were Clive and Tim Roberts, founders of Original Organics Ltd, and proud inventors and manufacturers of the 'Original Wormery' and other recycling and gardening products, whose company outgrew two units and had to move to much larger premises at Uffculme.

The stores at M.S.T., Normans Green

Above: A Fordson Standard stands abandoned in the M.S.T. yard at Normans Green.

Above right: This Massey Ferguson 185 was completely re-built by M.S.T. after it had rolled over a number of times.

Right: The old Fordson Standard salvaged by George French and later refurbished by him.

Chapter 5: Plymtree Church

There is some evidence to show that Plymtree Church is the second to have been built on the site, and that the present building was begun in Saxon times. Firstly, the Yew Tree Campaign have certified the tree to the south of the chancel as being over 1100 years old (i.e. before AD895), and yews were always planted in Saxon churchyards. Secondly, there is a blocked doorway in the north wall (uncovered during the 1902 work to underpin it) of Saxon or very early Norman shape. Most importantly, when the floor of the church was dug up and re-set in 1910 the rector reported that, 'a portion of an old wall, with plaster face, was found about a foot inside the present North wall near the pulpit', which clearly indicates that an earlier building – almost certainly a church – occupied the site before our present one was begun.

Towards the end of the 13th century, probably because it was the oldest church in the area, Plymtree was the 'mother church' of the parishes of Blackborough, Bradninch, Broadhembury, Buckerell, Butterleigh, Clyst Hydon, Clyst St Lawrence, Cullompton, Feniton, Kentisbeare, Payhembury, Rewe, Silverton and Talaton, which together made up the Deanery of Plymtree. And from this time on we know the names of the Plymtree rectors.

By the late 1300s, Plymtree was rich enough, due to the wealth created by the cloth industry, for the parish church to be re-built. Almost certainly this would have been largely funded by the lords of the manor at that period, Sir Thomas Courtney, or Thomas and Margaret Peverell. The rebuilding produced the nave and chancel which are the basis of the present church. The main material was trap, a locally-available dark red, volcanic stone, with Beer freestone windows and doorways. The barrel (or wagon) roof was made from locally-grown oak and would originally have been thatched, though it was roofed with slate (then known as 'hele-stone') from at least 1600.

Churches in medieval times had no furniture other than the altar, font and a lectern for the Bible, with perhaps a chair of some sort for the priest, and a bench for the lord and his wife; the peasantry stood or knelt on the beaten earth floor to hear the Mass said in Latin. Many churches had their walls plastered, and painted brightly with pictures of saints: although there is no direct evidence of such paintings at Plymtree; the walls of

Plymtree church, c.1890, with the ancient Church House to the right.

the chancel have typically-medieval plaster, which may just cover some earlier glories.

It is difficult in this day and age to understand how completely the church was the 'hub of the universe' for each parish in the Middle Ages. As well as being God's house, it served as the parish hall, and at times the village pub: for 12 days at Christmas the church was filled with people watching plays, and enjoying church-ales; and similar festivities were held at Easter and on May Day. At harvest-time, or when the plague threatened, villagers would take comfort from the Host being paraded to bless the crops, or to ward off the illness. If the church then had some sort of a bell tower (the present one was not built until the 15th century), the bell would have been rung to call the people to prayer, and to announce important matters such as a visit by the lord of the manor, the marriage or death of a parishioner, etc.

In the 1420s the bell tower was added to the church, four bells being cast by Robert Norton of Exeter. Chancery proceedings were taken in 1432 against Norton and John Forde (of Woodbeer) by the parishioners, who accused them of fraudulently misrepresenting the weight of bell-metal used, and of appropriating the extra money charged; there is no record of the result of this action, but from the claim we can see that the people, rather than the lords, had paid for the bells, and that Plymtree was still a wealthy parish (due to continuing revenue from the cloth industry).

The south window showing the portrait sculptures on either side.

The Forde aisle and the south porch also date from about the same time, the window finials bearing representations of their creators, John Forde and his wife. The shield charged with a St Andrew's cross (being the arms of Bishop Neville) carved on the capital of the western response [the arch joined to the wall] between the nave and the Forde aisle, date the work fairly accurately, as Neville was Bishop of Exeter only from 1458 to 1464. The reconstruction incorporated a 'rood-stair' – a small staircase set into the north wall, giving access to the top of a rood screen, built across the width of the church separating nave from chancel, and surmounted by a carving of the crucifixion. It is not known whether such a screen was then installed, but if so it was not long before it was supplanted by the beautiful one in situ today.

It is likely that the eastern end of the aisle (now the vestry) was originally used as the private chapel of the Forde family. According to a paper read to the Diocesan Architectural Society in 1850, it was separated from the chancel by a parclose (a wooden screen), with a carved, single-leaf door in it, but this was removed in 1883 to make room for an organ. The present windows at the east and west ends of the Forde aisle were cut down from three panels (of the same design as those in the south wall) to two; possibly the set was obtained ready-made when the aisle was built, but for structural reasons – either then or later – the end windows had to be reduced by one panel.

The Stafford Knot (the sign of Isabel, widow of Humphrey Stafford, Earl of Devon) and the Bourchier Knot (representing Sir Thomas Bourchier, who she then married) are both carved in the rood screen, and it seems likely that one or both paid for its creation some time after 1470.

The porch was an important part of the church, and of the life of the community. There the churchwardens dispensed charity, made loans and collected debts; wills were read in the church porch (since these came under Ecclesiastical, not Common Law); and there penitents stood on a white sheet while they made a public confession of their sins.

The windows in the north wall are clearly of Tudor design, and their insertion must have required a patron willing to spend a great deal of money on the church. It is possible that this patron was George, Earl of Huntingdon who, as lord of the manor in 1532, gave the land for the building of the Church House.

In 1548 Protector Somerset (in the name of the infant king, Edward VI) ordered the removal of all 'papist images' from churches and chapels. It is probable that this order resulted in the removal of the rood (the wooden crucifixion scene above the screen), and the smashing of the Holy-water

The scouts and guides celebrate Mothering Sunday at the church in 1988 (above), while nearly 100 years earlier in 1899, Plymtree school pupils gather on Ascension Day. To the left of the picture is the restored preaching cross which had been re-dedicated to the memory of Rev. George Gutteres. (Rev. Edgar Hay and Master Richard Rowley are standing beside the cross.).

stoop (set in the wall to the right of the south door within the porch) and the niches (containing statues) which formed part of two columns between the nave and the Forde aisle.

By his will in 1697, John Land, who had been born at Woodbeer Court but had made his fortune in London, ordered his executors to sell:

...my two silver tankards, two silver plates, a silver-gilt salver, caudle cupp and porringer, a silver boate and taster, a little silver box, two dozen of silver spoones and one dozen of silverguilt spoones and all my other plate whatsoever. And also my large gold seale ring, a large plaine gold ring, three diamond rings and eight other mourning and hair rings. And the money to be raised thereby I order to be laid out by my Executors in the purchase of plate for the Communion table of the Church of the said parrish of Plymtree and a velvet cushion for their pulpit. And it is my desire that the Minister and Churchwardens and four of the principall Inhabitants of the said parrish of Plymtree for the time being doe take all due care of the Charity of one hundred pounds, Communion plate and cushion.

These items were collected from London by the rector, who claimed expenses of £1.-17s.-9d. for his trouble. The large communion plate given to the Church is still in its possession, and the velvet cushion almost so: the velvet deteriorated with age and had to be renewed in 1890, when the original initials and date 'I 1697 L' in gold thread were transferred on to the new material, which now does duty as the pulpit fall.

A large gallery was erected at the back of the church in 1719, to provide room for the musicians and choir needed to lead the singing of the metrical psalms which became popular at about this time. At some point – then or thereafter – another gallery was built against the south wall of the church, for the use of children.

During George II's reign the royal coat of arms, now to be seen in the ringing chamber, was painted and fixed behind the altar. At different times it has been behind the altar, fixed over the small window above the south porch, and in the parish school.

In 1815 either the churchwardens were very caring folk, or the services

went on for a very long time, since there was a thatched 'privy' in the churchyard, the lime in the pit being replenished regularly, and the 'night soil' removed.

The Rev. Dornford, a High-Churchman and rector from 1832, introduced carved woodwork (the wall-panels around the altar), metalwork and old pieces of painted glass into the church. He also had the foot of the east window of the chancel raised, by inserting some stonework,

A heavily re-touched postcard of the church, c.1907 with children lined up along the raised pavements. Above is the interior of the church in 1895.

apparently to provide a dark back-drop for a large crucifix and candle-holders: the window was restored to its original proportions in 1927. In the return for the National Religious Census in 1851, Dornford mis-described the dedication of the church as being to 'St Mary the Virgin', rather than St John the Baptist, further indicating his High-Church sympathies.

In 1873 the ancient Deanery of Plymtree disappeared, being replaced by the Deanery of Ottery St Mary.

Old postcards show how the church looked internally. In 1895, the end wall of the chancel was in poor condition, with cracked and stained plaster. On each side of the east window were mounted the boards painted (in 1635) with the Ten Commandments, now at the other end of the church. The chancel was lit by two hanging oil lamps and similar lamps were suspended within the arches separating the nave from the Forde aisle, with two further lamps on brackets on the north wall; these were obtained at a cost of £9-1s. (plus 12s. for fitting) and were installed ready for the Lent services in 1893, allowing winter evening services for the first time; they were also loaned out for village functions.

Part of the rood screen across the south aisle.

The pulpit was twice as high as the present one, but sported the pulpit fall donated from the estate of John Land in 1697. In the Forde aisle were box pews in simple Georgian style, while the pew ends in the nave show that woodworm had already done their worst. The north wall leaned outwards, as it still does, and external photographs show the wall had, by then, been buttressed (although it had to be underpinned and further strengthened later); they also show the high brick chimney flue for the large, square-cast iron stove, set between the pews beside the north wall, which was the only heating for the church. High on the north wall was fixed another painted board (now on the wall of the vestry room) recording donations for the poor of Plymtree.

Externally, in 1880, the tower had only one strengthening bar pierced through it, just below the bell-chamber, rather than the huge amount of ironwork inserted in 1895. The door to the tower was then obviously very old, but its present replacement is of the same design. The yew tree to the north of the tower, now huge, was then only eight feet tall; it stood against the then wall of the gardens of Redgate Cottages, the end 15 feet or so of which are now part of the churchyard.

Rev. George Gutteres, the new rector, noted in 1894, 'The Parish Church has for long been suffered to fall into deeper and deeper decay, and except for the energetic case of the Rev. F. B. Blogg who some 11 years ago spent £100 in strengthening and repairing the roof, very little has been done to the sacred edifice, its fabric or furniture for many years. I have consulted Mr Geo. H. Fellowes Prynne, Architect of Westminster, London, who has made a careful survey of the Church and issued a Report, from which I give brief extracts:

The floor is in an extremely bad state. The flag stones are laid without concrete, on the natural soil, with the inevitable result of being uneven and damp. The vaults and graves under have caused the floor to sink several inches from the level in many places; especially is this the case near the Screen in the South Aisle. The platforms under Seats and Pews are rotten and damp. The North Nave Wall is 8 inches out of the perpendicular and settling outwards, and the Buttresses in their present condition are insufficient to prevent further settlement... The Roof of the Porch is entirely rotten and in a falling condition. The Belfry Stage of the Tower shows large cracks right through the walling on three sides, and I am strongly of the opinion that it will be shortly, if it is not at present, absolutely unsafe to ring the Bells with the walls in the present state; the cracks are of a really serious nature and are liable to increase rapidly. The Clock floor is in a very rotten condition. The 'worm' has greatly damaged, and is still damaging, the old Oak Seats, and some immediate steps should be taken to prevent the complete destruction of this really fine work. The Screen is suffering also from the same defect.

Prynne estimated the probable cost at £1,050, which sum did not include the tower and the tower arch – 'which is a separate Estimate, and if rebuilt from the higher string course would cost £500-£600, or if repaired and strengthened £250-£300'. The parish opted for strengthening rather than rebuilding the tower (and at the same time had both of the galleries removed from the church), but the debt for building work was not fully discharged for five years.

After the death in Algiers of Rev. Gutteres, the ancient preaching cross was re-dedicated by the Bishop of Crediton in 1898 in his memory: the cross' head had been found in the foundations of the Church House when it was cleared after the fire there (showing that it had fallen before that building existed), while the shaft had been built into the Rectory garden wall.

The lamp which stands beside the lych-gate steps was given in 1901 by a friend of Rev. Hay, and 'the solid and graceful stand' for it was made by Tom Bray at John Sanders' workshop at Normans Green. The rector wrote in the parish magazine that he hoped that people would donate oil for the lamp, so that it could provide light for the village during the week as well as on Sundays.

In 1902 there was more work on the church. The whole of the north wall of the nave, which had been forced outwards by the weight of the roof, was given new, deep foundations – it was found they had 'consisted only of large pebbles' – and its centre was filled with concrete in place of the original rubble filling: the roof was stabilised with new trusses of English oak. The Flemish alabaster depicting the Resurrection, which had formed part of the reredos, was moved to the western wall of the Forde aisle.

The church porch, the roof of which had rotted, was completely refurbished in 1905 as a lasting memorial to the late 'Squire', Thomas Henry Baxter of Greenend: it was during the course of this work that the broken Holy-water stoop was found under the old plaster finish.

In 1910 the floors were re-laid on a bed of cement concrete and dry rubbish, the old seats were re-fixed, and new seats and seat-backs of English oak were added to some old oak pews. Repair of the windows was begun, though the glazing was not completed until 1927. The interior plaster was also repaired and colourwashed.

After the Second World War the roofs of the nave and Forde aisle were remade; and in 1948 the lych-gate was completely restored as a memorial to Rev. H.C. Onslow, Rector of Plymtree for the previous 19 years: it was again refurbished in 1994 in memory of Edwin Martin. Land for an extension to the burial ground was purchased and, after it was cleared, levelled, pathed and walled by various groups from the village. It was consecrated by the Bishop of Crediton on 2nd May 1957.

The yew tree (rear of picture) that shades the church is over 1100 years old.

Above: Four of the painted panels at the base of the screen – the Adoration of the Magi.

Right: Close-up showing the beautiful gilded carving of the cornices and pan vaulting.

Rectors of Plymtree

The fact that Plymtree had rectors (rather than vicars) shows that it was always an independent parish, not controlled by, nor reliant upon, another religious foundation. Johel Walerande, a Sub-Deacon of Exeter Cathedral, is the first rector we know of, appointed in April 1261 under the patronage of Lady Albreda de Botrelle by Bishop Walter Bronescombe.

A year later, in May 1262, Lady Albreda appointed Gundi, a priest. Though perhaps a good rector initially, in 1284 a 'Co-adjutor' (a sort of receiver) was appointed as 'Gundi was wasting the goods of his church'; the same year Bishop Bronescombe granted his licence to Master Robert de Evesham, Archdeacon of Exeter, to receive the rents of the church lands for five years, and to have the rectory 'unless he could find a dwelling in which to live'. By 1291 the land was worth £5-6s.-8d. per annum, according to the Taxation of Pope Nicholas IV (which allowed benefices to be taxed to raise expenses for a crusade).

At some time before 1327, William atte Pole took over as rector, serving as such until his death in 1335. That December Sir (the medieval equivalent of 'Reverend') Gilbert de Sheptone, priest, was appointed under the patronage of William de Pillaunde, Parson of Kingstone, Dorset. He was also the patron of Sheptone's successor, John de Pillaunde in September 1340, who, within a week of his appointment, obtained permission from Bishop Grandisson to go to study at Oxford: he was successful in his studies, and in 1371 was appointed Penitentiary for the Deanery of Plymtree and five years later Penitentiary-General for the Archdeaconry of Exeter. (A Penitentiary was responsible for penances and dispensations.).

Sir John Tregrenewil (or Grenwyll) became rector in March 1393, his patron being Thomas Peverell, who was married to Margaret, a daughter of Sir Thomas Courtenay (a son of the Earl of Devon, who had been lord of the manor of Plymtree since 1345). Tregenewil was a typical medieval rector, being seen in the parish only to collect his tithes and rents, and leaving all pastoral duties to badly-paid curates. His two successors, from 1417, Thomas Job and Sir James Job, were in the same mould, the former vanishing for study at Oxford almost as soon as he had been appointed.

Walter Hungerford, first Lord Hungerford, married Catherine Peverell in 1422, she having become Lord of Plymtree by descent. Five years later she was patron of the new rector, Sir Robert Dunnynge. As he was 'instituted' to the Rectory in London, it seems doubtful that he ever came near the parish, unlike Sir Richard Smarte (or Smert) who followed him in June 1435. Smarte is described as 'the earliest recorded Devon musician.' It was during Smarte's rectorship that the Forde aisle was added to the church. Smarte retired in 1477 on a life pension of £4 per year 'from the fruits of the Parish Church'.

By 1477 the Hungerford/Peverell estates were in other hands as a result of the Wars of the Roses. Following the execution for treason of Thomas Hungerford, Lord of Plymtree, all his lands and rights had not, as was usual, been estreated to the King, but were 'committed to the care of his widow Alianore and his children under the trust of John, Lord Wenlok', a great Yorkist leader. But Lord Wenlok rebelled against the King and was killed at the Battle of Tewkesbury in 1471, and it would seem that Edward IV then appointed John, Lord Dynham – a special favourite – to administer them. It was Dynham who was patron of the next rector, William Reynye, who remained as such until his death in 1521.

The Hungerford family had by this time regained the lordship of Plymtree, and the next rector, Sir John Lylle, was presented under the patronage of Sir Richard Sacheverelle, second husband of Mary, Lady Hungerford. Lylle's incumbency covered the tumultuous years of the Reformation, and the Prayer Book Rebellion of 1549. He responded to Thomas Cromwell's demand to know the value of all church property, reporting in 1536 that Plymtree's church land was worth £21-18s., and the tithes £2-3s.-9$\frac{1}{2}$d. per year.

In 1554, during the reign of Mary, another Hungerford appointee, Richard Hayward, became rector. He must have followed 'the religion as set forth by her Majesty', and revived Catholic services until Queen Elizabeth succeeded in 1558. Henceforth all rectors were members of the Church of England. During the Reformation the Hungerfords sold the manor of Plymtree to Thomas Goodwyn, 'a merchant of Plymtree and London', and he passed the advowson (the right to appoint rectors) to other gentlemen in London.

Their first choice in 1567 was James More, who obviously lived in the parish since he collected all the loose sheets which since 1538 had comprised the records of baptisms, marriages and burials, and copied them into a parchment book. More died ten years later, and Master Henry Stephins took over as rector.

Thomas Payne became rector in 1591, serving for 55 years until his death in 1646 (during the Civil War). One of his daughters, Suzanna, a widow, had married his successor, the most notable of all Plymtree's rectors, Nicholas Monk. Monk was the brother of George Monk, the most effective of all Cromwell's Generals, and the key to national unity when Parliament descended into anarchy. Royalist supporters used Nicholas as go-between to pass messages to his brother enlisting his support for King Charles II's Restoration. Nicholas Monk's rewards were first to be Provost of Eton and then Bishop of Hereford; he is buried in Westminster Abbey.

Some time before 1662 John Glanvill took over the rectorship from Nicholas Monk, and on his death in 1680 Richard Long was presented by Mr Thomas Trosse, son of Nicholas Monk's wife by her first husband. The same patron presented Roger Eveleigh as rector in 1685. By 1688 the patron was King James II, 'his' choice being Mathew Mundy, who served the parish until his death in 1736; his son, also Matthew Mundy (born in the parish), followed his father and remained as rector until his death in 1759.

In order to provide livings for its married fellows, Oriel College, Oxford, had purchased the advowson for £900 from Matthew Mundy junior in 1737. Their first nominee, in 1759, was James Beaver. He obviously reverted to medieval practice since, in 1771, despite being Rector of Plymtree, he was living

John Durno Steele, appointed rector of Plymtree in 1954.

in Oxfordshire - and no doubt paying a pittance to a curate to carry out his duties. He held on to the Rectory until his death in 1777, being succeeded by the next Oriel College appointee, John Fleming. Fleming died eight years later and was followed by Daniel Veysie, who served the parish until his death in 1817.

The next rector was Edward Offspring Holwell who, in 1820, sued Thomas Blake of Greenend, John Harris of Sanguishayes, and other landowners, for failing to pay their tithes – which amounted in total to less than £200 a year. The case took ten years before being decided in his favour: the defendants had to pay his costs as well as their own, being an incredible £1948-9s.-9d.

His successor from 1832 was the colourful Joseph Dornford. In his youth he ran away from his Cambridge home to join the army, and while fighting in the Peninsula War (under Wellington), he was commissioned – a most unusual thing in those days when commissions were almost exclusively obtained by purchase. After the war he entered Oriel College and received Holy Orders. In 1847 he was honoured by being made Prebendary of Exeter Cathedral, while retaining the rectorship of Plymtree. He was apparently a High-Church man, who tried to convert the parish

but failed – except for the women; he was a big, handsome man, and unmarried, and his introduction of carved woodwork (such as the wall-panels around the altar), metal-work and old pieces of painted glass into the church (and in the Parsonage House) apparently attracted the ladies. He had firm ideas about how the parish in general should be run, and Parish Vestry meetings were described as 'tumults'. The village men took direct action, candlesticks vanished from the altar, and lads were encouraged to despoil the shrubs and pines in his garden.

In 1868 Dornford died, to be succeeded by Thomas Mozley, whose wife was the sister of Cardinal Newman. Mozley supplemented his income by writing leaders for *The Times*. Each day he would drive to Sidmouth Junction (now Feniton), receive his subject by telegraph, write his piece in a nearby hotel, and despatch it by the 5 o'clock train to London. He was so well thought of by the publisher that, when he retired in 1880, he was granted a pension of £800. Mozley was so appalled by the lack of education among Plymtree's poor, that he paid over £1600 to build and equip a school and master's house, and then paid the teacher's wages.

The splendidly-named Fowler Babington Blogg took over from Thomas Mozley in 1880, but he only stayed for three years before his brother Arthur replaced him. Arthur continued to support the school, and was generally well thought of.

George Gilbert Gutteres took over when Arthur Mozley died in 1892, but after an extremely busy and effective five years, during which he started repairs to the church, and founded the *Parish Magazine*, he exchanged rectorships to move to Suffolk: however, before taking up his new post he went on holiday to Algiers, where he died. The ancient parish cross was discovered shortly afterwards, and re-erected in his memory.

The parson from Suffolk was Edgar Hay, a man with a great interest in local history, who transcribed the parish registers and many of the contents of the parish chest. Despite becoming Archdeacon of Barnstaple, he maintained contact with Plymtree after he was succeeded by Humphrey Cedric Onslow in 1929; in 1940 Hay published his transcript of the Parish Registers, and he was buried in the churchyard in 1950. Onslow saw the parish through the war, filling many of the parish offices and handling the affairs and problems of evacuees. He worked hard to build up funds for the church roof, and was a keen proponent of Christian unity. He remained rector until his death in 1948, when his many friends and parishioners restored the ancient lych-gate in his memory.

Crichton Willoughby McDouall followed him. A New Zealander, McDouall and his wife had served as missionaries in China for 40 years, being imprisoned by the Japanese for 3$\frac{1}{2}$ years at the end of his work there. They retired to Dorset in 1953 (though they, too, had their remains interred at Plymtree), and Mr McDouall's short-lived successor in January 1954 was Gilderoy Davison, former Vicar of Bocking, Essex, then well-known as a writer of popular fiction, who died in May of the same year.

It was not until August 1954 that a new rector was appointed, in the person of John Durno Steele (*pictured on page 35*), who had previously ministered in the Falkland Islands. He was an extremely popular and active rector, who received many gifts on his retirement.

In 1963 R.I.N. Edwards (a Welshman, whose first names were never used, being always referred to as 'Rin') became rector. He was a brilliant scholar, fluent in many living and dead languages – he had helped to translate the Dead Sea Scrolls – and never happier than when engaged in intellectual debate: any subject would do. To supplement his stipend, he taught at Exeter Cathedral School and, since he had no transport of his own, would invite himself to travel with any parishioner driving to or from the city. He was very well-liked, but something of a 'fish out of water' in a rural parish. When he retired he lived at 2 Greenend Cottages until his death in 1985.

George Ridding was Rev. Edwards' successor in 1981, becoming the first rector of Plymtree to take charge also of the parishes of Broadhembury and Payhembury. Alan Roberts, who had served as a Royal Navy officer in submarines, came to serve Plymtree (and also Broadhembury and Payhembury) from a Birmingham parish in 1989.

One of Rev. Smert's 11 carols of the 1440s, Reproduced by kind permission of Stainer & Bell Ltd., P.O. Box 110, Victoria House, 23 Gruneisen Road, Finchley, London.

Church Music

In 1435 Richard Smarte (or Smert) became the rector for Plymtree. Smarte is described as 'the earliest recorded Devon musician; with John Truelove, of whose origins nothing seems to be known, he composed carols to be found in a manuscript in the British Museum.' In all there are 11 of Smarte's Carols in the B.M. manuscript [ref: Add.MS.5665], which were published in 1952 in the volume *Medieval Carols*, edited by John Stevens for the *Musica Britannica* series (*see left*). These works, later known as the Plymtree Carols, were sung at the annual carol service in the Parish Church until fairly recently.

A large gallery was erected at the back of the church in 1719, to provide accommodation for the musicians and the two-part choir needed to lead the singing of the metrical psalms then in vogue.

The churchwardens' accounts give an indication of the development of music for church services. In 1781 John Critchett, the Parish Clerk who seems also to have been the music master, purchased 'strings for the Bass Viol' (now known as a cello), and in 1786 he spent 12s. on music. A hautboy and bassoon are mentioned from 1790, and 32 years later clarinets joined the band. The hautboy seems to have been particularly hard on reeds, as the churchwardens had to buy new ones two or three times a year.

It is likely that there was a choir in the church from at least the Restoration of Charles II in 1660 until the rectorship of Joseph Dornford. Though fond of giving long and powerful sermons, the choir encroached more and more on his time and one Sunday in the 1840s he took advantage of a pause in their singing to exclaim, 'Enough of that': the choir walked out, never to return during Dornford's time. Not until Rev. Thomas Mozley took over the Rectory in 1868, was the choir to be reinstated.

After the death in August 1883 of Charles Mozley of Derby, brother of both Rev. Thomas Mozley and his near successor, Rev. Arthur Mozley, an organ was presented to Plymtree Church by his representatives, 'knowing that this destination would be much in accordance with his wishes'. This instrument was believed to have been made in the 1700s by Samuel Green, a famous organ builder. From 1892 the organist – who was paid a salary of £2 per year – also acted as choir mistress. Young members of the congregation were paid a small sum to pump the organ, and may have joined the annual choir outings. By 1906, Miss Agnes J. Robinson was paid £6 per annum as organist, and the choir, led by Mrs Eva Trefusis of Hayne House, were members of the East Devon Choral Union. In 1917, Miss Rosamund Huyshe of Clyst Hydon Manor became organist and when she retired in 1957 there was a special service for her at which Mrs Alice Farnell (a member of the choir for 60 years) presented her with a bunch of flowers.

Throughout the inter-war period choir outings were a highlight, and with the help of subsidies from church funds, the members travelled far and wide. Photographs taken on these outings show that hats were essential accoutrements in the 1920s and '30s.

The 1883 organ was fitted with an electric blower on New Year's Day 1958, rendering 'redundant' Ron Cleal and Michael Hill – the last in the line of some 50 young people who had spent their Sundays pumping away to help the organist make music. But the old organ had by this time seen better days, and the following year Kenneth Burge, of Rickmansworth, Herts, kindly offered to give the church one of the 'Precentor' electronic organs he manufactured, in memory of his late uncle William Farnell. He installed the new organ on 1st July 1959, and it was dedicated the following day when it was played by a famous organist, Mr J.E. Swift, who also gave a recital after evensong. The old organ was later removed to Shirwell, near Barnstaple.

Two decades later another replacement was required, and one was found for sale at Shaldon United Reformed Church. The rector, Rev. R.I.N. Edwards led an appeal for money to buy it, over £2000 was raised by parishioners and this, with other donations, enabled it to be purchased and installed in 1979. After Rev. Edwards died in 1985, a brass plate was fixed to the instrument in memory of him and his efforts.

Today, despite the fact that the organ is in perfect working order, guitars and synthesisers are in vogue, and *Hymns Ancient & Modern* have been displaced by more trendy ditties, to the discomfiture of traditional Anglicans.

Plymtree Church Choir

Mrs Hay with the choir after the First World War. Left to right – top row: Ellen Pratt, Ivy Ford, Mrs Hay, Dorothy Knight, Elizabeth Cross; bottom row: Kathleen Pratt, Florence Clarke, Annie Clarke.

The choir c.1922. Left to right – back row: Frank Knight, Lou Pratt, Nell Pratt, Mr Hamlin; middle row: Alice Burge, Myrtle Leigh, Lizzie Kant, Lily Leigh, Ivy Vinnicombe; front row: Marjorie Marshall, Annie Clarke, Kathleen Pratt, Elsie Pratt.

*A choir outing to Teignmouth, c.1925. Left to right – back row: Ted Widgery, Kathleen Pratt, Nellie Gilliland;
bottom row: George Minifie, Gertrude Minifie, Annie Clarke, Phyllis Minifie, Eniz Nichols.*

Plymtree choir outing to Teignmouth on 9th July 1928.

The Church Tower

Judging by the date of the first bells, the tower was probably added to the church in the 1420s. Like the rest of the building, it was built of Thorverton trap and 'local rubble', with Beer freestone doorways and windows. It rises to nearly 60 feet, has slightly buttressed corners and a crenellated parapet, also of Beer stone. According to answers given in a questionnaire returned from the parish to Dean Milles in the 1750s, the trap-stone was 'brought from a hill between Plimtree & Cullumbton.'

Half-way up, on the east side, is a niche containing a statue of the Virgin and Child, the head of the latter being missing; it fell to the ground in 1953, and Rev. McDouall put it in 'a safe place' – now unknown. When the statue was restored in 1993, a crown which was found behind the main work was placed on the Virgin's head; also found were a wooden top, a small leather-bound ball, and a number of stones: village tradition has it that the statue was, at the turn of the century, used for target practice by small boys.

There are three stages to the tower and a small ancient door in the south wall gives access to a clockwise-circular staircase (the correct rotation for defence by a right-handed swordsman!) of 40 very irregular stone steps leading to the former ringing chamber, which now contains only the clock and the weights which drive it.

This has an even more ancient wooden door, on which the marks of the adze used to form it can clearly be seen. This room is lit by a small window and the great thickness of the wall is obvious. From here a steep wooden ladder rises to a trap door giving access to the bell chamber: it is very dangerous to enter this chamber, even when the bells are 'down' (i.e. at rest, hanging downwards). Ten feet along a 6-inch wide beam, with bells close by, is another short, steep ladder rising to the trap door to the roof, which is lead-covered. Some of the stones forming the parapet of the roof have initials carved into them - i.e. 'WNC' and 'AR', probably stonemasons; the name 'J. Dimond' and initials 'BP' (for Benjamin Parris), both church-wardens in 1830, also appear.

In the 1780s, the Rev. Richard Polwhele wrote to all incumbents and gentry in Devon to obtain data for a *History of Devonshire*, which he published in 1793. Plymtree rector John Fleming M.A. wrote that the tower was 'square built, and crampt round the top with iron, being very much shattered'. At that time the tower had only four bells.

Three of the walls were found to have large cracks through them in 1894, so the tower had to be further strengthened with heavy cast-iron beams, inside and out, held together with 2-inch diameter iron studding and massive nuts: the whole job cost £359, plus £15 for a lightning conductor. Despite all the ironwork, the tower still sways slightly when the bells are rung – though perfectly safely.

The 1895 refurbishment included the creation of four new pinnacles at the corners of the tower, the original ones having weathered too much to be safe; much of the stone-work of the large west window was also re-carved. The present ringing area on the ground floor was described as 'little short of a disgrace; for some time it has been used chiefly as a tool shed and a coke-hole'; this was cleared out and a new, wind-tight tower door was fitted.

Ted Widgery raising the flag on St George's Day, 1993. Then aged 82, Ted had for many years taken responsibility for the flag and winding the clock.

The Bells of Plymtree Church

We know that there were three bells in the tower from at least 1432, since in that year the parishioners brought an action in the Court of Chancery, alleging fraud against them by John Forde, who on their behalf had ordered three bells from Robert Norton of Exeter, and paid him £31-6s.-8d., being £1-7s. per hundred pounds weight of bell-metal. The parishioners were doubtful that the bells weighed the 2322 pounds claimed, and found that their weight was in fact 1800 pounds. They alleged that the two had, 'by ontrewe ymagynacion coveyn and disseit' conspired together to defraud them of the £7 extra that had been paid. Sadly, we do not know the result of this action.

Following the 'Prayer Book' or 'Western' Rebellion in 1549, Edward VI's Protector Somerset, sent Sir Peter Carewe, Sir Gawen Carewe, Anthony Harvy and Thomas Haigh to the county as his commissioners, to make sure that no Popish books or objects were to be found in parish churches. In the 'Return of Church Goods for the County of Devon', dated 3rd March 1553, they recorded, 'Parochia de Plymptree: iiij belles yn the tower their.' Three of these bells were those mentioned above; the fourth was cast in 1549 by Roger Semson of Aish Prior's foundry in Somerset; weighing 690 pounds (6cwt:0 qrs:18 lbs), it is still in use as the fourth bell, bearing his mark and the legend 'Ave Maria Gratia Plenia, R.S.'. Polwhele's history describes the church as still having four bells in the 1780s.

A new bell, weighing 863 pounds (7:2:23), was cast in 1669 to replace one of the older ones; it bore the legend, 'Christopher Baker, John Tilley, church-wardens. TP Exon 1669', the initials being those of Thomas Pennington III, a member of a family which cast bells at Exeter for two centuries.

In March 1826 the wooden bell-cage needed replacing, and the parishioners were invited to consider adding a fifth bell: they decided that the expense would be too great to be raised by a rate, but authorised the churchwardens to make room in the new frame for an extra bell, and to raise money by the church rate for the installation of the extra bell if such could be purchased through voluntary subscriptions. By the following month the churchwardens had received estimates from Messrs. J. Mears of London for the re-casting of one bell, and the supply of a new one, and these were accepted. The lighter bell of the original four weighed 678 pounds (6:0:6), and that was re-cast to 555 pounds (4:3:23); Mears charged £17-9s., allowing 1s. per pound for the old bell and charging 1s.-4d. per pound for the new one. The new bell of 648 pounds (5:3:4) was paid for by public subscription, of which there is no record: on the assumption that Mr Mears charged 1s.-4d. per pound weight, the cost would have been £43-2s.

The bell cage (described in the accounts as the 'ringing gallery') cost £9, plus £1-1s.-1d. for ironwork; two clappers added £2-2s. and five new bell-ropes £1-8s.-6d.; the erection of the bells cost £24-1s.-7d. All these expenses caused the church rate to rise dramatically.

Both the 1826 bells are marked 'Edward Offspring Holwell, rector', and bear the maker's name. The lighter one, hung as the new treble, names Charles Harward and Thomas Griffin as churchwardens, and states, 'Erected and raised by subscription 1826.' The other names William Brice and Edmund Middleton as churchwardens. Three years later the 1240-pound (11:0:8) tenor bell was re-cast, being marked 'J. Mears of London fecit 1829. Revd Edward Offspring Holwell, minister. John Dimond, Benjamin Parris, churchwardens.'

Until 1895 the five bells were rung from what is now the clock chamber, but when in that year the tower was strengthened, with room for a sixth bell, it was decided that it was better to use longer ropes and to ring from the ground floor. A Mr Harry Stokes of Woodbury built huge new frames of elm for six bells, resting on oak, 12-inch square beams, for £88-1s., and added a new treble bell of 546 pounds (4:2:14) for £35-13s. The other bells were re-hung as 2nd [1826]; 3rd [1826]; 4th [1549]; 5th [1669] and tenor [1829] in this pattern:

```
    4 |   | 5
  3  _    | 6
  2  _  _  1
```

The 'Re-opening of the Bells' was combined with the Harvest Festival on Thursday 26th September 1895. Mr Stokes had obviously not yet been paid for the sixth bell, as there was a collection for the new bell fund. The Plymtree ringers were: treble, Charles Knight; 2nd, William Bickley; 3rd William Salter; 4th William Stiling; 5th Richard Pratt; tenor, Walter John Salter. Ringers from Clyst Hydon, Ottery, Feniton, Talaton and elsewhere also rang. A tea was provided by Mr Jarvis (the village baker) at the Rectory, where there was dancing to the Payhembury Band, and games for the children. In the evening another dance was held at the school.

From October 1937 John Taylor and Co. of Loughborough removed and tuned the bells, and added roller-bearings, at a cost of £179 raised by voluntary subscriptions. They were re-dedicated at a special service on 30th April 1938.

On 23rd June 1985 a full-height screen dividing the ringing chamber from the nave was dedicated to the memory of Gordon Lear and William Persey, churchwardens 1939-1946 and 1947-1971 respectively. The screen shields the waiting congregation from the 'calls' of the ring-leader, and from the mechanical noise of the bell-ropes moving through their guides.

The main purpose of church bells was, of course, to call the parishioners to services, but it was also the custom for the sexton to toll the tenor bell every minute for an hour after a death. At the funeral, the bell was likewise tolled for an hour – striking 4, 4, 4 for a male and 4, 3, 4 for a female. He was paid by the relatives or, if the deceased was a pauper, by the overseers: the cost was 1 shilling (the same as his charge for digging a grave). As well as ringing the bells, the sexton was paid to keep them well greased.

On 9th October 1746 the overseers of the poor paid 6s. 'for a hogshead of cider for the ringers' – possibly because they had rung a peal or more to celebrate the end of the Stuart threat – Bonny Prince Charlie having escaped to France the previous month.

As in the majority of churches in Devon and Cornwall (and, for some reason, in Barnsley, Yorkshire) the ringing style practised in Plymtree has always been 'call-change ringing', where the team leader calls each change in the order the bells will 'speak' during a peal. When call-change ringing is practised perfectly there is a clear rhythm, the interval between each bell speaking being the same, even though the 'melody' changes. (The 'method' system of ringing concentrates on the ringers changing the order of their bells in the ring with every pull of the rope, and the rhythm counts for little; the tower captains of Plymtree have given 'method' short shrift.).

When the sixth bell was added in 1895, competition ringing became a possibility, and Rev. George Gutteres decided that the ringers' activities should be regulated. At a meeting at the Parsonage on Monday 7th October that year the following rules were agreed to by the then ringers:

I. All new members shall be elected by a majority of existing members, subject to the approval of the Rector. The Rector reserves to himself the right to exclude from the ringing anyone guilty of misconduct.

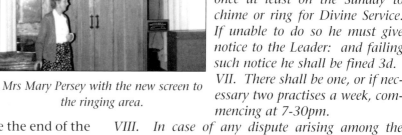

Mrs Mary Persey with the new screen to the ringing area.

II. That there be an Annual Meeting of members within a month of Christmas, at which the accounts for the past year shall be presented, and the Committee for the ensuing year elected to carry out the spirit of these rules. The Committee to consist of the Rector as President, Bellman as Leader, and three members to be elected by the members. One of the Committee to be chosen as Treasurer.

III. All monies received by the Treasurer shall be put into a Common Fund and divided as the Majority of the Ringers decide at the Annual Meeting. In case of a member leaving without notice, no share to be allotted.

IV. That the Leader shall have sole management in the belfry during the time of ringing and shall prevent any irreverence or unseemly language or behaviour.

V. Every ringer who is in the Belfry during the time of ringing or chiming for Divine Service shall attend that Service.

VI. Every Ringer shall attend once at least on the Sunday to chime or ring for Divine Service. If unable to do so he must give notice to the Leader: and failing such notice he shall be fined 3d.

VII. There shall be one, or if necessary two practises a week, commencing at 7-30pm.

VIII. In case of any dispute arising among the Ringers the matter shall be referred to the Committee whose decision shall be final.

IX. That these rules shall be agreed to and signed by every member in a book kept for that purpose.

X. These rules shall not be altered but by a majority of members at a meeting.

The rules were amended on 29th December 1902 to include the fine of 3d. in rule VI, and an additional rule was added and agreed to by the then ringers.

XI. Money received for ringing at Weddings shall not be put into the Common Fund, but shall be divided at once among those who ring the peals and these shall be appointed by the Committee. Ringing at Weddings shall cease at 7-30pm.

They were amended again on 31st January 1925 when, apart from the 3d. fine being abolished, rule VII was changed:

VII. That practises shall be arranged as necessary, commencing at 7-30pm and ending not later than 9pm.

It is clear that the Common Fund referred to

in rule III came from a collection made among the principal church-goers in the parish. There are records of 'Subscriptions' being collected every year until 1990. In 1902 they amounted to £2-19s., while £116 was given in 1990: an interesting donation appears in the 1910 accounts, when 2s.-6d. was given by 'an English Catholic'. Originally providing an honorarium for the ringers, from 1925 the money mainly helped to fund transport for an annual outing, and to competitions. Some who were Plymtree ringers until recently have happy memories of convivial evenings spent going from farm to farm collecting subscriptions, and being offered liquid hospitality at each one.

The practice evenings paid off in May 1935, when the team of Harry Baker, Tom Bray, Bill Bray, Frank Pratt, Ted Robinson, Frank Goff and Ted Widgery went to Kingsteignton to ring for the Devon Shield. On the 4th they got through to the final, which they won on the 25th. The total cost to the Common Fund was £4, but the value to the team was inestimable.

But success was not very regular: on 30th April 1960 at Upton Pyne the Plymtree team of George Knight, Roy Cleal, Bill Lovering, Ron Wright, Bill Radford and Ted Widgery won the John Leach Cup; and on 1st June 1968 George Knight, Roy and Ron Cleal, Bill Lovering, Herbie Minifie and Walt Radford brought home the Dunsford Shield.

That some of the ringers were exceptionally dedicated to the art was recognised in 1980 when the rector, Rev. R.I.N. Edwards, presented commemorative plates to Bill Lovering, Ted Widgery, Herbie Minifie and George Knight to mark 50 years of their ringing together. The following year George Knight's contribution to ringing in the county was marked by his being made President of the Devon Association of Bellringers.

Competition ringing eventually led, as it has done in many other towers, to a lack of fresh blood; the Captain, George Knight, saw that because age was catching up with the competition team, ringing at Plymtree could cease, and he began to recruit and train new ringers. This is not easy today with the many pressures on everybody's time and it has been an uphill struggle to assemble sufficient people to form a team. George retired from the Captaincy in January 1998, and Ron Cleal carried on the work he had begun. There is now confidence that there will be sufficient Plymtree Ringers to ring a peal on the first day of the new millennium – and bells will ring out over Plymtree 568 years after they were first heard here.

Top: The Plymtree Ringers display the Devon Association Shield they won at Kingsteignton on 25th May 1935. Left to right – top row: Ted Widgery, Fred Goff, Harry Baker, Bill Pratt, Bill Bray; bottom: Tom Bray, Ted Robinson.

Centre: Ringers' Dinner at Hayne House, c.1968. Left to right – standing: Herbie Minifie, John Hussey, Gordon Blackmore, Ron Cleal, John Baten, Roy Cleal, Ken Blackmore, Walt Radford, Ted Widgery. Seated: General Schreiber (churchwarden), George Knight (Tower Captain), Rev R.I.N. Edwards (rector), Bill Persey (churchwarden).

Right: Winning back the George Facey Shield at St Paul's, Tiverton, 13th May 1978. Left to right – top: Bill Lovering, Ron Cleal, Ted Widgery; bottom: John Bambury, George Knight, Roy Cleal.

The Plymtree Ringers for the Coronation of King George V, 1911.
Left to right – top row: unknown, Tom Bray, Jack Churchill, Richard Pratt, Rev. Edgar Hay;
bottom row: Fred Pearcey, Bill Pearcey (his son in front), Bill Bickley, Charles Knight, Walter John Salter.

50 years of ringing together. Left to right: Bill Lovering, Ted Widgery, Herbie Minifie, George Knight with commemora-
tive plates presented to them by Rev. R.I.N. Edwards on behalf of the Parochial Church Council in December 1980.

The Church Clock

The tower clock was constructed and installed in 1792/3, at a cost to the Parish of £27-6s.-0d. It was made by William Upjohn (1754-1812), one of a family of silversmiths, clock- and watch-makers of Fore Street, Exeter, and it seems that ours is the only tower clock he made for a Devonshire church. It is probably the oldest working example of a wrought iron, horizontal-framed 'birdcage' tower clock in the county – there are other similar clocks (e.g. at Modbury) but they have been taken out of use and are merely on display. Originally it was driven by stone weights attached to ropes, and needed to be wound every day by the Sexton, but in 1896/7 a Mr Reid of Exeter converted it to an eight-day movement, powered by iron weights suspended on wire ropes in double pulleys. (One of the original stone weights survives in the clock chamber.).

The frame consists of two rectangles 30 feet by 12 feet, made of iron strips about $1^1/_2$ feet wide and $^1/_4$ foot thick, 'welded' together at the corners by a blacksmith. These are separated horizontally by 24-foot corner pillars made of 1-foot square iron, into which bearings have been forced to take the driving-rope wheels and gears, and eight hand-made nuts hold the whole thing together. All the other gear shafts for both the going and striking trains run in huge brass bearings set into iron straps bolted vertically to the long sides of the top and bottom frames: one pair of these straps is 'T' shaped, to take the 'scape wheel shaft'.

The anchor escapement runs in a fixed bearing at the rear (above the frame) and a bearing bolted to the top of the front of the frame, which also supports the pendulum. This gives a beat of 2.7 seconds. The going train works through 9:1 and 10:1 gears to a brass gear, supported in a moveable bearing clamped to the bottom frame at the back of the clock, which makes one revolution per hour. A short shaft runs through a bearing (screwed to the wooden frame below the front of the clock) to a carden (universal) joint.

Since the clock is mounted on the north wall and the face on the south, a span of some 10 feet has to be crossed. A 4-foot rod runs from the front of the clock to a carden joint, mounted on a suspended beam; this is connected to a bevel gear which could take another drive to a face on the east or west sides of the tower. A 6-foot shaft then continues across the tower to another universal joint forming part of the system which controls the hands. There is a large rod bolted to the shaft in opposition to the minute-hand to act as a counterbalance. The hour-hand is mounted on a tube which runs through the 4-foot thick wall from the face to this assembly, while the minute-hand works through a rod, driven directly by the clock shaft and running through the hour-hand tube. A gear on the end of the minute-hand shaft drives the hour-hand tube through a 60:1 gearing system bolted to the inside of the south wall: this assembly also acts as the inner bearing for both hands. The striking side is activated by a complex set of levers, and when released operates through a count-wheel and then several levers and wires to cause a heavy iron hammer (about the size of a carpenter's mallet) to strike the outside of the tenor bell when that bell is 'down'. The hammer is held slightly off the bell by a short leaf spring, thus allowing a clear note: when the bells are being rung, a cable in the ringing chamber allows the hammer to be pulled back out of harm's way. Only the hours are chimed, there being no mechanism to ring the quarters.

The following letter appeared in the *Parish Magazine* for April 1924:

'Dear Friends and Neighbours,
My good friend, Mr Frank Knight, can do no more for me, as I am very run down and worn out. Will someone kindly take round the hat for me and collect a nice little sum to set me going, and let my voice be heard once more.
Your faithful friend and servant,
THE CHURCH CLOCK.'

Edward Coe took up the plea, and collected £20-5s., which was sufficient to pay for the clock mechanism to be overhauled, and he also paid for the face to be re-painted.

The clock was re-bushed and overhauled in 1995 by *(left to right, below)* Tony Eames, Will Roberts and Derek Mason, but the striking mechanism was not then replaced. In 1998 the clock stopped, due to a dry outer bearing for the hour hand: a huge ladder had to be hired, and Dave Barrow spent several hours forcing grease into the bearing. The hour chimes will be ringing out by the millennium.

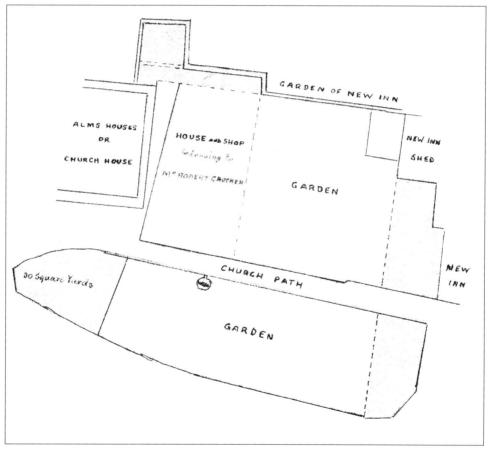

Top: Plymtree Church Houses c.1910. (The publican's daughter, Marjorie Marshall, appears to the left with her pony.).
Above: Plan annexed to the conveyance of when the Feoffees purchased 80 square yards of the shop garden in front of the Church House, and access for the occupants to the well owned by the shop (1899).

Chapter 6: Church House and Charities

On 20th September 1532, George, Earl of Huntingdon (also Lord Hastings, Hungerford, Botram and Molens), then lord of the manor of Plymtree, granted a piece of land lying in the east and south parts of the churchyard and measuring 200 feet by 100 feet, to seven 'worthy men' in the village. They were Richard Webber, John Sanders, John and Richard Tye, Richard Crosse, John Salter and Robert Whyte, and the grant was in the form of a lease for 100 years at a rental of fourpence per annum, payable at the Feast of St Michael the Archangel (29th September). No purpose is stated in the deed, but it is clear from later deeds that the Church House was then built there.

This was described by Rev. Edgar Hay, rector, in notes he made in 1905, as follows:

Church Houses filled the place of the modern parish room, and this one consisted of a central hall, where the guild meetings, and feasts, Church Ales, and village entertainments were held, with a kitchen at one end, in the huge fireplace of which old people tell of a sheep being roasted whole on the coronation of William IV, and at the West end a buttery with above it the Vestry Room, entered from outside by a bridge and stairs from the churchyard.

Because the land was 'leased', new lessees were required when the majority had died. Thus on 1st January 1558, in the reign of Philip and Mary, John Salter as the sole survivor of the original grantees assigned the lease 'of the said pece of Land and all Edyfyces and buyldings made & putt upon the same' to eight new trustees. They were John and Robert Crosse, William Holman, Edward May, Robert Webber, Charles Harward, Robert Rowland and John Salter the younger. (This deed quotes the term granted by Lord Huntingdon as being 'XX hundreth [i.e. 2000] yeares', but this seems to be an error).

By the 1st June 1597, with Queen Elizabeth I on the throne, William Holman, Robert Crosse, Edward May and John Salter 'the sonne' were the surviving lessees. By a deed they granted a lease to John Middleton for 35 years (or his life or the lives of his wife 'Elenore, or of his daughter Mearie Middleton or of Elenore Drewe, daughter of John Drewe of Plymptree'). This was in respect of 'one Sufficiente Dwellinge house' newly erected at John Middleton's own expense on a plot 70 feet 'easte

fromc the chimney of the Churchehouse' and 'ffortie foot from the Northside of the same land'. Middleton paid £4 for the lease of his house 'and Arbegarden [presumably an orchard] theire unto adioyning', and an annual rent of 6s.-8d. Since Rev. Hay described the great fireplace as being at the east end of the Church House, this house must have been built on the site now occupied by the village post office. Part of Middleton's lease, however, included 'all that Chamber ...erected over the great Churchehouse lytching...in the afterend of the same Churche-house' – this was, perhaps, what later became the Vestry Room described by Rev. Hay.

Robert Crosse and John Salter were the last surviving lessees when, on 20th May 1607, they assigned their lease to new appointees, being their sons Robert Crosse and John Salter, Thomas Tye, Andrew Holman, James Harwoode, John Wright and Abraham Webber. It is not clear what happened to these lessees.

Some 11 years later, on 10th November 1619, Charles Ford, Gent, and Phillipp Salter, Yeoman, both 'of Plymptree', purchased for £12 a 2000-year lease of the Church House land from the successors in title of George, Lord Hungerford, being Sir Fulke Buttrie of Marston St Lawrence, Northamptonshire and Sir John John Powlet of Hidestreat, 'Southamptonshire'. The yearly rental was to be £2, payable at the Feast of St Michael the Archangel 'if it be demaunded'; since the deed gave no right of re-entry for non-payment, it is clear that the grantees had no intention of demanding the rent. The most interesting point of this deed, however, is that it locates the buildings then on the site, viz 'that building on the East side of the Church stile, commonly called the Church House' and 'all that shedd or cottage on the West side of the said Church stile, together with the Garden thereunto adioyning lying on the West and North sides of the said Cottage'.

Of this cottage on the west side of the lych-gate, nothing physical now remains, but there is a tiny faded photograph from the last century which shows the end of a small two-storey thatched cottage there, with a man in a stove-pipe hat standing outside (*see page 12*). In 1780, John Pollard paid land tax on a value of 1s.-0d. for the 'Parish House', which may have been this property. The Tithe Apportionment of 1842 describes the 'Poors Cottages' in the plural, while the accompanying map shows the building divided into three. The 1851 census records four families, including one with five children, and four elderly single women (one of whom was bedridden), squashed into what the enumerator called the 'Alms Houses': life there must have been very unpleasant.

Rev. Thomas Mozley, rector 1868-1880, has recorded that he purchased 'some wretched hovels' from the Feoffees during his rectorship (in order to widen the road by the church), which were certainly these cottages, for which it appears he paid about £140.

The next deed relating to Church House is dated 20th April 1637 – towards the end of Charles I's reign – when Philip Salter as surviving lessee appointed as his successors Charles Ford, Robert Land, Robert Webber, John Salter, William Lane, William Pratt, Richard Harwood and Thomas Boucher (alias Skinner).

In 1662, by the will of Mrs Mary Crosse, widow of Robert, the Elmore Meadow was left upon trust for ever 'to aid and support Two Poor People and towards apparelling the same'. This small field of three-quarters of a statute acre was farmed by the owners of Greenend, who provided cloth in excess of its true rental value to be given to two poor men, chosen at a parish meeting each Christmas. Robert Land and Thomas Boucher (alias Skinner) survived their co-lessees, and on 1st October 1691 passed on trusteeship of the Church House land to George Ford, John Land, John Salter, John Harward, Richard Moxey, John Boucher (alias Skinner), Robert Salter and Ames Wilcox.

John Land, one of the younger sons of Robert Land of Woodbere Court, was apprenticed in the 1640s to a goldsmith in Fleet Street, London. There he learned not only that skill but also the art of banking, since goldsmiths' shops were well-protected and had strong-boxes, and were thus safe places for merchants to deposit their working capital. Mr Land became wealthy, and in 1676 he leased a house he owned at 1 Fleet Street to personal friends, who founded Childs Bank there. When he died in 1697, he left many bequests, including some to Plymtree. He gave £100 'to be put out at Interest on good security for the benefitt and use of three poor honest men and two poor honest women inhabitants of the parrish of Plymtree... And the interest thereof to be paid to the said five poor people halfe yearly Equally for ever.' (That interest usually came to £2-10s., in those happy days of 'steady money', so each pauper chosen by the Parish Vestry received the considerable sum of 10s.).

Land's instructions led to the creation of the Plymtree trusts for the poor, and the Feoffees (the old name for trustees) have continued as a body to this day. A painted board, formerly on the north wall in the church but now in the vestry room, records '1702: William Hole, Robert Veryard, Robert Salter, William Helman, Joan Helman, Bernard Wright, Richard Ford, George Harward, John Skinner, Roger Ford, Rev'd. Nicholas Monck and Robert Salter, in different donations gave £85.' It is clear that this is a list made in 1702 of donations given over previous years, since Nicholas Monck died in 1662.

That money, together with £40 from the poor rate and John Land's £100, a total of £225, was used to purchase land at Clyst William. The Feoffees still have a copy of the deed by which that land was sold in 1641 by Katherine Farrant of Feniton to her son Bernard Wright of Broadhembury, for £40. The land consisted of four fields, two called the Marlespitt, one named Pickinhill and one the Beathaye, in all totalling $16^1/_2$ acres. The rental from these fields was 'to be given away in Linen at the Discretion of the Feoffees together with ye Minister of the Parish, after Mr Land's Donation be fulfilled.'

The same painted board records other donations for the poor:

1720 Andrew Crosse, Esqr, by his last Will, gave the REEVE MEADOW towards the Relief of the Poor for ever. The Rent to be distributed annually.
[The Reeve Meadow was a small field of 3 roods, 7 perches]
Anne Veysie bequeathed £100 to the Poor of the parish of Plymtree, the interest of the same to be distributed on the 25th August annually at the Discretion of the Rector of the Parish.

It is strange that the board does not record a bequest of £20, made in 1772 by Dorothy Mundy, daughter of the Rev. Matthew Mundy, who directed that the interest from the money be expended in purchasing shoes for two poor women of the parish, though it includes that of Miss Ann Veysie, whose gift was made by her Will as late as 1857. Miss Penelope Gertrude Veysie added a bequest of a further £100 in 1891, both women directing that the interest be distributed 'as directed by the Rector and Churchwardens'.

The Charity Commission intervened in 1867 to ensure that all the Plymtree charities were tightly-run, setting out a scheme which had to be followed; they also allowed the Elmore Meadow to be sold, for £70, and the proceeds invested. The last of the Victorian bequests was from Mrs Mary Dyer, who in 1894 gave £200, the interest to be used to purchase blankets and warm clothing to poor parishioners at Christmas.

From the general funds, 48 paupers benefited at Easter 1898 from gifts of dowlas (coarse linen for sheets or shirts), and two of coats, at a cost of £12-3s. A similar number of gifts was distributed each Easter and winter.

In 1908 Rev. Hay convinced the Feoffees to sell all the lands held in trust (with the exception of the Poor's Meadow at Clyst William) to Devon County Council 'to provide smallholdings for small farmers'. The £520 received was invested in government Stock, the interest of about £13 per year being spent on gifts of blankets, flannel and boots, which were distributed by the rector at Christmas to children attending catechising, to widows and to aged men. (All the fields sold to the County Council were sold on to larger farmers within a few years.). That these various charities continued to be distributed into modern times, however, is shown by the churchwardens' accounts for them for 1916-1923.

On 10th June 1895 the Church House (by then including three dwellings for the poor, plus the vestry room) was destroyed by a fire, and with it six cottages next door – some incorporating shops – where the village stores now stands. The Church House was replaced by a red brick building, providing a vestry room and subsidised accommodation for elderly villagers – originally for five, but after remodelling in 1970, for three.

Strangely, the new building had neither garden nor water supply, so in 1899 the rector and others negotiated with Robert Crocker, the shop owner, and for £1 secured both 80 square yards of his garden situated in front of the Church House, and the right of the occupants to draw water from the well (which still exists) outside the shop door; although the garden only cost £1, a total of £31-18s.-3d. was then spent to fence it.

The Feoffees still manage the Church House, aided by their Clerk, Lesley Pettitt, and provide comfortable, modern accommodation for three senior citizens with connections with Plymtree.

Given its small size – under 400 people live in the parish – Plymtree is most generous to charities; over £15,000 has been raised in the past 25 years by Molly Tronlin and her Friends of the Imperial Cancer Research Campaign, and when the Devon Scanner Appeal was run in the 1970s, a Plymtree function raised £900 in a single night. David Tancock, a fine local musician (after work as a builder), hosted a 'Rock Night' with his band 'One Night Stand' at the parish hall in 1992 to raise money for the Special Care Baby Unit at the Royal Devon and Exeter Hospital, which had saved the life of his son; a barrel of beer was auctioned by Ian Wilson to boost the income, and an amazing £800 was passed to the Unit. A repeat performance the following year made £900.

Dyer, Mundy and Veysie Charities
ACCOUNT FOR THE SEVEN YEARS, 1916-23

RECEIPTS

	£	s	d
Seven Years' Interest to 5th October 1923, at £3 5s. a quarter on £520 stock 2½ per cent. Consols	£91	0	0

PAYMENTS

	£	s	d			£	s	d
Balance advanced by the Rector, Dec. 31st 1916		14	7					

James Pearse & Co., Exeter, for Blankets, Sheets, Flannel, &c.:				T. Redwood & Sons, Wellington, for Boots:				
Xmas, 1917	6	10	5			6	5	0
Xmas 1918	6	17	6			6	2	6
Xmas 1919	5	10	10			5	17	6
Xmas 1920	6	1	3			5	12	6
Xmas 1921	8	9	8			3	12	6
Xmas 1922	8	5	0			8	0	0
Xmas 1923	7	17	6			5	0	0
				Balance in hand			3	3

	£	s	d
Total expenditure	£91	0	0

Xmas 1917 -	38 gifts, viz.,	20 pair boots,	18 flannel, &c.
Xmas 1918 -	35	18	17
Xmas 1919 -	29	17	12
Xmas 1920	30	16	14
Xmas 1921	31	11	20
Xmas 1922	34	17	17
Xmas 1923	28	10	18

These gifts, to the value of £13 a year, are distributed by the Rector at Xmas to children attending catechising, widows and aged men.

An extract from the churchwardens' accounts book as printed in the Parish Magazine.

Chapter 7: Nonconformists

Until 1850 we know little of non-conformist worship in Plymtree, due largely to the wartime demise of most Devon probate records.

The Compton (religious) census of 1676 elicited the response from the rector that there were '200 conformists and only one non-conformist' in the parish. Given the round figure of 200, one must conclude that Rev. John Glanvill failed to carry out a true head-count, and minimised the number of nonconformists so as to keep his post-Restoration bishop happy. Certainly, 19 years later the Exeter Assembly of the United Brethren of Devon and Cornwall (the governing body for Presbyterians and Congregationalists) was so concerned about the activities in 'Plimtree' of Anabaptists (the most fervent of Puritans) in the absence of one of their own ministers on the circuit, that they agreed to a petition from the village to provide £4 yearly from their funds to pay for a minister; this was reduced to £3 in 1706, when Richard Evans was on the circuit; payments ceased in 1711.

Edward Skinner of Plymtree, sergemaker, by his will of 13th February 1729/30, directed that he was to be buried as a Quaker. His father lived at Wills' tenement in the parish: his wife was Mary Skinner, and he named Thomas Skinner of Plymtree, sergemaker, as his executor. He had a house at Uffculme let to a woolcomber tenant, and ordered that all his property (except Wills') be sold to provide for his wife and the settling of his and his father's debts. Mary Skinner was buried at Plymtree on 23rd May 1733, but Edward Skinner's burial does not appear in the Plymtree Register, and it is likely that he was buried by the Quakers in their burial grounds at Uffculme or Cullompton. (Until the 1850s there was a 'Wills' Cottage' in Greenend Lane, approximately where the bungalow 'Casa Mia' now stands.).

In his book *Devonshire Characters*, the Rev. J. Baring-Gould wrote of self-proclaimed prophet and farmer's daughter, Joanna Southcott:

In 1792 she had a serious illness and went to Plymtree to recuperate. When she recovered she set to work with renewed vigour. She pretended to have found, while sweeping the house, a die with 'JS' between two stars on it, and this she henceforth used for sealing her prophecies and her 'passports to heaven'.

The then occupier of Woodbeer Court was one William Southcott Young, so it seems likely that that was where she remained. Whether or not she preached in the parish, or had any effect on religion locally, is not known.

When Bishop Carey was preparing to make a visitation around his diocese in 1821, he sent out a set of queries about each parish, to be answered by the incumbent. Rev. Holwell replied that there were 80 families in the parish (the national census of the same year counted 77 families, a total of 381 souls), 'and no Papists or Dissenters'.

Some 27 years later, on 28th February 1848, Rev. William Marker Anstey, Minister of the Independent Church at Kerswell, commenced preaching at Plymtree in the morning and afternoon, and at Kerswell in the evening. The Sunday School at Plymtree began on 12th March, and 15 children attended. They were formed into classes by Mr Anstey, with volunteer teachers.

At that time the Independent Church at Plymtree consisted of four lady members – Eleanor Bickley, Ann Parris, Elizabeth Daniel and Elizabeth Sarah Lawrence – and that at Kerswell of four men and three women. On 12th August 1848, a joint meeting of members was convened at Kerswell, and it was resolved that the two churches should be constituted as one.

From its founding, the new church at Plymtree held its services in a cottage at Normans Green, and this was continued until 1850. Since the arrival of the High Churchman, Rev. Joseph Dornford, at the Rectory in 1832 there had been dissatisfaction with the form of services at the Parish Church, which, by 1849, had reached crisis point. Many of the congregation – mainly farmers in the parish – then decided to join forces with the independent church at Normans Green.

As a consequence of this influx a decision was taken to build a church at the corner of the crossroads there. The land for the building was given by Miss Ally Slater, the owner of Fordmoor farm, and the church was built of stone from the Blackdown Hills, hauled in carts by the farmers of the new congregation. The timber for the roof and for the interior was cut by hand with pit saws on the green. Most of the work involved in building the church was done by local tradesmen.

The result, a 'neat and commodious chapel, containing schoolroom', was officially opened at Norman's Green on Good Friday, 18th April 1851. It seated 200 and, according to the national religious census return, signed on 10th March 1851 (before the official opening by Henry Dowell, manager of the chapel), an average of 70 persons attended service, plus 20 Sunday School children – from which it is clear that religious dissent had grown strongly since the 1820s.

It is not clear when the Independent Church joined the Congregational Church Union though it was certainly before 1894. The most notable of the many Ministers who served the chapel was Rev. Hampden Garibaldi Classey, who served from 1888 until his death in 1935: his wife, Hephzibah, devotedly assisted him in his parish work, but died in 1925. The interior of the chapel was renovated in 1895, when a new floor was laid, new seats and a new pulpit installed, and a large porch built at the main entrance. At the other end of the church a new two-storey extension provided suitable accommodation for the Sunday School, at a cost of £225. The money was raised by a two-days sale, for which all sorts of articles were donated, including poultry, pigs, sheep, calves, and other farm produce.

In 1900 it was decided to enlarge the burial ground. The owner of the adjoining field, Mr Sanders, gave a strip of it large enough for the purpose and, with the exception of the brick wall and fencing, the work involved was done voluntarily by the young men connected with the church.

In about 1947 a private electricity supply was installed to provide power for lighting and, when a new organ was obtained in 1950, it was powered by an electric blower. All the equipment and materials were again donated, and all of the installation work was done by the young men of the church and a few other helpers, therefore costing the church nothing. Part of the work was 'an engine house and a coal shed adjoining'. It is interesting to note that only once did the electricity supply fail, when the preacher was little more than half-way through his sermon – on 'The Light of the World!' He managed to finish in the darkness, the engine was restarted and the light came on for the last hymn. The electricity plant did its work well until the church was connected to the South Western Electricity Board's supply in 1953.

When mains water came to Plymtree in 1957, voluntary help was again given by the young men of the church, who dug a trench and laid a pipe from the mains to bring water to a tap in the engine shed (a great help to the ladies who needed water for church flowers, for social occasions etc.), and also into the church building to feed the storage tank for the (coal-fired) heating system.

Although villagers remember tensions between church-goers and chapel-folk during the inter-war period – amazingly, a member of one tradition would not enter the village shop while someone from the other was there – today there is more consideration for the beliefs of others. The church is now a part of the United Reformed Church, and is well-supported.

Above: The Rev. Hampden Garibaldi Classey preaching from his mobile van which visited villages in the Exe and Culm valleys, c.1905.

Left: Plymtree United Reformed Church, c.1978. The Rev. Gladys Smith (centre) hosts a party for the children in the Sunday School.

Devon. To the Church-wardens and Overseers of the Poor
to wit. of the Parish of *Broadwoubury* ———————— as also to the
Church-wardens and Overseers of the Poor of the
Parish of *Plymptree in the said County* Thefe

WHEREAS Complaint hath been made by you the Churchwardens and Overseers of the Poor of *Broadwoubury* ———
aforefaid, unto us whofe Hands and Seals are hereunto fet, Two
of *our* Majefty's Juftices of the Peace ————————————
for the faid County of *Devon,* ~~That~~ *one being of the quorum, that willi*
pring eldeſt his wife Henry John and william their fo

lately intruded *themfelves* into your faid Parifh of *Broadwoubury*
there to inhabit as ——— Parifhioners contrary to the Laws relating to the Settlement of the Poor, and *are likely to* ——— become Chargeable there : And
whereas upon due Examination and Enquiry made into the Premifes by us the
faid Juftices, it appears unto us, and we accordingly adjudge, that the faid ———

william pring eldeſt his wife, Henry John and william
their fony

are likely to become Chargeable
and that *their* laft legal Place of Settlement was in the faid Parifh of *Plymptree*
——— where *they* ought to be removed, as the Law in that Cafe
directs

THESE are therefore in *his* Majefty's Name to order and require you
the Church-wardens and Overfeers of the Poor of *Broadwoubury* ———
——————————— aforefaid, That you or fome of you, do forthwith remove
and convey the faid *william pring eldeſt his wife Henry John*
and william their fony ———————
from your faid Parifh of *Broadwoubury* to the Parifh of *Plymptree* ———
aforefaid, and *them* deliver to the Church-wardens and Overfeers of the Poor
there, or fome or one of them, together with this our Warrant or Order, or a
true Copy hereof; whereby they are likewife required in *his* Majefty's Name,
and by Virtue of the Statutes in fuch Cafe made, forthwith to receive the faid
william pring eldeſt his wife, Henry John & william their
fony
into their faid Parifh of *Plymptree* ——————— and provide for *them* ———
as their own Parifhioner according to Law. *Given under our Hands and*
Seals, the *fourain* ——————— *Day of* *June* ———— *in the*
twelfth ——— *Year of our Sovereign* *Lord George the Broad King* —
over Great-Britain, and fo forth, and in the Year of our Lord God One Thoufand
Seven Hundred *and thirty nine.*

Removal order for William Pring and his family, 1739.

Chapter 8: Overseers of the Poor

Until the dissolution of the monasteries they and the churches dealt with the relief of the poor as a charitable obligation, but thereafter the responsibility was placed on the parish. When there was a need the churchwardens would hold a 'church ale', having a fête and selling ale and food to raise money, or approach wealthy parishioners for donations; this no doubt worked fairly well in a small community like Plymtree, but not so well in the fast-growing towns, and as a result a compulsory parish rate was introduced from 1572. Indolence was not to be encouraged, however, so in 1576 parishes were required to provide materials to set the poor to work.

From 1598 (reaffirmed by the great Poor Law Act of 1601) Justices of the Peace were required to appoint overseers of the poor in each parish to assess and collect the parish rate and apply monies for the relief of the poor. The parish officers of Plymtree seem to have ignored these laws, and the churchwardens continued to look after the poor without formally declaring themselves to be overseers. The first record we have of an officer described as such is in 1652, and we know the names of most of those who served as such from then until 1868.

A book – used by the churchwardens from 1621 to note monies received and loaned to paupers (without interest, but secured by a guarantor for the money) and to farmers and other wealthier men (when the interest charged was applied for the use of the poor) – was taken over by the overseers from 1678 to record their accounts. From this date we know the parish poor rate was collected in a regular way – as had been required by law for the previous 96 years!

One result of this system of parish support was that the 'needy' tended to move to parishes where there were a lot of landowners to pay to support them, so in 1662 an Act of Settlement was passed which restricted the 'right of settlement' in a parish to those who were born there, or married such a person, or owned land there; it also allowed the overseers to ignore paupers who they could prove not to be 'settled'. Later laws permitted legal action to remove such people back to their own parish.

Being one of the overseers (three until 1698, then two) was not an easy job, and although in theory every literate person (usually men, but not always) took their turn, in practice the rector and large landowners would arrange for one of their tenants to do the work. They were appointed by the Parish Vestry, a meeting open to all ratepayers, held monthly or quarterly, which carried out the functions of a Parish Council but also set the poor rate and decided which paupers should receive relief; any parishioner in difficulty could apply to the Vestry for help. The overseers' first task was to ride to the nearest Justice of the Peace to buy two warrants – one to confirm their appointment and the other to collect the poor rate. The rate was based on land-holding, and the 'monthly' rate varied from 1s. (paid by the rector) to $^1/_4$d. The rate could be collected 'as often as the Necessity of the Poor shall Require' however, and never seems to have been collected 'monthly': in 1712 it was gathered 38 times, while in 1812 there were an amazing 464 calls on the ratepayers; as a further illustration of the variable nature of demand, in 1735 there were 72 'Rates', the following year 120, and the next only 60.

Collecting such rates cannot have been easy, but the overseers also had a regular stream of needy parishioners coming to their doors for money for subsistence whenever they could not work, or were ill. They were responsible for finding the putative fathers of illegitimate children, to obtain money from them to pay for the child until he or she was aged eight: they also found 'apprenticeships' for poor children. Each overseer had to keep accurate accounts, and swear to the truth of them at the Vestry meeting at Easter, at the end of their year, and then again before two Justices of the Peace. For their year's service, each overseer received one guinea.

In 1703 the overseers paid out £37-13s.-$10^1/_2$d. in 'pay', of between 4s. and 6s.-6d. a month to 11 poor parishioners who clearly had no other income. In accordance with an Act of Parliament designed to prevent people claiming poor relief in more than one parish, people in receipt of poor relief had to wear a large badge, marked with a 'P' and the first letter of their parish, on their left upper arm.

The death of a pauper was also a strain on the poor rates: for example, when Catherine Otton died in March 1703 the overseers paid 2s. for her laying out, 3s.-5d. for a shroud, 2s.-6d. for making her grave, carrying the bier and ringing the bell,

1s. for the required affidavit (that she had been buried wrapped in woollen cloth) to be written and sworn, and then 4s. for the Queen's Tax – a total of 11s.-11d – nearly as much as she had been expected to live on for two months. The death, in the same year, of Rose Carnell incurred additional expenditure of 8s. for a coffin. Also in 1703 the overseers had the Church House re-thatched, paying 5s. for the straw, the work being done by Ames Wilcox and Robert Salter, for which they were paid £1-7s.-8d. and £1 respectively.

Another problem (since the Civil War) was that of roaming dogs, Elias Haycraft being paid 5s. in 1704 'to keep dogs out of the Church'.

The following entries in the Poor Book, made by John Andrew, Overseer for 1743, show just how costly 'intruders' from other parishes could be, what with providing cash, a bed and food for them, and then having to pay lawyers and court costs to obtain an order from the Justices that they return to their home parish, and a further order that that parish pay (some of) Plymtree's expenses. The total loss to the parish ratepayers for sending the Tapscots back to Culmstock was £7-11s.-5d.

But people were also 'removed' from other parishes to Plymtree, some becoming a drain on

1743	Disburstments Extraordinary	£	s	d
May	To Tapscots family	0	2	0
	To a bed stead bed tye and met[meat] for Tapscot family	0	6	3
	To a Rugg for Tapscot	0	1	6
	To Tapscot	0	1	0
	To Tapscot	0	1	6
	for Retaining 3 Councilers [lawyers] about Tapscot	1	11	6
	Pd. the money that was upon Tapscot Kittle [large pot]			
	[*He seems to have got it on credit!*]	0	1	3
	To Tapscots family	0	1	0
	To Expence when we went to Retain Council	0	2	6
June	To Tapscots family at 4 several Times	0	5	6
	for a man & horse to goe after Tapscots Kittle & Turn [spinning wheel]	0	2	0
July	To Tapscots family	0	1	0
	To Tapscots family	0	1	0
	Pd. at a parish meeting	0	4	0
	To Eliz Trump with a suppena [subpoena] about Tapscot	0	1	0
	To Expences upon Mr Brutton when we went for brefets [breakfast?]	0	0	8
	Pd. the Clerk of Broadhembury for Taking out/ The Examination of Tapscot and expences	0	1	3
	Pd. for Entering the appeal against [parish of] Culmstock	0	1	0
	To Eliz Trump for witness against Culmstock	0	2	6
	To 3 Councellors fees	3	3	0
	Pd. for the order against Culmstock	0	3	0
	To Expences at Sessions	0	3	9$^{1}/_{2}$
	To a horse and man to Carry home Tapscot & Expences	0	3	0
	Pd. Grace Knight for Empting Tapscots Bed / & bread for the family }	0	0	2$^{1}/_{2}$
	Pd. Mr Fortiscue for himself and horse several / Times about Tapscot}	0	5	6
	My own horse and Expenses several Times	0	5	6
		9	13	6

Receipts

Received of Culmstock people		2	2	0

the rates. In 1739 William and Alice Pring and their three sons were removed back to Plymtree from Broadhembury, where, having become unemployed, he was likely to become chargeable to that parish. He obviously found some work back home in Plymtree, as only occasionally did he receive parish relief: but when he died in 1746 the parish paid for his burial and his wife was unable to support the family; she was given monthly poor pay, and her three sons were put out as apprentices as soon as they were old enough (*see the order for their removal, page 52*).

The overseers' duties did not extend to physically removing people found by the Justices to be unlawfully settled; that fell to the parish constable, although he only had to take the 'intruder' to the next parish. On Christmas Eve 1753, for example, Anne Richards, a Plymtree-born orphan, aged 22 and pregnant, was arrested at Ross-on-Wye for begging in the street; she was examined by a justice, and ordered to be removed to Plymtree forthwith under escort from parish to parish. (She was lucky; for such an offence she could have been sent to the House of Correction.).

Some items from the Poor Book for 1745 give a flavour of the work of the overseers at that time. At least one wall of the Church House needed urgent attention, and they spent £30-3s.-5d. in rebuilding it with stone and bricks, but mostly cob, bonded with lime and horsehair; their accounts show that each layer of cob was allowed to dry for a month before the next was laid, and the whole work took from May to the following March, when the thatching was completed.

The overseers then managed to remove Ann Finnimore from the list of parish paupers. She had been a drain on funds for many years, having had two 'base' children in the previous ten years (one of whom had died within a year, to be buried at parish expense); she was also on monthly Pay. They looked for a man from another parish who was willing to marry her and take her away. Humphrey Ware of Cullompton was the man, and they married on 3rd October 1745: 20 days later he was paid £5-2s. for his trouble. Whether they lived happily ever after is not known!

Another means of reducing the poor rate was to apprentice the children of paupers to landowners, usually when they were between the ages of seven and fourteen years; they had to serve their masters until a girl was 21 (or married) or a boy was 24. The youngsters were to be taught appropriate 'mysteries' – of husbandry (farming) for the boys and of housekeeping for the girls, and in many cases the landowners were happy to take on these children, since they would get work from them merely for the cost of their food. John Harward, the richest landowner in Plymtree, took on Elizabeth Salter, aged 13, and she no doubt

fitted easily into his large household staff at Hayne House. Whether Melior Skinner, just six years old, was so happily absorbed into Henry Anning's family at Clyst William is more doubtful. The overseers also decided that Edward Baker, holder of a very small tenement, should have Jane Baker (age unknown) as his parish apprentice; unhappy, he refused to sign the necessary indentures of apprenticeship, and it took a summons from the Justices of the Peace to force him to do so.

A new face in Plymtree in 1745 was Andrew Hannaways (elsewhere written as 'Hannibus'), 'he having been a prisoner in France and thereby become a Cripple'. He did not appear to have been born in the parish, or have any other right to a settlement, so the overseers presumably took him on as a patriotic duty towards a former soldier or sailor. They gave him clothing, lodging and 'drink', and put him on Monthly Pay, and he stayed for 11 months before travelling to Bath with his brother: the parish paid 10s.-6d to hire a horse for them, plus £1 expenses for the journey.

By 1795 the cost of living had increased so much that the day-labourer's pay was insufficient to provide for their families. Justices in Berkshire agreed to subsidise their wages out of the poor rate, and the system spread rapidly; by an Act of 1796 the amount to be paid to those on outdoor relief (i.e. not living in a workhouse) was tied to the cost of bread, which accelerated the numbers applying for it. Farmers liked the system since it really subsidised them, their labourers' wages being partly paid by all the ratepayers of the parish. But the system destroyed the shame of 'going on the parish', and therefore injured the self-pride of working men and women.

Sir Frederick Morton Eden reported on 'The State of the Poor' in 1797, describing the nearby parish of Clyst St George, whose agricultural day-labourers probably lived under conditions similar to those in Plymtree:

No labourer can at present maintain himself, wife and children on his earnings. All have relief from the parish in money, or corn at a reduced price. Before the war wheaten bread and cheese, and about twice a week meat, were their usual food: now barley bread and no meat. They have of late made great use of potatoes. An industrious healthy man can earn 8 shillings a week by piece work on an average throughout the year. Labourers' children are often bound out as apprentices at 8 years of age to the farmers. Prior to the present scarcity a labourer, if his wife was healthy, could maintain two young children on his 6 shillings a week and liquor without any parochial relief. A very few years ago labourers thought themselves disgraced by receiving aid from the parish, but this sense of shame is now totally extinguished.

Under the New Poor Law of 1834, parishes had to join into unions, with an elected Board of Guardians establishing union workhouses; Plymtree then became part of the Honiton Union, and henceforth the truly poor were sent to the workhouse there, which was not only extremely unpleasant but also brought shame on the family.

'Outdoor relief' was supposed to be abolished overnight but, since each parish still set its own poor rate and the local overseers could see the misery caused by its removal, many parishes still provided local relief: the poor in Plymtree were also lucky to have the Feoffees of the Plymtree charities to help them 'in extremis'.

1897 Poor Rate-payers

The following list comes from the Poor Rate set on 11th May 1897. The six cottages at 'Village' which burned down with the Church House in 1895 had not yet been rebuilt – they were replaced by the present Post Office Stores. Robert Lear farmed Tyes (and looked after the gardens of Hayne House) for Thomas Baxter, who owned 808 acres in the parish, including Greenend, Tyes, Hayne, Middle Woodbeer, Little and Middle Clistwilliam, Pencepool and Bowling Green.
Not everyone was so well off: each of those marked with an asterisk received financial help (between 4 and 10s. each) from the Feoffees of the Parish Charities during the first half of the year.
So also did (non-ratepayers) Mrs Cape, Polly Clarke, Thomas Clarke, John Quick, Hannah Salter, Samuel Salter, Walter Salter, Joseph Wilcox and Sarah Wyatt.

William Aplin *	Greenend Cottages	John Norrish	Danes Mill
Charles Baker *	Hayne Cottage	Wm. John Norrish	Pencepool Farm
James Baker *	Knights Cottage	William Parris	Hayne Farm
Thomas H Baxter	Greenend	Aaron Pearcey	Hern Farm
Herman Bickley	Cooks Farm	Charles Pearcey	Stocklandhead Farm
Frank Boundy	Cottage at Fordmoor	George Pine	Lower Woodbeer Fm.
Wm. Henry Boundy *	Bondsbridge Cotts.	John Pope *	Mots Lane cottage
Sarah Burge *	Cottage at Village	Charles Pratt *	Cottage at Colliers
Elizabeth Burnell *	Bondsbridge Cotts.	James Pratt	Sanguishayse
William Burnell *	Bowling Green	John Pratt *	Cottage at Fordmoor
Charles Carnell *	Raymonds Cottage	Mary Pratt *	Cott. at Pencepool
Harry Causeway *	Perhams Green cott.	Richard Pratt *	Greenend Cottages
Mary Churchill	Cottage at Colliers	W. & Philip Prouse	Clistwilliam Barton
William.H. Clarke*	Greenend Cottages	James Quick	Knights Cottage
Rev.Garibaldi Classy	Normans Green Cott.	Henry Rice *	Redgate
W.Donaldson Clavell	Blampins Cottage	Anna Salter	Cottage at Pencepool
James Cligg	Middle Woodbeer	John Salter *	Cottage at Fordmoor
F. James Cligg	Little Clistwilliam	Thomas Salter	Cottage at Colliers
Ben Cook	Weaver House Farm	William Salter	Cottage at Village
Thomsine Cook	Park Cottage	William Salter sen.	Beach Cottage
William Cook	Weaver Farm	John Sanders	Post Off. (Old Forge)
Fred Daniels	Cottage at Fordmoor	Richard Sanders	Perhams Green
Henry Ellicott	Cottage at Fordmoor	John Scribbins *	Redgate
Henry Farley *	Bondsbridge Cottages	Ann Stamp *	Cottage at Fordmoor
Grace Farnell *	Cottage at Pencepool	Jane Stiling *	Cottage at Colliers
Franks	Bowling Green	William Stiling *	Clarkes Cottages
Harry Glanvill *	Cottage at Fordmoor	William Stiling sen. *	Hayne Cottage
William Glanville *	Bondsbridge Cottages	Samuel Summers *	Clarkes Cottages
Rev. George Gutteres	Rectory	John Veales *	Mots Lane cottage
John Henley *	Greenend Cottages	John Veales sen. *	Pencepool Cottages
Thomas Hussey	Woodbeer Court	Elizabeth Vinnicombe	*Farcey's Cottage
Walter Hussey	Brewers Cottage	James Vinnicombe *	Raymonds Cottage
Rebecca Ireland *	Cottage at Pencepool	Simon Vinnicombe *	Cooks Farm cottage
Willie James *	Cooks Farm cottage	Lewis Ware	Redgate
W. Arthur Jarvis	Bake House Cottage	Maria Ware	Middle Clistwilliam
Charles Knight *	Redgate	James Webber	'New Inn' PH
Ann Loman	Lower Weaver	Henry Wheaton	Fordmoor Farm
George Loosemore	Rose Cottage	John White *	Cottage at Colliers
Edward Middleton	2 cotts at Pencepool		

Care of the Sick

Ellis Veryard, born 1657, who lived at Perhams Green, was the third generation of physicians in Plymtree. In 1702 and 1704 his name appears in the accounts of the overseers of the poor for fees for treatment. Shortly after this he moved to Cullompton, where he died in 1714. But apart from the Veryard family, doctors do not seem to have lived in the parish until the 1930s, when the much-loved Dr Russell Shove moved into Perhams Green Cottage.

We can guess that the more wealthy landowners, living at Hayne House, Fordmore, Woodbeer Court and Greenend, would have a doctor on a retainer, while their tenant farmers would pay for one if his attendance was really needed. The poor were catered for by payments to others for their treatment and, if they could not work, by money given to them for their and their family's subsistence. From 1688 the payers of the poor rate had to contribute to the county 'Hosipitall' (which payment was lumped in with the charge to support the county gaol – invariably spelled 'goal'). No doubt the prospects of anyone taken there were not very good; having said that, only two villagers were hospitalised in the following century and a half, and both returned home.

Most of the payments recorded in the account books found in the Plymtree parish chest relate to injuries caused by accidents. Thus the first such payment I have found was in 1681, when 9s. was paid 'for cureing of Connett's boys heade'. That such a large sum (being about four weeks wages) was paid tends to indicate that it was a doctor who gave the treatment on this occasion, although that was unusual. In 1691, Richard Buckle was paid 5s. 'when his Sons Bone was Broken'; that payment may have been for him to buy bandages and suchlike, or possibly to pay a doctor's fee.

More common was the paying of a village 'dame' (or 'Gamer' – the dialect word for Grandma) to undertake the work. Thus in the year 1682 Sarah May was paid £1-10s. – 'for Cureing of Agnis, Mary & Eliz: Shobrookes scald heads'; the treatment must have lasted quite some time to justify that sort of remuneration.

1700 was a bad year for illness in Plymtree. The overseers paid John Shirfield £1-9s.-4d., John Colman 11s.-6d., Henry Taylor 9s.-6d., Joan Tippet £1-5s.-6d. (including her burial costs), Richard Whitrow 15s., John More 10s., John Lee 14s. and Joan Stabback 5s. – in each case for their 'sickness'.

Three different doctors looked after poor parishioners in 1727: Dr Salter (who lived and practised at Clyst Hydon, 'cured Venn's child'; Dr Mills 'looked after the two Morrises and old Richard Drew', and Dr Baker was 'paid 3s. for what he hath done for the old Lackington'. Furthermore, Bridget Fortescue was given £6 'for going to Dr Salter', though for what is not made clear, and Michael Coome was to 'have one shilling to pay the Doctor', – his medical emergency was obviously less than that of Mrs Fortescue.

The overseers records, which are detailed from 1707, show that small-pox regularly affected the parish. The most common treatment (as with many other maladies) was 'bleeding', and Tom Pratt was clearly a past-master at the technique, since he was paid handsomely 'for bleeding the poor people' between 1739 and his death in 1778; he was so professional that in half of the entries he is called 'Doctor' Pratt.

The effect of illness on the population was severe. In 1731, for example, there were 21 burials, seven of which, including those of three small children, resulted from small-pox. One of the sick, Mary Richards, was provided with some provisions as she could not work: she received (cost), 'Butter (1s.-10^3/$_4$d), Sugar (6d), Milk (2s.-6d), Butter & Bacon (3s.-8^1/$_2$d), Shop goods (6s.-11d), and Bread and flower (4s.)'. The parish paid to treat poor people for the disease in 1711, 1731, 1732, 1735, 1741, 1756, 1757, 1771, 1775 and 1795, the year before Edward Jenner proved that vaccinating with cow-pox serum prevented the more serious infection.

In 1802 six families were infected with the disease, and the parish overseers went to Bradninch to hear about vaccinations. One of the yeoman farmers, William Trump, showing his faith in the new treatment, immediately paid 2s.-6d. to have his child vaccinated. Thereafter, there were occasional outbreaks; in 1822 the four children of Robert Luxton, a labourer, were vaccinated at the cost of the parish, followed in 1829 by '30 poor children', each at a cost of 2s.-6d. There is no indication that the disease struck Plymtree thereafter, at least as far as the poor were concerned.

Mental illness was not apparently a great problem, but when it did occur it was treated with all the sensitivity one expects of the 18th century. In 1775 one Richard Davy became ill, and the overseers paid him regular sums until 10th September, when things became too much for his wife, Sarah. She was given some money for people to look after him, but that didn't work, and the following entries appear in the Poor Book:

To a Fetter & Chaine when Richard Davy was put in the Church House - 1s.-6d
To a Staple for the Door – 2d
To a Pint of Cyder for Richard Davy when he was put into the Church House 1^1/$_2$d

Well, at least they kept him happy while they chained him up! The parish paid for a stream of people to look after him – including the good 'Doctor' Pratt – for a time, but he seems to have recovered fairly quickly, and went back to live quietly with his wife. It is also clear, however, that he could not work, as he was paid a monthly allowance by the overseers for at least the next five years.

The School Log Book, begun in February 1873, immediately noted a whooping cough epidemic in the village. Between March and May 1875 scarlet fever was 'raging', and there was also an outbreak of measles. July 1881 was very hot, and 'nearly half the children in the neighbourhood are suffering from measles'. These three diseases, plus mumps, chicken pox, ringworm and 'croup' (which killed five-year-old Emma Pratt in 1890), appear in the books with great regularity, while diphtheria, which was responsible for the deaths of young George Summers and Mabel Grabham in 1897, was, thankfully, more of a rarity.

Nearly 80 people attended a social dance held at the Schoolroom on Thursday 20th December 1906, and £4-10s. was raised for the Cottage Nursing Scheme; Col. the Hon. J. S. Trefusis (of Hayne House) and W. B. Franklin (of Fordmore) acted as stewards.

The Hon. Mrs Eva L. Trefusis explained the scheme, by which she hoped to obtain a trained nurse for the parishes of Plymtree, Broadhembury and Clyst Hydon:

The Cottage Benefit Nursing Association provides working women, brought up in cottages, who have been given Hospital training and are capable of nursing any case of illness or accident. In confinements they are not allowed to act without a doctor. They go and live in the cottage where the illness is, and if it is the woman who is laid up, the nurse does all the work of the house, lights the fire, cooks the meals, sends the children to school and does everything for the family except the washing. If there is no room for her in the cottage she is lodged with a neighbour, or is provided with a camp bed for her to sleep in the kitchen. All that cottagers or labourers have to subscribe is 1s. a year, and 1s. per week and her food when they want the nurse: trades-people pay 3s. a year and 3s. per week and her food: farmers subscribe 5s. per year and 5s. week and board.

Nurse Eleanor David was appointed in April 1907, and was immediately almost fully employed. It was reported in March 1909 that:

There were 124 Members and 14 Associates during 1908. The following is the list of cases Nurse David has attended since April last year: in all cases she has been much appreciated and has done her work to the satisfaction of both doctors and patients. List of cases: Confinements – 7; Rheumatism – 2; Paralysis – 1; Hemorrhage – 1; Enteric fever – 1; Typhoid fever – 1; Internal ulceration – 1; Tuberculous meningitis – 1; Bronchitis – 1; Various visits for wounds, stings, bad eyes, legs, etc – 10.

Nurse David was replaced in July 1911 by Nurse Jarmain, who also served for four years until leaving to work in a London hospital in July 1915: due to the demand for nurses caused by the war, it was not possible to find a replacement for her, and the Association was then wound up.

The influenza pandemic of 1914 claimed the life of little Herbert Willmott, 'a bright, loveable boy', but luckily no-one else succumbed.

Between the wars the doctor used a pony and trap to visit his patients, and when the weather was bad he was often treated to a cup of tea and a warm by the fire before continuing his round. The doctor knew his patients and their families well, and he was held in great respect by all.

Until the advent of the National Health Service, medical treatment had to be paid for. In 1897 the rector had hoped that Queen Victoria's Jubilee celebrations would raise a surplus of £25, 'enough to endow the parish with two annual Tickets for the Exeter Hospital'. There were a number of savings schemes to cover such costs, but the favoured one in Plymtree was the National Deposit Friendly Society, whose local representative was Mr E. J. Robinson. In 1920 males aged five to forty five and females five to forty could be covered against doctor's fees, the cost of medicine, and also get sick pay of 1s. per day, all for a regular 4d. a week (or 3d. if weekly wages did not amount to 15s.).

Chapter 9: Schools in Plymtree

Until 1873 there was no generally-available educational facility in the parish, though there were a number of privately-funded schools at different times.

In January 1792 Mrs H. Bennett advertised vacancies at her 'Boarding School for Young Ladies' in Plymtree through the *Exeter Flying Post* newspaper. She engaged 'to instruct the Ladies in all sorts of Needlework, Tambour, Dancing, the English Grammar, Writing, Arithmetic, &c., &c., at the very moderate rate of ten guineas per Annum.' This advertisement appeared at regular intervals, but in 1800 she was obliged to insert a special notice to the effect that rumours about her school's closure were false: nonetheless, thereafter details of her establishment no longer appeared in the newspaper.

Aerial view of Plymtree School, 1967. The original layout is unchanged apart from the removal of the fence that originally separated the juniors from the infants.

In 1818 the then rector reported to the parliamentary 'Select Committee on the Education of the Poor' that 27 children were being educated at a private day and Sunday school, 12 of whom were paid for and clothed by a private family, and that there were 40 more children 'desirous of education'. In 1827 a 'Parochial Day & Sunday School' was reported as having been established, admitting 42 children (24 boys and 18 girls), 4 supported by subscribers and 4 by school fees. Another return to parliament in 1833 stated that a further four small day schools had been established in the parish since 1818 to educate a total of 16 boys and 15 girls, all at the expense of their parents. Where these schools were held is something of a mystery.

From about 1841 a small 'Day School' was run in the village by Mrs (and Miss) Mary Ann Veysie, and from 1876 a 'Ladies School' was run by Mrs Jane Brice at Rose Cottage.

White's Devonshire Directory for 1850 and *Morris's Directory* for 1870 both refer to a 'Day School' (run by Louisa Scovern) as well as a 'Ladies' School' in the village. It is doubtful whether the 66 children (generally aged 4 to 9 but with a few older), described in the census of 1851 as 'scholars' could have found room in either establishment.

What is known for certain is that the rector from 1868, Thomas Mozley, and his wife were deeply interested in education, and he was worried by the apparent lack of concern for the subject shown by villagers: the 1871 census recorded 109 children aged 3 to 14 years, but only 26 were described as 'scholars'. He paid £1400 to have Plymtree Mixed Elementary School built, and it was opened on 10th February 1873; he equipped it and paid for its teachers, and he continued to teach scripture and direct the work of the school until his retirement in 1880.

School attendance was not free, as parents had to contribute 2d. a week for each child if they were poor and came from the village, and 4d. otherwise. The 'three Rs' were taught, as well as singing, and the older girls had to practice sewing for three, and younger ones two, afternoons each week.

At its opening, the school had 44 children over the age of 7 years, taught by headmaster Edwin Gale and his wife Caroline. As the school established itself, a number of children, aged between 12 and 15 who had not previously received schooling, came along. Since the vast majority of village children were both illiterate and innumerate when they began their education, the two teachers must have had their work cut out.

In April 1874, two 'monitoresses' were selected from the First (eldest) Class of the school, to assist the teachers; they were Sarah Eveleigh and Hannah Salter, each paid 1s. a week, and their appointment being the first step a poor rural child could take towards becoming qualified as a teacher. In 1877 two assistant monitoresses were also appointed, teaching the younger pupils for $7\frac{1}{2}$ hours per week, and being themselves taught for a similar amount of time. By 1881, the school had expanded and the census listed 98 'scholars' out of 130 children in the parish aged between 3 and 14 years.

Hannah Salter had to give up her training after four years, when her grandmother moved out of the district, but Sarah Eveleigh managed to win a scholarship to a training college in Truro after seven years as a monitoress at Plymtree, and went on to become an assistant mistresss at the Central School, Exeter. A later successful monitoress (by then called a 'pupil-teacher') was Rosina East, who was appointed in 1881 and qualified as a teacher in 1886.

During the harvest holidays in 1884 a school was started by Rev. Classey at the Chapel, and

Left: Plymtree schoolchildren, c.1907.

Below: Plymtree School, c.1920 showing the infants' side on the left, fenced off.

William and Ellen Manfield, and Bessie Lane, were sent there. The reason given to the Headmaster of the village school by Mrs Manfield was that 'it is such a bad road for them in the winter'. Since the Manfields lived at Hayne House, religious preference seems nearer the mark, the journey to the school being the same distance as, and probably easier walking than, that to the Chapel.

The cost of teachers' salaries, equipment, the upkeep of the building, and an annual rental of £24-5s.-0d. to the rector, were all raised by a 'voluntary rate' – part of the parish rate paid by male householders Vestry – and by school fees. At a meeting of rate payers in 1890, 'Some expressed their intention of not paying the Rate for the current year unless the additional £5 yearly, granted to the Master and Mistress of the school by the managing committee, was revoked'; it was.

In addition to the rate and fees there were, until 1900, Government payments made according to the numbers of children in the school and on the results achieved in examinations set by Her Majesty's Inspectors during their annual visits, which concentrated on the 'three Rs'. Later, the grant was solely based on pupil numbers – 17s.-0d per annum per infant, and 22s.-0d per older child – although the HMIs still inspected and tested the school.

The old 'voluntary rate' which had formerly been used for church purposes had become the Parish Council rate in 1894; the ratepayers, especially the nonconformists, objected to continuing to pay the rates to support a school under the control of the Church of England, and a certain amount of bitter debate followed. The rector (Edgar Hay) therefore began to encourage the villagers to raise money to buy the school from Mrs Mozley, who was apparently content to accept whatever sum the village could afford. They raised £425 by a half-crown rate and donations, and in 1899 the school was conveyed in trust to the Church of England, the trustees being the Bishop of Exeter, the rector, and Mr Thomas Baxter. A list of subscribers was printed in the *Parish Magazine*.

The village then raised further money to build a new school house for the Master; the old one, in front of the school, was demolished in 1902 to create a larger playground for the children, and the new house was built on a half-acre site next door: a photograph of the opening ceremony, performed by the Bishop of Exeter on Moday 28th July, 1902, survives (*below*).

Children had to stay at school until they reached the age of 13, and had passed the national 'Standard IV' tests in reading, writing and arithmetic. In the early days however, many boys (and a certain number of girls) left school illegally to take up paid employment with local farmers.

Even by the 1930s the school provided all the education most village children received. There

were two teachers, and children started in the little room at age 5; at 10 they moved to the big room, where they stayed until they were 14.

During the Second World War, a Catholic Primary School from Southwark in south London, complete with their teachers, Mr and Mrs J. Moan, was evacuated to Plymtree. They held their classes in the parish hall, and the rector permitted them to use the vestry room for their services. They returned to London in February 1943, donating their books and other materials to Plymtree School.

The number of children attending Plymtree School began to decline in the 1960s. Miss Millett,

who had led the school from 1943 retired in 1966; her successor, Mrs Park, had to face the prospect of the school being closed almost as soon as she arrived. The village rallied in support of the school, and the threat of closure was lifted.

But by 1982 the future of Plymtree School was again at risk, with only 14 pupils on the roll. The Parish Council called a meeting; Alan Barnett agreed to lead an 'action committee'. The then teachers, the Misses Hayman, resigned and the County Council sent in a new Head Teacher, Chris Thornhill, to finalise the inevitable closure. The villagers had other ideas, however, and with the support of all the governors, and making great

Left: Raising money for Plymtree School: (left to right) the Rev. George Ridding, Phillip Horsfield, Chris Thornhill (head teacher) and Alan Barnett (Chair of Governors) taking part in the sponsored North-South Dartmoor Walk, 1983.

Below: Florence Gallagher and George Valvona model the new Plymtree School uniform.

Parents and pupils joined together in 1982 to demonstrate against the proposed closure of Plymtree School.

use of the expertise of Alan Barnett, they joined together to keep their school. Chris was totally committed to making the school a success and, under his leadership, it went from strength to strength.

This community effort resulted in the founding of the Friends of Plymtree School, whose fund-raising efforts have since provided vital financial support for the work of the school while adding to the social life of the village. A new uniform was designed for the children, consisting of the slogan 'PLYMTREE – Life in the Country', the 'Y' in 'PLYMTREE' being enlarged and embellished as a tree.

As the numbers expanded, the old buildings were unable to cope, and more were needed. An incredible £3000 was raised, a redundant sectional classroom (below) was located at Stoke Canon School, and Chris got the Royal Marines to

dismantle and re-erect it at Plymtree; this effort won commendation in the Village Ventures Contest for 1987/8. A second, similar, classroom was later erected with the aid of a great deal of parental labour.

One of Chris Thornhill's great delights was music, which he used to build the self-confidence of every child in the school. In 1995 the Plymtree School Choir was invited to join the Devon and Cornwall Constabulary Band for their annual charity concert at the Grand Hall of Exeter University. So well did they perform that they were – unprecedentedly – invited again the following year.

Unfortunately, Chris Thornhill's health deteriorated, and he was on sick leave prior to retirement when the school celebrated its 125th anniversary on 13th February 1998; on that day the 111 children and all the staff and governors dressed in Victorian costume for a day of joyful celebration.

Also in 1998, OFSTED inspected the School, and found it to be well above average in all respects: its glowing report on the quality of education provided in Plymtree rightly reflected the dedication of all the staff, now led by Head-teacher Mrs Pat Fay. In 1999 the amazing results for the tests of Key Stage II children were published: Plymtree's pupils' results were the fourth best in Devon, putting the school in the top 200 in England and Wales.

Above: The school having expanded its numbers needed further teaching space for the children. Alan Lock, Bill Tingle and Mick Purves dismantling a redundant classroom for removal to Plymtree, June 1986.

Right: Head teacher Chris Thornhill (with beard) and the children of Plymtree School pose in front of the newly transferred school-room, the obtaining and re-erection of which was entered for the Village Ventures contest run by Shell (UK) in 1987/8, and which Plymtree villages won three years earlier in 1984 for their efforts in saving the school.

School Sports

Above: School Sports Day at the recreation ground, 1997. A competitive round of 'tunnel ball' proves a far cry from the refined lessons in country dancing of days gone by.

Left: Miss Millett (on the right, with gramaphone) instructs the girls in just such a lesson, c.1948.

Below: Plymtree School at the Culm Valley Schools Association Sports Day at Willand, 1986. From left to right – top row: Alex Hancock with Robin, Jean Lock, Chris Thornhill;
3rd row: Simon Barnett, Neil Purves, Joseph Hancock, Mark Bowles, Robert Coombes, John Thornhill, Timothy Lock;
2nd row: Rebecca Batten, Sara Bird, Angela Bowles, Julie Churchill, Emily Thornhill, Deborah Todd; bottom row: Raul Bowles, Daniel Copplestone, Jennifer Eaglestone, Rachel Horsfield.

Below: Chris Thornhill leads a sing-song in the school garden after Sports Day, July, 1985.

Special Days Past and Present

Left: Plymtree School, c.1948 with a song written by the head teacher, Miss Millett.

Right: In 1953, Coronation year, Miss Millett led a school trip to London which, of course, took in a visit to Buckingham Palace. Members of the group included Lorna Piper, Virginia Lovering, Hester Blackmore, Monica Lock, Phyllis Cleal, Ron Cleal, Diana Slater, Rosemary Alpin and Michael Hill.

Below: School concert at the parish hall, 1995.

Below: The school play, 1979 – 'The Midnight Thief'. Of the 22 pupils attending Plymtree School at the time, every one of them took part.

Plymtree schoolgirls, c.1922:
From left to right – back row: M. Widgery, H. Hussey, M. Burnell, A. Cooksley, D. Jarvis;
middle row: R. Saunders, E. Bird, F. Clarke, K. Pratt, F. Widgery, D. Holsgrove;
bottom row: J. Lock, W. Clarke, G. Jarvis, M. Bird, P. Minifie, J. Jarvis, P. Bird.

Plymtree schoolboys, c.1922.
From left to right – back row: G. Knight, R. White, F. Trivett, L. Glanville, J. Vinnicombe, G. Roswell;
3rd row: G. Minifie, G. Pratt, W. Bird, E. Widgery, R. Franks, W. Clarke, H. Minifie;
2nd row: J. Franks, A. Rowsell, C. Holsgrove, T. White, F. James, G. White, W. Lovering;
bottom row: F. Lock, A. Kellaway, A. Rosewell, H. Glanville.

The Passing Decades

Plymtree School in 1948. The children included: Rosemary Aplin, Hester Blackmore, Ken and Ron Cleal, Malcolm Churchill, John Gratton, Maragaret White, Michael Hill, Alan, Monica and Tony Lock, Malcolm Jones, Virginia Lovering, Roger Mason, Diane Salter, Iris and Marion Smith, Wendy Salter, Charles Vicary and Malcolm Williams.

Plymtree School, 1965
From left to right – back row: Stephen Peters, Christine Hellier, Peter Crane, Diane Luxton, David Tancock, Philip Batten;
middle row: Pamela Blackmore, Jill Clarke, Nigel Tancock, Roger Shere, Gillian Delves, Roy Lang, John Batten, Margery Crane, Lynda Lock;
bottom row: Jonathan Page, Ruth Peters, Wendy Franks, Janet Blackmore, Josie Kynaston, Geoffrey Delves, David Kynaston, Edwin Holmes, Yvonne Hellier, Trevor Hellier, Jocelyn Campbell, John Blackmore.

Victorian Day, 3rd February 1998

Above: Venda Gay and Pat Fay with Reception Class. Present are: Sarah Bloomfield, Katy Clark, Laura Derek, Matthew Frost, Jack Gimber, Joshua Jenner, Oliver Jenner, Laura King, India Langley, Hayley Lapthorne, Katie Maguard, Georgina Roberts, Emma Robertson, Robert Selway, Peter Thomas, Martyn Tolly, Joanna Williams, Alexander Wise, Benjamin Wooff, David Yendell.

Sally Whittel's Class 2 (and some of Class 3). Present are: Matthew Barret, Matthew Bere, Megan Bere, Aimee Blatchford, James Burgess, Sarah Caller, Harriet Chambers, Julia Harris, Kester Davids, Lee Derek, David Hammet, Nichola Hammet, Edward Higgs, Emily Holway, Leo Hopper, David Newcombe, Alexander Newman, John Paiva, Robyn Paulson, Tom Pettitt, Jacob Pring, Nicholas Roberts, Elena Rusalen, Jason Shelbourne, Christopher Reddaway, Laura Reed, Sam Ryder, Sunny Selway, Carolyn Yendall.

Victorian Day, 3rd February 1998

Dr Alison Browning and Fran Batten with Class 3 at Plymtree Church. Present are: Matthew Bere, Rachel Blackman, Killy Bloomfield, Danielle Chambers, Eamon Fayers, Bettany Griffiths, Holly Gyger, David Hammett, Matthew Hammett, Robin Harding, Laura Holway, Ania Honey, Megan Langley, Alex Newman, Clare Piper, Steven Reed, Janice Tolly, George Valvona, Nichola Williams, Katy Wooff.

Janet Barnett and Class 4. Present are: Ella Barnes, David Bewick, Laura Bewick, Harriet Bryant, Catherine Caller, Christopher Daniels, Tace Daniels, Christopher Edwards, Florence Gallagher, Timothy Gibbs, Megan Gimber, Stephen Gordon, Christopher Griffiths, Holly Higgs, Holly Hopper, Felicity Maries, Laura Newcombe, Kate Pettitt, Tim Piper, Jane Shere, Stuart Smith, Jessica Spencer, Kayley Thomas, Virginia Tidball, John Wilkins, Sarah Williams.

Victorian Day, 3rd February 1998

Left: Maggie Palfrey with some little ones.

Right: The staff at Plymtree School don their regalia to take part in the Victorian day, 1998.

Chapter 10: Law and Order

English society has always been controlled by law. The Saxon king, Edgar, divided the country up into shires, and he ordered that 'tythings' (groups of ten families) should be responsible for the actions of every member, and to pay a fine if any offended. He went on to create units with administrative and criminal jurisdiction, called 'hundreds', from groups of ten tythings. Plymtree was originally part of the hundred of 'Silfretone' (Silverton), but by Norman times it was called 'Hayridge', which name survived until 1834.

The royal courts of King's Bench and Common Pleas were in theory available to all, especially when the king's justices began to leave London and go on circuit around the country. They visited Devon in 1238, and in each hundred they held an 'Eyre' where, sitting with 12 jurors, they heard 'presentments' (allegations) about various wrongdoings, deaths, etc. One such presentment was that 'John Billes de Plimtre was found drowned in the River Culm'; the jury found he had died by misadventure. The name of William de Widebeare (Woodbeer) appeared twice, once as complainant and once as defendant; but he did not appear before the Eyre in either case, and both presentments were dismissed.

The Court of Chancery was another royal court, and in Tudor times it had a sister court, Star Chamber, which was part of the monarch's Privy Council. These courts dealt with personal outrages which could affect the 'King's Peace', and had the power to issue writs of sub-poena ('under pain') to force defendants to appear. In 1543 it heard arguments between Charles Coplestone and Thomas Stukeley, two claimants to the freehold of Woodbeer Court: Stukeley claimed that he had purchased the premises from a Jasper Horsey, and that Coplestone had entered the property and 'pulled downe a grete parte of the saide house, Suffrynge the resedue of the house to Rest in Greate Ruyne and decaye', while Coplestone claimed Stukeley was a liar and that Horsey only held the property against a debt owed, and that he had continued to live in the house until Stukeley 'with one William Cruse and John Frenston, persons of yll fame and name' and armed 'with swords, bucklers, bylls, staves, bowes and arrowes' had arrived and forcibly ejected him. It is not clear who won the case.

Ecclesiastical jurisdiction ran alongside the other legal systems, regulating all matters of marriage and death, as well as exercising control over the church's lands and property, which were extensive. Thus in 1529 John Salter, his wife Thomasine, and their son John purchased a 98-years lease of a parcel of land at Clyst William from the Prioress of St Katherine's Priory, Polsloe. The land included a close called Crosse Park, occupied by John Goodwyn, and a cottage with a right to graze cattle 'throughout the whole land late of Robert Swythynge'; the whole parcel was subject to a sub-lease for the life of William Salter and his wife Margery, and an annual rent of 35s.-4d. was payable to the Priory.

An intriguing note in Bishop Laud of Exeter's Common Register, dated 1st February 1449/50, instructed the Dean of the cathedral 'to enquire into an alleged pollution of the cathedral by bloodshed between William Raynold and William atte Ford, both of the parish of Plymptre'. Further details of the men and the cause of their fight are unknown but, had they been arrested by the Dean and his men, they could have been taken before a Church court and punished severely.

Another parallel judicial system was that of manorial courts. From the time of Domesday the lords had huge estates and, through their local stewards, extracted as much as they could from their tenants in money, crops or unpaid labour. Robert Hungerford, lord of Plymtree (and many other manors in various parts of England) died in 1459, leaving his estates to his son, also Robert. At the time, Robert junior was being held hostage, having been captured while attempting the relief of Chastillon in Aquitaine seven years earlier in 1452; he was only released on payment of a ransom of 12,000 marks plus a similar amount for the expense of keeping him (a total of about £16,000, equivalent to many millions of pounds in today's money). This money was raised by the sale of wool from his father's lands – which shows how extensive they must have been – though no doubt his tenants here and elsewhere also 'contributed' to the pot. Robert's bad luck continued, for he took the losing side in the Wars of the Roses, and was eventually beheaded.

Although by Tudor times most lords' estates were much smaller, the system of holding manorial courts continued. Whenever a tenant married or died a 'fine' had to be paid, and a change of

The magistrates' warrant appointing special constables, 1847.

tenant of a property owned by a lord also involved a 'fine'. A record of one such survives:

Court Roll of the Manor of Plymptre of Humphrey Smith, esq. [who had purchased the manor from Thomas Goodwin], *and Anne his wife, held on 15th September 1577. To the Court came Elizabeth Crosse, widow of Robert, together with Thomas West and Joan his wife, and surrendered lands which she held by Custom, and the land was then passed to her sons, Robert junior and John, for their lives, on payment of a £100 fine. Enrolled by John Maydon, Seneshal.*

The manors existed within their parish, of course, and the parish within its hundred, each of which had constables to enforce the law under the supervision of the Justices of the Peace of the county. The Justices were drawn from the county gentry, and hundred (or head) constables tended to be yeomen; but every ratepayer was supposed to serve his year as parish (or petty) constable – though the richer ones tended to pay others to serve in their stead. Perhaps because of this, entries in the poor books seldom name the petty constables, though they often identify those of the hundred.

Each of these officers had many administrative, as well as law-enforcement functions. When all the justices met at their Quarter Sessions, much of their work was to do with regulating trade and wages, with setting rates to raise money for bridges, the county gaol and hospital, and the like, but they also heard appeals from decisions made by single justices and, sitting with a petty jury, minor criminal cases. Likewise, the constable's job consisted largely in chasing away strangers not carrying 'passes' from a justice, arresting the alleged fathers of bastard children, and escorting families who had illegally tried to settle here back to their own parish.

That checking foodstuffs was part of the Parish Constable's duty is shown from an entry in the first poor book, probably written shortly after the Civil War: 'There was bought by Robert Crosse, Constable, a pare of Scales w'ch the p'yshe paydde for and it cost iiij.s 8.d. – it was to waye Bread as so said'.

An earlier entry, in the churchwardens' accounts for 1625, shows that informal justice, using social pressure, was also practised: 'Collected among the youth towardes th'amending of the glass of the north window of the Church next the tower – 10d.'

But Plymtree was also required to have its own means of formal punishment in the shape of the stocks. They had to be replaced in 1704, when 12s. was laid out on them; John Hawkins was the carpenter and Richard Palmer provided the ironwork. Intriguingly, there are no extant records of these stocks being used for punishment; were they utilised by the petty constable as a threat, to encourage parishioners to be good, and vagrants to move on, or were they merely there because the law required them?

Plymtree had no lock-up in which to keep prisoners until they could be taken before the local justice, so they were kept in private homes: the constable was paid by the overseers for his time spent guarding them, and the householder was paid for his trouble. Thus, in April 1727 the constable was paid 3s.-6d. 'for carrying Baker to Bridewell' and 3s. for 'his Charges & at Kifts' – Kift being the 'lucky' householder. Will Baker was just the sort of parishioner the overseers didn't want; it seems from the records that he consistently failed to support his wife, Elizabeth, who would 'fall on the parish' as a result. When released from the Bridewell the same year, he offended again, and it cost 5s. to transport him back there. Four years later 2s. was spent on obtaining a summons for him, issued at his wife's instigation.

All summonses and warrants had to be paid for at this time and, since everything the churchwardens or overseers did required legal authority, quite a lot of the overseers' rate money went 'to the Justices Clark' every year.

Before the establishment of a regular constabulary, the Justices of the Peace for the county dealt with public disorder by calling out military forces – either regular or militia units – or by appointing special constables from among local men of good reputation. In 1847 agricultural and other wages were depressed, but the price of food had reached an all-time high: 'bread riots' began to break out not only in the towns, but also in villages.

In May of that year the two justices for this area heard a statement on oath from a gentleman that a 'tumult' was likely to take place at Uffculme; fearing that such disorder may spread, they visited Plymtree on 28th May and issued a precept by which they appointed 24 men to be special constables for the following four months 'for the preservation of the Public Peace and for the protection of the Inhabitants and the security of the property in such parish'.

The chosen men were Samuel Bearn, Richard Blansford, Thomas Brice, John Cook, William Cook, William Cook junior, William Crook, John Davey, John Dimond, Samuel Granger, William Hockey, James Hussey, Thomas Hussey, William Lawrence, Thomas Mean, Benjamin Parris, Abraham Potter, Joseph Quick, Robert Reed, John Richards, John Salter, Thomas Salter, John Shiles and James Stamp. In the event it is believed that no such 'tumult' occurred, so their services were not required.

Violence is uncommon in Plymtree but on 12th May 1859 the *Exeter Flying Post* reported:

...an inquest held on William Clarke, aged 31, a mason of Plymtree. On 14th April 1859 he, with his father and brother [both named Joseph], John Trapp and others were drinking in the 'New Inn'. Late in the evening, Trapp challenged Clarke to fight; he eventually agreed to do so for a sovereign. No blows were exchanged. At 11pm they left for home [at Fordmore]. About a quarter mile from the inn, they removed their coats and began to fight. Somehow Clarke sustained a compound fracture of the leg. One of the Salter family helped his neighbour Clarke, who was later taken to the Devon & Exeter Hospital, where he died on 8th May. The verdict was 'accidental death'.

When the Devon Constabulary was first established in 1857, Plymtree was policed from Cullompton. Over time village bobbies began to appear, being billeted in local homes, but it was not until the 1920s that purpose-built police houses were put up all over the county, not only to provide dwellings but also police offices, where people could go to get assistance at any time of night or day. The local Constabulary House was at Langford, though that was sold off in the 1970s. However, it is still occupied by its last official tenant, ex-P.C. David Head, well-known for his light touch in dealing with problems in Plymtree and the surrounding area.

Nowadays, Plymtree is policed by officers in motor cars; happily they are seldom called upon to visit the village.

The men of the Plymtree Company, 3rd (Cullompton) Battalion, Devon Home Guard.
From left to right – back row: Fred Richards, Sid Lock, George Willmington, Fred Daniel,
Percy Batten, Herbie Minifie, Sidney Daniel, Gilbert Daniel, Edwin Widgery, Jack Turner,
Bill Lovering, Ernie Perry;
middle row: Robert Trickey, Bill Smith, Bill Jarvis, Miles Tidball, Gilbert Pratt, Les Sanders,
Fred Widgery, Fred Hussey, Jack Smith, Edward Langdon, Frank Blackmore;
front row: Frank Dymond, Earnest Pearcey, Jack Slater, Harold Franks, Ted Widgery,
Frank Hellier, Maurice Mulcahy, Humphrey Chattey, Edwin Martin, Jack Baker,
George Knight, Fred Franks.
(Absent: Bill Broom, Cyril ('Ike') Daniel, William Farnell, George Minifie, Percy Hill, Fred Slade)

Chapter 11: Times of War

Ancient times

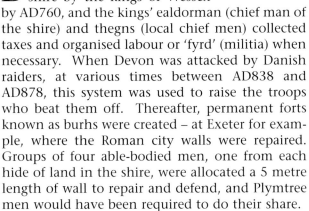

Devon had been recognised as a shire by the kings of Wessex by AD760, and the kings' ealdorman (chief man of the shire) and thegns (local chief men) collected taxes and organised labour or 'fyrd' (militia) when necessary. When Devon was attacked by Danish raiders, at various times between AD838 and AD878, this system was used to raise the troops who beat them off. Thereafter, permanent forts known as burhs were created – at Exeter for example, where the Roman city walls were repaired. Groups of four able-bodied men, one from each hide of land in the shire, were allocated a 5 metre length of wall to repair and defend, and Plymtree men would have been required to do their share.

Under King Edward the Elder (AD899-924), England became united, and King Edmund (AD939-46) created a new system of sub-county areas known as hundreds; Plymtree became a village in the hundred of Hayridge. Each hundred had its own thegn, but the new units cut across old loyalties, and began to weaken the defence system. When the Danes next attacked in force in 988, the fyrds managed to fight them off without great damage to English property, but further attacks in 997 and 1001 led to great plunder. Exeter held firm during the latter assault, but the Danes then beat the local fyrd at Pinhoe (where there is still Danes Wood), sacked Broadclyst and moved off across country to the East. Whether they came and sacked Plymtree is an open question, but we do have Danes Mill in the east of the parish (*below*) which may indicate that they did – and perhaps one of them stayed.

Tudor times

In 1509, at the age of 17, Henry VIII became king. He knew there were threats from the alliance of Scotland and France, and from Spain, and almost immediately set about strengthening the nation's war-preparedness: he re-organised the Royal Navy, ordering the building of huge new double-decker ships carrying 70 cannon, and he required all men under the age of 40 to possess bows and arrows and to practice archery every Sunday.

When Queen Elizabeth's throne was being challenged by Mary Queen of Scots and her supporters, the sheriff and five commissioners were ordered to find the military strength of the county by mustering all men aged 18 to 48 available for fighting, and to ascertain what arms and equipment they had. Richer persons unable to fight were required by the Statute of Armour to provide horses, arms and equipment according to their income from land or value of goods. The most important inhabitants of each parish were sworn to present the muster, and parish and hundred constables prepared the roll. All then mustered, with those of local parishes (to ensure that the same arms and/or men were not presented as being from different parishes), at a convenient place before one of the commissioners.

In 1569 the men of Hayridge hundred paraded at Cullompton, and those from Plymtree produced weapons in the shape of four bows, four sheafs of arrows, three pikes, three bills, and a harquebut (a primitive, long-barrelled gun), while their armour was three corslets, one murrion, one almen rivet and four stele caps. Six archers, three harquebusiers, four pikemen and ten billmen declared themselves trained and ready. Older men, and women ratepayers, were ordered to provide another harquebut for the use of the fighting men.

Throughout the 17th century the churchwardens' accounts include payments for taking the parish armour to a town or village in the hundred, and then for repairs to the pike, or sword or armour, as directed by the local Justices. In 1635 they also paid for 'repairs to the butts', showing that archery practice continued.

The PROTESTATION OATH RETURN for PLYMTREE [1642]

Babercombe, John	Holwill, John	Salter, Charles
Backer, John	Huckeway, Francis	Salter, Charles
Backes, Thomas	Isacke, William	Salter, John
Beadon, Allen	Irish, William	Salter, Philip
Bevis, Joseph	Juell, Robert	Salter, Robert
Bouden, Richard	Kent, John	Salter, Thomas
Burrow, Robert	Kent, William	Salter, William
Cash, William	Kinge, George	Sheiles, John
Cate, Robert	Kiston, John	Shore, Emanuel
Clarke, John	Knight, George	Smith, Ellis
Coocke, Robert	Knight, George	Smith, John
Crosse, Andrew	Knight, George	Squier, Michael
Crosse, Edward	Knight, Richard	Stacke, John
Crosse, William	Lane, Edward	Stanicke, Nicholas
Dawe, Thomas	Lane, Nicholas	Toser, Thomas
Denninge, John	Langbridge, John	Tucker, Nicholas
Domet, Thomas	Lee, James	Tucker, Thomas
Drew, Richard	Lee, Thomas	Turner, Fortin
Ducke, Humphrey	Loveing, John	Tyllard, John
Dyer, Humphrey	Manie, Richard	Tyllard, Thomas
Elicot, Roger	Maningeton, John	Vearne, Richard
Elles, George	Manly, John	Veriard, Ellis
Facy, Henry	Manly, Robert	Veriard, Robert
Forscue, Andrew	Manly, Robert	Veriard, Robert junior
Forscue, Christopher	May, Henry	Veriard, William
Forsecue, Edward	Michell, Nicholas	Vilven, James
Forsecue, James	Middleton, George	Warre, Rigilow
Forsecue, John	More, Charles	Warrior, William
Forsecue, Roger	Norcott, Henry	Wats, Nicholas
Foyle, Samuel	Oton, William	Way, Humphrey
Gent, William	Palmer, Peter	Webber, Robert
Godfrey, Francis	Parre, Thomas	Wescot, Thomas
Godfrey, Hannibal	Payne, Thomas - Minister	Wescote, Thomas
Godfrey, Thomas	Pearce, Robert senior	Wescote, William
Godfrey, William	Pearce, Robert junior	Westerne, George
Greedy, Edward	Potar, Henry	Whitny, Francis
Greedy, John	Potter, Thomas	Whity, Thomas
Greedy, Nicholas	Pound, Christopher	Woodford, Richard
Greene, Robert	Pound John	Woodson, John
Haeward, John	Pound, John	Wright, Henry
Harvy, Richard	Pound, John	Wright, Henry
Harward, Richard	Pound, Robert	Yeewe, Philip
Harward, Richard	Pound, William	
Hill, Jasper	Pounde, John	
Hill, John	Pounds, Bartholomew	Non-takers of the oath:
Hodge, John senior	Radford, Philip	
Hodge, John junior	Richards, Robert	May, Thomas (sick)
Hole, Edward Richards,	Richards, Tibbet	Pearce, Andrew
	Tibbet senior	(not at home)
Holway, William	Roads, Richard	Warren, Francis (sick)

[Signed]   Thomas Payne, Rector
Abraham Webber, Church Warden   William Pratt, Constable

The English Civil War

As part of their political and religious struggle with the king, the Commons and Protestant Lords took an oath in the spring of 1641 'to live and die for the true Protestant religion, the liberties and rights of subjects, and the privilege of Parliament'. To begin with they decided not to impose this Protestation Oath on the populace, but changed their minds when, in January 1642, the King tried to arrest five M.P.s. Every man aged 18 and over was required to take the oath, and lists were made of those who signed, as well as of those who refused to do so. In Plymtree alone 143 men signed, 3 were sick, but none refused; the list is signed by the rector (Thomas Payne) and the then churchwarden (Abraham Webber), and also by the constable, showing that the Oath was taken under the superintendence of the hundred. However, the fact that nearly every man signed did not mean they would support the parliamentary cause against that of the King.

On the whole, East Devon was slightly more royalist than parliamentarian when the war proper began in 1642, and recent research shows that while whole parishes tended to favour either the King or the parliament, the distribution of such loyalties was very patchy. Broadclyst, Bradninch and Ottery, for example, were strongly in favour of the king, while nearby Cullompton and Broadhembury maintained equally strong support for the parliament.

Plymtree does not figure in surviving records as supporting either side, though we do know of three men who were wounded while fighting on the King's side, as they later received pensions. They were William Blewett (or Bluett), gent, a Captain of Foot in Col. Sir John Acland's regiment; Abraham Doble, a foot soldier in Col. Richard Arundell's regiment; and Robert Melhuish, whose regiment is not stated. (Interestingly, none of these had signed the Oath at Plymtree in 1642.).

Throughout the war, Exeter (the parishes of which were split 50/50 between king and parliament) was almost constantly occupied by one side or the other, and beseiged by the opposing side, whose troops would then forage the country for provisions, wreaking havoc in local villages. It is possible that Plymtree escaped these particular depredations due to its isolated position and its distance from the city.

An interesting rumour dating from this time was reported in the 1750s, in answer to the Dean Milles questionnaire, which asked about, among other things, 'ancient Preaching Crosses'. The rector responded: 'I have heard that there was an ancient Cross in the Church yard & can make out that it was removed by one Land, an old zealous Committee Man in ye Civil wars; ye Base or Sockett of it I have seen & is now in being.' (The 'Land' mentioned as a 'Committee man' – i.e. a Puritan – would have lived at Woodbeer Court: however, a Robert Land supported the Royalist Capt. Bluett when he applied for a pension. In any case the rumour seems to have been untrue, as the head of the cross was discovered in the foundations of the Church House, which had been built in Tudor times.).

The Monmouth Rebellion

In February 1685 James II succeeded his brother Charles II; although the new king accepted the constitutional position of the Church of England, the fact of his being a Catholic increased the friction between the Crown and Protestant dissenters. The Duke of Monmouth (Charles II's illegitimate son, and therefore a contender for the Crown), called for James's removal, and 730 East Devonians joined Monmouth when he landed at Lyme Regis.

The rebels marched through Axminster to Taunton and then towards Bristol before retreating to their final defeat at Sedgemoor at the hands of the king's professional army. There followed the Bloody Assizes in September at Exeter and elsewhere, when Chief Justice Jeffreys meted out scant justice and hard punishment to those captured, a total of 26 men being executed, and many more transported to the West Indies.

Two of the Devonshire rebels were from Plymtree: Thomas Cookney was a woolcomber, who was imprisoned at Taunton and then 'presented' at Dorchester Court, but was proposed for a pardon; Thomas Stone was a worsted comber, who was imprisoned in the High Gaol of Devon, but who also appears to have been pardoned, as he was buried at Plymtree in 1732.

The two men were typical of Monmouth's 'army', one third of whom had hitherto been engaged in the cloth industry. It may be that there were also Plymtree men in the Devon Militia, who failed to engage the rebels but instead contented themselves with keeping an eye on them. (At least the Devon Militia did not run away or desert to the rebels, as the Dorset and Somerset Militias did!).

The regular army

Local training in firearms apparently continued, at least until the end of the 17th century, since the overseers paid the constable £2-6s. for ammunition in 1697. But the king needed more than the militia to fight England's enemies, and a regular army began to be established from 1660.

Apart from foreign mercenary troops, young English soldiers were always required. One such was Richard Venn, born in Plymtree in 1702, who joined the army at 24. During his service he would have fought against the French and the Jacobites, but he survived to become an out-pensioner of the Royal Hospital, Chelsea; he retired home to Plymtree in 1749 and married a widow, living peacefully until his death in 1791.

SCHEDULE

Return to be made by the Constable to the Clerk, of the Subdivision Meeting.

A list of the persons within the Parish of *Plymtree* between the ages of 18 and 45 liable to serve in the Militia, taken the *3* Day of *January* 18 *17*.

No.	Names	Description	Age	Whether any Child and if any whether under or above 14	Exempt or not exempt from the Militia	Grounds of Exemption	Volunteer or Yeoman
1.	Griffin, Thomas	Loger	21		Not exempt		
2.	Salter, Charles	Lodger	21		Do.		
3.	Cook, William	Housekeeper	37	1 Child under 14			
4.	Potter, William	Sarvent	35		Do.		
5.	Wolcott, Henry	Lodger	21		Do.		
6.	Quick, Edward	Lodger	24		Do.		
7.	Vinicomb, John	Sarvent	23		Do.		
8.	Brice, John	Housekeeper	21		Do.		
9.	Brice, William	Lodger	23		Do.		
10.	Richards, John	Sarvent	21		Do.		
11.	Harris, Francis	Lodger	42	1 Under 14			
12.	Dimond, John	Housekeeper	43	1 Under & 1 Above			
13.	Dowell, James	Housekeeper	27	1 Under 14			
14.	Clarke, William	Housekeeper	28	1 Under 14			
15.	Baker, Henry	Lodger	28	None	Exempt		Yeoman
16.	Salter, John	Lodger	28	Do.	Do.		Do.
17.	Griffin, John	Lodger	23	Do.	Do.		Do.
18.	Parris, Binjimen	Housekeeper	35	4 Under 14	Do.		Do.
19.	Sanders, John	Sarvent	21	None	Do.	Serving in the Local	
20.	Hussey, Thomas	Sarvent	24	Do.	Do.	Do.	Do.
21.	Gard, William	Lodger	25	Do.	Do.	Do.	Do.
22.	Clarke, John	Lodger	23	Do.	Do.	Do.	Do.
23.	Salter, Thomas	Lodger	22	Do.	Do.	Do.	Do.
24.	Richards, William	Sarvent	24	1 Under 14	Do.	Do.	Do.
25.	Hockey, William	Housekeeper	31	None	Do.	Served 4 years in the Local	
26.	Ireland, John	Housekeeper	33	1 Under 14	Do.	Do.	Do.
27.	Hines, John	Housekeeper	32	2 Under 14	Do.		
28.	Fouracers, James	Housekeeper	43	1 Under, 1 Above	Do.		
29.	Bennett, Gorge	Housekeeper	40	6 Under 14	Do.		
30.	Petters, John	Housekeeper	40	3 Under 14	Do.		
31.	Woodbery, William	Housekeeper	34	2 Under 14	Do.		
32.	Ellis, William	Do.	34	4 Under 14	Do.		
33.	Bray, Richard	Do.	35	4 Under 14	Do.		
34.	Stiling, Thomas	Do.	32	2 Under 14	Do.		
35.	Blake, Humphry	Do.	27	2 Under 14	Do.		
36.	Veysie, William	Do.	35	5 Under 14	Do.		
37.	Deaner, William	Do.	35	3 Under 14	Do.		
38.	Stiling, William	Do.	42	2 Under 14	Do.		
39.	Bennett, William	Do.	35	5 Under 14	Do.		
40.	Tucker, Charles	Do.	43	3 Under 14	Do.		
41.	Saulter, John	Do.	24	1 Under 14	Do.		
42.	Jared, John	Sarvent	34	None			
43.	Gredy, Robert	Sarvent	25	Do.			
44.	Lake, John	Sarvent	23	Do.			
45.	Truckey, James	Sarvent	21	Do.			
46.	Harnal, Henry	Sarvent	23	Do.			
47.	Stark, Gorge	Apprintice	19	Do.	Do.	Apprintice	
48.	Stiling, Joseph	Apprintice	19	Do.	Do.	Do.	
49.	Salter, William	Apprintice	19	Do.	Do.	Do.	

The 1817 militia list. The final column, for 'Licensed Teacher not carrying on Trade', was blank and has been left out.

1745-1914

France unsuccessfully sent a fleet to invade England in 1744, in support of Bonny Prince Charlie, and war preparations began; they were to continue almost constantly until the defeat of Napoleon in 1815. This called for an increased supply of all sorts of crops and livestock, cider and wool, and farmers grew rich.

The income from farms was valuable to the parish and, since everyone aged between 18 and 45 was liable to be called (by ballot) to serve in the militia, from 1781 we find the overseers paying other parishes who were supporting the wives and children of men acting as substitutes for these valuable parishioners. Hence, 'To the Overseers of Bradninch for John Veyseys Family being a Substitute for Wm. Fulford in the Supplementary Militia home to the 3rd Day of December 1799 – £7-4s.', and in 1808 'paid John Lenden Ten parts of thirteen towards a Substitute in the Militia being the part of this Parish to pay which was Drawn for Cadleigh – £7-13s.-9d.'

The navy also needed men, so a bounty was offered for volunteers. In 1795 Mr Thomas Blake, overseer, paid one William Baker £5-9s. for joining up. Baker was released by 1804, when he was unluckily balloted for the 'Army of Reserve'.

The First World War

The Great War led to a considerable increase in agricultural production and employment for Plymtree people. The Devon War Agricultural Committee ensured that sufficient grain was being grown to meet the national requirement: of 1988 productive acres in 1918, wheat was grown on 278 acres, oats on $183^1/_2$, barley on $43^1/_2$ and potatoes on $8^1/_4$. The rest of the land, apart from that occupied by orchards, was presumably used for livestock.

There was no conscription into the Services until 1916, but many men volunteered to join up, and others were reservists who were called to the colours: two of them died. Frederick Stiling joined the 7th Battalion of the Devonshire Regiment as a volunteer, then transferred to the Royal Artillery, and survived most of the War only to die on 6th June 1918, in a prisoner of war camp in Aulnoy, France, five months before the Armistice. Sam Bird, the father of six at Normans Green, was serving as a driver (of horses) with the Royal Field Artillery in France when his lungs were so damaged by a poison-gas attack that he was repatriated to a military hospital in Ripon, Yorkshire; he died there on 22nd August 1918.

Various Militia Acts were passed by Parliament during times of hostility, with the aim of training soldiers to defend the country. The Local Militia Act of 1807 was one such, and we have the 1817 return of all 49 Plymtree men liable for service. Despite the fact that this was peace-time, John Sanders was already a militia-man, and William Hockey had previously served his four years.

In 1906 the Rector reported to the parish:

'The proposal to form a Plymtree Rifle Club has, chiefly owing to the good influence of Mr A. Marshall [the publican], led on to something far better, namely, the enrolment of a Plymtree detachment of Captain Lilley's Honiton or 'D' Company of the 3rd or Volunteer Battalion of the Devon Regiment. About 25 have enlisted, and are being drilled by Sergeant-Instructor Greenslade, in the old Tithe-barn at the Rectory, where also a Morris-tube range is being fitted up. Every able-bodied man ought to take the opportunity, which Volunteer corps give, of fitting himself to defend our country, if need be, against foreign aggression. The best, indeed the only, guarantee of peace is to be prepared for war.'

Despite regular Church parades (and presumably further training) thereafter, peace was not in fact guaranteed.

A third man, Joe Dyer, who joined the Coldstream Guards from Plymtree at the outbreak of war, was killed in a training accident in France in 1915. (In fact, he was a Broadclyst man, working only temporarily in Plymtree.). The needs of the army, due to the wholesale slaughter on the Western Front, became so desperate that the schoolmaster, William Gale, was conscripted.

We know that there were at least 36 ex-servicemen from the village who survived the war, since that number was invited to a supper and entertainment at Greenend on Saturday 4th October 1919, organised by the Peace Festivities Committee. Absent was Percy Prouse, youngest son of Mrs William Prouse of Clyst William, who was working on the railway and living at Folkestone. It was there that he was presented with the Military Medal, the citation reading:

On March 21st 1918, while serving with the Machine Gun Corps on the Somme, after being surrounded by the Germans, he fought his way single-handed to his own lines with a machine gun, two hours after he repulsed an attack.

The same Committee had previously arranged a Peace Sports, involving all the men, women and children of the village, each of whom had been given a 'tea', and every child some chocolate.

The Second World War

Some 27 Plymtree men served in the armed forces during the war, and two of them lost their lives. Private Harold George Franks died on 13th November 1943 while fighting the Germans with the King's Own Royal Regiment in Greece, his death being recorded on the military memorial at Athens: Sergeant Air Gunner Francis Sidney Knight, R.A.F.V.R., was killed on 16th August 1944 while flying with No. 148 Squadron R.A.F. against the enemy in Italy, his body being buried in the war cemetery at Assissi.

At the outbreak, the Plymtree Local Defence Committee was formed, later re-named the Plymtree Invasion Committee. *The Plymtree War Book* (its cover bearing the note that, 'If hasty evacuation be necessary, this book must be destroyed') shows that almost every villager was involved. There were air raid wardens, fire guards, first-aiders, A.R.P. and other messengers (some of them 16-year-old girls like Barbara Cross, and Freda and Hilda Mary Daniel), a Rest Centre Committee, and a 'Housewife Cleansing Service', all set up against the day when the bombs began to fall, or the village was invaded by German troops.

The first line of defence against such an event was, of course, the Plymtree Company of the 3rd (Cullompton) Battalion of the Devon Home Guard. Firstly under the command of Major Frank Sanders and then Captain Maurice Mulcahy

(licensee of the 'New Inn'), loudly assisted by Sgt. Major Frank Hellier of Clyst Hydon, the Plymtree volunteers included: Jack Baker, Percy Batten, Frank Blackmore, Bill Broom, Humphrey Chattey, Cyril

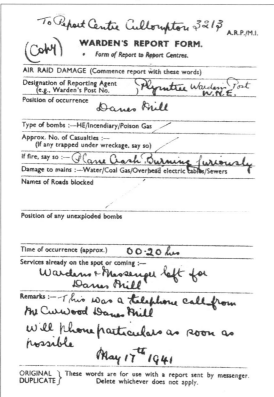

The Wildish family who lodged with the Husseys at Oaklands while father was in the army.

('Ike') Daniel, Fred Daniel, Gilbert Daniel, Sidney Daniel, Frank Dymond, William Farnell, Fred Franks, Harold Franks, Percy Hill, Fred Hussey, Bill Jarvis, George Knight, Edward Langdon, Sid Lock, Bill Lovering, Edwin Martin, George Minifie, Herbert Minifie, Ernest Pearcey, Ernie Perry, Gilbert Pratt, Fred Richards, Jack Salter, Les Sanders, Fred Slade, Bill Smith, Jack Smith, Miles Tidball, Robert Trickey, Jack Turner, Edwin Widgery, Fred Widgery, Ted Widgery and George Willmington.

Their only moment of real excitement came at 12.20am on 17th May 1941, when a German Junkers 88 bomber was shot down by a Beaufighter night-fighter of 600 Squadron from R.A.F. Colerne, near Bath, crewed by F/Lt. A. D. McBoyd and F/O. A. J. Clegg. The bomber had flown from Rosieres in France to bomb Birmingham, but broke up in the air as a result of the attack and crashed behind Danes Mill with its load of 12 bombs, killing its crew of four: the bodies of Oberfeldwebel Fritz Preugschat and Unteroffiziers Heinz Kretschmer, George Feus and Franz Mitzkah were buried at the Higher Cemetery in Exeter. The A.R.P. (Air Raid Precautions) Warden's report of the incident still survives (*left*).

It is possible that the searchlight battery sited in Woodbeare Coppice field (at what was judged to be the highest point in the parish) played a part in the destruction of this enemy bomber. The battery was manned by 40 men of the Royal Artillery, who lived in nissen huts near their searchlights: they apparently joined in the local social life of the village whenever their duties allowed and, despite the strength of local cider, there was never trouble of any consequence.

The Home Guards' normal duty was night patrols on their bicycles, at the end of their day's work on the farms or in local factories, to hunt for German parachutists and saboteurs. One special target of their interest was a house at Normans Green, rented by a couple who many villagers believed to be of German origin, and from which it was alleged that lights were shown at night. The couple vanished one night, and a room in the house was 'found to be full of wires'. Were they spies? We shall never know!

It has been alleged (by one of the Home Guard) that the consumption of cider was undiminished during their deeds of daring-do. Everyone smoked in those days, and at the end of a spell of duty one of the company disposed of his fag-end out of the back of their truck: unfortunately their brand-new rifles were in a trailer behind, and gun-oil proved to be highly inflammable!

As there was great fear of aerial attack, farmers followed the lead of the army and repainted their brightly-coloured tractors dark green, so as to make them less of a target.

Early on in the war many evacuees from the cities arrived in the parish, including the Wildish family from Kent (*see opposite*). A Catholic primary school was evacuated *en masse* from Southwark in south London, with their teachers, Mr and Mrs J. Moan.

German ex prisoner-of-war, 'Blondie' Schmidt looking after Roger and Elizabeth Persey at Fordmore, 1947.

The U.S. Army Air Force had arrived in Devon by then, and G.I.s from the Dunkeswell base were often to be seen driving their jeeps around the lanes, usually heading to or from the pub: they loved Devon cider.

Charity fund-raising continued during the war. A newspaper report of one held at Hayne House in 1942/3 to raise money for the local Nursing Association shows just how much effort was poured into such an event.

When the war was over, the Parish Meeting formed a Welcome Home Committee for the returning servicemen. A May Queen election was held, at a penny a vote; Mary Martin won with 10,300 votes, and she presided on 18th May 1946, when a fête and dance was held at Greenend. £325-9s. was raised, from which the War Memorial tablet in the church was funded: each of the returning servicemen, and the next of kin of those who had died, was given ten guineas as a 'thank you' gesture from the village.

Miss Mary Martin, 'May Queen' at the 'Welcome Home' celebrations for ex-servicemen, with her supporters at Greenend, 18th May 1846.

The Cullompton Fire Brigade, 1911.
A posed picture, taken after they had fought the fire at Plymtree Rectory on 10th August 1911.
Captain Brooks is sitting behind the driver.

Chapter 12: Fires

The then rector, Rev. Edgar Hay, writing in about 1930, noted that: 'during the past 50 years at least eight out of about twenty-five houses bigger than cottages have been burned down. They had lasted for hundreds of years, though thatched and built of timber and cob: the fatal change was fitting modern stoves with forced draught into old chimneys with wooden beams built into them.' He was writing with some knowledge, since it is believed that such a forced-draught stove had led to the terrible destruction of the Rectory nearly 20 years earlier in 1911.

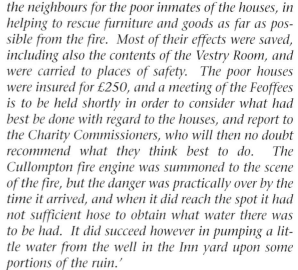

Firemen tackling the roof fire at Buckhurst Cottage, 1st April 1997.

In earlier days, when most buildings (and hay-ricks) were thatched, fires were fought by friends and neighbours, using buckets of water from the nearest stream or pond, and by pulling down burning thatch with long hooks. Some grand houses, such as Hayne, Fordmoor and Woodbeare Court, had fire insurance which entitled them to call out the insurers' fire brigade – though given that a message would have to be sent by hand, and the brigade assembled and galloped to Plymtree before it could begin work, the utility of this arrangement must have been somewhat doubtful.

The *Exeter Flying Post* recorded the odd fire at Plymtree. Thus on 21st March 1850 it blandly reported that 'A fire destroyed one old house belonging to William Hockey.' (Not for the first time, the newspaper got it wrong: William Hole was the owner, and William Hockey the occupier, of the end cottage at Pencepool, beside the stream. It was very quickly re-built).

The Rector, writing in the *Plymtree Church Monthly* for July 1895 described the fire which destroyed the Church House and other cottages:

Monday June 10th will be remembered as the date of a fire in Plymtree Village. From the Church lych-gate up to the New Inn there now remain but ruins of the cottages once standing there. Fire broke out just before noon, and in three hours it was all over. It broke out in the premises of Mr Lewis Ware, Carpenter and Wheelwright, almost in the centre of the block, and spreading right and left soon held all the cottages. The men working at the Church were of the greatest help and, joined by others, succeeded in checking the fire before it seized the Inn. The three Church Houses with the Vestry Room could not possibly be saved, and being thatched ignited all the more quickly. Mr Ware's premises, including dwelling house with shop at the front, store-houses and carpenters' shop, were almost entirely burnt out. Much help and sympathy were shewn by the neighbours for the poor inmates of the houses, in helping to rescue furniture and goods as far as possible from the fire. Most of their effects were saved, including also the contents of the Vestry Room, and were carried to places of safety. The poor houses were insured for £250, and a meeting of the Feoffees is to be held shortly in order to consider what had best be done with regard to the houses, and report to the Charity Commissioners, who will then no doubt recommend what they think best to do. The Cullompton fire engine was summoned to the scene of the fire, but the danger was practically over by the time it arrived, and when it did reach the spot it had not sufficient hose to obtain what water there was to be had. It did succeed however in pumping a little water from the well in the Inn yard upon some portions of the ruin.'

The same newspaper also reported the fire, but failed to mention the loss of the Church House.

The Cullompton Fire Brigade (*left*) often fought fires in the parish, their first Plymtree call being when an oil lamp was left standing too close to a bedroom partition at Middle Weaver farm. However, the occupier, Mr J. Pratt and his workmen dealt with the fire before the brigade arrived.

A local newspaper report, of 27th August 1909, gives a flavour of the way they operated:

At 1.15pm on Thursday the Brigade received a telegram asking them to attend a hayrick fire at Greenend, the residence of Mr J. N. Franklin, JP. Captain George Brooks, sub-captain F. Sweet, firemen W. Sweet and J. Pring were soon on their way to Plymtree with the engine, drawn by three horses, the other firemen following close after on bicycles.

They used three hoses to prevent the fire spreading to nearby barns, and had to remain at the scene until 11pm that day. The next month they tackled another rick fire at Tyes Farm 'believed to have been caused by an incendiary'; and in May 1911 lightning was the cause of a fire in outbuildings at Woodbeare Court, which took the firemen nine hours to extinguish. But by far the most serious fire this century was that on 10th August 1911, which destroyed the Rectory. This is the newspaper report of that fire, which includes many fascinating details of the old building:

FIRE AT PLYMTREE
RECTORY DESTROYED

In the recollection of the oldest inhabitant of the pretty village of Plymtree - a small rural parish about four miles south-east of Cullompton - there has never been such a devastating fire as that which occurred in their midst an hour before noon on Thursday last when the ancient, thatched Rectory, occupied by the Rev E. H. Hay and family, was totally demolished. By lucky chance, the Rector and his gardener, Mr W. Pratt, were at home at the time of the outbreak.

When our representative visited the grounds of Plymtree Rectory on Friday afternoon, a scene of devastation presented itself: bare walls of cob in some cases over 3ft thick, and huge charred timbers of oak were all that remained of one of the oldest and most picturesque rectories in Devon. The Rector was then standing almost in the middle of the debris with Captain Brooks, of the Cullompton Fire Brigade....

RECTOR'S NARRATIVE

In reply to condolences as to his loss, the Rector said:-"Thank you. It is indeed a great catastrophe. I was just discussing with Captain Brooks the probable cause of the conflagration. On the morning of the fire I had a bonfire of weeds in the kitchen garden. But I cannot think that a spark from that was the cause of the outbreak, because the wind was East and blowing towards it and away from the Rectory."

The Rector proceeded to "pace out" the distance from the spot where the outbreak occurred to the heap of charred weed in the garden, and found it was 30 yards. He also pointed out the high laurel bushes over which a spark would have to be carried in order to reach the Rectory, and added: "No, I feel convinced the fire did not originate from that source: it must have been started by a spark from the kitchen chimney falling on the thatch, which after these weeks of record heat was as dry as tinder." Captain Brooks took a similar view.

Asked to give a few details connected with the fire; the Rector willingly consented and suggested that we might find a comfortable seat on an old oak settle, which with many other articles of furniture, mostly oak, was then standing on the edge of the lawn fronting the charred walls of the Rectory. Our representative commented on the excellence of the carving on the back of the settle whereupon the Rector remarked: "This settle was formerly an old oak bedstead which I purchased at a cottage sale for eighteen pence. I affixed the carving to the back. I am very fond of old furniture of any description." That that was so, was evident from the choice old furniture littered about the lawn. Near-by was a fine old Jacobean bench, unfortunately damaged by hurried transit from the house; a little further on were an old oak sideboard and a wardrobe of similar material. "That Jacobean bench really belongs to the Church," explained the Rector. "We had several things stored at the Rectory while the recent repair of the Church was in progress."

And then our conversation passed to the fire proper. "It broke out," said the Rector, "at the west end of the Rectory a little before eleven o'clock on Thursday morning. I was sitting in my study at the time, writing. I believe young Mr Veysey, butcher, of Cullompton, gave the alarm, but the smoke appears to have been seen by other people in the village about the same time, including Mr R. Lear, of Tye's Farm. Soon almost the whole village had come to the rescue, and every one set to work to get out the furniture; even the children lent a helping hand, and I am extremely grateful to all; also to the Cullompton Fire Brigade, who responded smartly to the call and did excellent work, sometimes at great personal risk. Mr R. Lear, Mr A. W. Marshall, Mr W. B. Franklin, Mr F. W. Minifie, and Mr F. R. Knight tried to cut off the flames on the roof. But the fire had such a hold of the thatch that it was impossible for the helpers to check its course.

"When the Brigade came, they at once endeavoured to isolate the fire by cutting into the thatch in two places. But it was of no avail, the fire had crept underneath the thatch in all

---

directions and as soon as the flames were subdued at one spot they burst out afresh in another part of the building. The thatch in some places must have been nearly ten feet thick. You see, when the roof was re-thatched, they did not remove the old thatch; why should they? It is less trouble to put new on the top.

"Thanks to the willing help of the people I have mentioned, and that of Superintendent de Schmid, who motored here, Police Constables Lewis, Gill and Densham, we managed to save nearly all the furniture. I am especially thankful to say that we saved the church plate; and the church registers, which date from 1538, and were stored in an old oak box. This is the second time this box has narrowly missed being destroyed by fire; the other occasion was at the time of the fire in the old vestry room in 1895. This oak box was formerly chained down to the floor in the old church house. We always kept the box with the church registers near the window of the drawing-room of the Rectory. I said to my wife one day, 'If ever there is a fire here and I am not here, be sure and try to save the church registers by bundling the old box out of the window.' So this is the second narrow squeak it has had; I suppose people will be afraid to have the box in their houses after this," added the Rector with a smile.

Referring to the structure of the Rectory, the Rector said the main portion was about 500 years old. It contained sixteen or seventeen rooms; the drawing-room was 43ft. by 16ft., with two huge fireplaces; immediately above was an oak-floored sleeping chamber. This chamber had been partitioned off in the usual way into three separate rooms, the inner for the maids, the middle for the rector and his wife, and the outer for the men folk. In modern times an annexe about six feet wide was built all along the western wall and a separate entrance into each bedroom pierced through the original outer wall.

"Since the fire," proceeded the Rector, "I have since discovered two or three old cupboards which were apparently bricked up near the old-fashioned fireplaces in the mediaeval part of the building. In one of the bedrooms there was an Adam mantelpiece. I was sorry not to be able to save some of the beautiful stained glass in the upstairs windows of the old part of the rectory. Some of the glass contained Dutch inscriptions, and dated from 1639. About eighty years ago, there was a rector here named Joseph Dornford, and it is said that these windows were put in by him."

FIRE BRIGADE'S GOOD WORK

About 11-30 on Thursday morning Captain Brooks received a telegram worded: "come at once, Plymtree Rectory on Fire. Hay." He at once cycled round to warn several firemen, and within six minutes of the alarm three horses drawing the manual engine were on their way to the scene of the fire. Capt. Brooks, in the course of an interview, said: "When we arrived at Plymtree the roof of the Rectory was well alight. We immediately got out about a thousand feet of hose, water being obtained from a pit (dug by Mr J. N. Franklin, of Greenend), into which water flowed from a spring situated about 800 feet from the Rectory.

"With the idea of isolating the fire, we cut and stripped quite four feet of thatch from the roof. It was then we discovered that the fire had crept between the ceiling and the roof, on to which we played water from four different positions. Sparks were flying about in all directions, and Mr Lear was fearful as to the safety of his straw and hay ricks, situated about twenty or thirty yards away from the Rectory. I sent word telling him to put his men near the ricks, and beat out all sparks immediately they settled thereon. It was impossible to spare one of the hoses at that time as the fire was gradually becoming fiercer every minute. Thursday was a hot day, and this together with the intense heat of the fire made our work exceedingly hard. At one time it almost seemed as if we were working within a circle of fire; the flames ran along the dry grass of the slope at the back of the house, burning laurel and other bushes en route. A fine old Weymouth pine was also badly scorched.

"Never in all my life" (continued Capt. Brooks) "have I had to contend with so fierce a fire; it almost needed half-a-dozen fire-engines to successfully cope with the flames, which spread to the outbuildings. Suddenly we found that the thatch of the old tithe barn, situated a few yards from the Rectory, had caught. But before the flames made anything like headway, we had stripped off the burning thatch and gave the roof a thorough damping down. The firemen worked splendidly; before they had been at the job ten minutes the perspiration was pouring from their faces like water from a pump; their shirts were as wet as if one had trailed them in a river. We kept pumping continuously for 12 hours - that is from about mid-day till midnight on Thursday. Even then it was not safe to leave the spot as little fires were repeatedly jumping up in all parts of the debris. Everything is so dry that to have left the spot would have *been to court great danger to surrounding property. We have now... three men in charge, Firemen W. Brooks, J. Whitfield and myself."*

OTHER DETAILS
Captain Oakes, of Hayne House, kindly placed his house at the disposal of the Rev. Hay and his family until the School House was ready for occupation. Mr Lear stored some of the Rector's furniture at his house.

Mrs Hay and daughter and servants assisted the Rector in saving as many as possible of the family relics. The Rector's chief thought was of

thankfulness that nothing worse had happened, and of sincerest gratitude to the host of kind friends who had helped him in his misfortune; but when all was done that could be done to save the historic old building, Mrs Hay collapsed. On inquiry on Friday we were glad to hear that she is rapidly recovering from the effects of the shock. Supt. de Schmid sustained an injury to his back while lifting an old oak chest. On inquiry at the Cullompton Police Station we were glad to hear that Supt. de Schmid was making good progress. It is understood that the damage, amounting to about £2,400, is covered by insurance.

The rector later noted in the *Parish Magazine* that the fire 'started in the kitchen wing, and was probably caused by some of the brickwork of the chimney having perished with extreme age.'

In 1923 the parish meeting voted to contribute £48-5s. as its share towards the purchase of a motor Fire Engine (for £1,050) by the Cullompton Fire Brigade: had they not done so, there would have been no assistance in fighting any big fires like that at the Rectory, although the householder or the parish still had to pay working expenses if the Brigade was called out.

That at the old Rectory was not the last fire in Plymtree, but it was probably one of the last resulting in the total destruction of a house in the parish. (Langford Court, nearby, was burnt out in June 1994 – it has since, happily, been rebuilt.). In

the case of a fire which occurred at Middle Clyst William in May 1959, for example, the blaze, despite being serious, was controlled in the traditional way, by pulling down the thatch.

Thatch remains an extremely combustible material but, despite the fact that we still have a number of thatched houses in the parish, roof fires are quite uncommon and, with the speed of communications and the efficiency of the Devon Fire and Rescue Service, they are quickly dealt with when they do occur. A recent fire is a case in point, for when, on 1st April 1997, the thatch of Buckhurst Cottage, Fordmore, caught alight, a host of fire appliances from Cullompton, Ottery St Mary, Honiton, Exeter and Exmouth arrived in time to ensure that Bryan and Jane Franklin's house was saved.

Above: The Rectory is consumed by fire on 10th August 1911.

Right: A newspaper clipping of the fire which destroyed part of the roof at Middle Clyst William on 23rd May 1959.

Chapter 13: Parish Politics

Until the 19th century 'political' tensions revolved around religion, money or personalities, and only rich men were involved in the 'great game' of politics with a capital P. True, some men had high ideals which they followed to the extent of fighting for them – in the Civil War and the Monmouth Rebellion, for example. But most taking-of-sides occurred for lesser reasons.

The poor books and other parish records record occasional arguments between villagers, but most were very minor. More serious were the legal actions fought between rectors and landowners over tithe charges, which must have caused a great deal of bad feeling in the parish. This problem was intended to be tackled by the Tithe Commutation Act of 1836, under which commissioners negotiated fair land values with landowners, which values formed the basis of a 'rent-charge' payable to the incumbent. At a meeting between Rev. Joseph Dornford and the major landowners on 27th January 1839, land values were agreed, as was the rent-charge of £282-17s.-4d. p.a., and everything seemed settled.

But the ownership of the Rectory was in the hands of Oriel College, Oxford, and they refused to accept the level of rent-charge: they got their own surveyor and valuer, who came up with a figure of £311-2s.-0d.; the landowners' man said £221; eventually the Commissioner imposed a figure of £290. It is not known whether anyone was happy with this figure but, when it was imposed on 6th May 1842, after three years of haggling, at least it brought an end to expensive court proceedings.

The old system of local government, based on hundreds and parish vestries, came to an end in 1894. Henceforth, Plymtree was administered by Honiton Rural District (based on the old Poor Law Union) and its own Parish Council; on 4th December Plymtree Parish Council was elected and held its inaugural meeting. Since 1872 the National Agricultural Labourers Union, aided by nonconformist preachers, had been agitating nationally, with some success, for better pay for land workers. In the 1880s they and other interests began working for rural householders' electoral rights equal to those already given to townspeople, and in 1884 they succeeded. Not only could a working man vote, but he could also stand for election – to the Parish Council at least.

Despite the fact that the chapel had flourished when the farmers transferred their allegiance from the parish church, it was also strongly supported by farm-workers. The old rift between church and chapel was exacerbated by this political advance.

The new Parish Councillors were Thomas Arbery of Perhams Green, farm labourer; Thomas Henry Baxter of Greenend, farmer; Hampden Garibaldi Classey of Normans Green, Congregational Minister; William Cook of Lower Weaver, farmer; Richard Pratt of Greenend, farm labourer; John Sanders junior of Normans Green, artisan; and Henry Wheaton of Fordmoor, farmer. The chairman was the rector, Rev. George Gutteres.

The 'voluntary rate' which had formerly been used for church purposes – including the School – became the Parish Council rate in 1894; the ratepayers, especially nonconformists, objected to continuing to pay rates to support a school under the control of the Church of England, and a certain amount of bitter debate followed. When Rev. Edgar Hay arrived as rector in 1897, he immediately tried to quiet this quarrel by encouraging the villagers to raise money to buy the school from Mrs Mozley.

New Parish Councillors were elected at a parish meeting on 6th March 1899. Those elected (with their votes) were: William Loosemore (27), William Prouse (26), H.G. Classey (26), Thomas Henry Baxter (24), John Sanders (24), Richard Sanders (22), James Cligg (13), James Pratt (9) – a total of 145 votes were cast. The rector noted in the *Parish Magazine*, 'Membership of the Council is no longer practically confined to Dissenters, and the Parish is to be congratulated on being more reasonably represented': the fact is that all but one of the new councillors was either a landowner or a farmer. At the Council's first meeting on April 15th, the rector was elected as Chairman, and Richard Rowley (the schoolmaster) was appointed Clerk at a salary of one guinea a year. In the same year Devon County Council came into being.

Apparently, the Parish Council could nominate two of the thirteen Feoffees (Trustees of the Plymtree Charities), and this led to some interfaith friction. In the years 1898-1900 dissenters were in the majority as Feoffees, but in February 1901 Rev. Classey was removed from the Trust by the Council, and churchmen then outnumbered the congregationalists. In 1904 the latter circulated a 'statement' in the parish, and claimed that the trustees were rashly spending money which would have the effect of cutting gifts to the poor by half. The rector responded in the *Parish Magazine*, showing that two of the three items of expenditure had been promoted by congregationalists, and that distributions to the poor in the following three years had in fact increased slightly.

A number of other disputes arose over the following years. Lewis Ware, owner of a row of cottages, had extended his garden out into the road between the New Inn and the church, creating a 'dangerous corner', and the owner of the new shop on the site (Mr Crocker) declined to remove the danger. In 1902, as a result of County Council intervention, part of his garden (and an enclosed area in front of the New Inn) was cut off and returned to the highway.

Two councillors, Richard Sanders of Woodbear and Philip Prouse of Clyst William, declined to serve after their election in 1901, and so did their co-opted replacements; both were chapelmen, and all sorts of allegations were made. At the next election, in 1904, the votes at the parish meeting were in favour of five 'Churchmen' and four 'others'. In the *Parish Magazine* the rector reported that 'Mr Classey' (he never gave the Congregational Minister his title as 'Reverend') 'demanded a poll' (of all those in the parish entitled to vote) 'on behalf of James Cligg and James Pratt' – each of whom had received only 13 votes at the Meeting, and were Chapel-men. He went on, 'Churchmen are asked to attend and vote for Messrs. Baxter, Cook, Loosemore, Prouse and [John] Sanders, and for no-one else. There are 75 voters on the roll, and we ought to give our candidates such a majority as will prevent the parish being ever again subjected to this wanton waste of money.' The poll cost £7-14s.-4d. to hold; James Cligg tied with E. N. Wheaton with 29 votes each, and Cligg became Councillor by the drawing of lots!

In 1908 the rector announced that he intended to sell the glebe land, in order to raise more funds for the poor by investment than could be achieved from rentals. He added that his, 'main reason for arranging this sale is, that the letting of glebe, and still more the enforcing of the conditions on which it is let, are too often sources of disputes and 'bad blood' between parsons and people.' The 33 acres of land was valued at £1,625, and several parish meetings followed where resolutions about whether to try to buy or rent the land for the parish were proposed, adjourned, lost and amended. In the event, the land was purchased by Devon County Council.

In 1919 Rev. Edgar Hay was not only Chairman of the Parish Council, but also the Chairman of the Housing Committee of Honiton Rural District Council. As such he was involved with implementing the Government Housing Scheme, which created the first council houses. He was passionately concerned that the six houses proposed for Plymtree be situated on good land in the centre of the village, not dumped on poor land out of the way, and he put himself up for re-election in order to achieve that end.

The day after the parish meeting at which his proposals for council housing were introduced (and derided by some), he wrote to George Leon of Hayne House, who had decided to stand in opposition to Mr Hay, in an attempt to dissuade him. While saying that he wrote 'in a friendly spirit', he suggested that some voters were 'conspiring to use (Mr Leon) for their own ends'.

Mr Leon took exception to this, publishing Mr Hay's letter and his reply, adding a covering letter to the electors, in which he quoted Mr Hay as having said: 'The kind of people who come to parish meetings are not very representative, though they thus get their way in matters which the majority don't think worth troubling about – such as, who shall be on the Parish Council.'

The Rector then went into print himself. He ignored the Hay/Leon correspondence, concentrating on his council house proposals. But the cause of the dispute can be seen from his words: 'I may be called a Radical and Socialist for standing up for the poor against a wealthy farmer, who grudges selling them even two acres of the eighty acre farm he has bought out of his war profits', and 'I demand that the [District] Council should use its powers of compulsory purchase.'

The land Mr Hay wanted for the houses was where Farthings Rise now stands, then owned by John White Hussey who, far from having bought the land 'out of his war profits', had in fact raised the money by borrowing it. In any case, Mr Leon obviously thought that landowners should be represented on the District Council, so as to protect them from such wild ideas as compulsory purchase. The Council did actually buy the land, but no building took place, and in January 1926 it was bought back by Mr Hussey. Shortly thereafter, on 5th March 1926, part of Little Normans field at Normans Green was conveyed by Mr George Sanders to Honiton R.D.C., and six council houses were built there: they were named 'Hillside'.

Rev. Hay also talked himself out of involvement with the supper and entertainment for ex-soldiers, held on Saturday 4th October 1919: the Committee formally asked him (as chief School Manager) for the use of the school during the evening but – he having responded that he would only agree if he received a written invitation to attend – they decided to hold it at Greenend instead!

Chapter 14: High Days and Holidays

In the old days the centre of social life in the village was always the Parish Church and the adjacent Church House, where the churchwardens brewed beer for 'Church Ales', and where that beer (and cider, of course) was sold to the people. Other parties were held there; for example, we know that a whole sheep was roasted on the fire in the Church House to mark William IV's Coronation in 1830.

From at least the Middle Ages, charters were granted to hold 'Fairs' in various towns and villages: primarily a sort of super market-day, they were usually held after the harvest, when almost everyone would have earned extra money, and provided the opportunity for working people to 'let their hair down'.

While Plymtree never had one, Langford had its own fair, probably on the basis of a medieval Royal charter, which was important until the last century: when Mary Moore, 12-year-old daughter of Robert, was voluntarily apprenticed to Fitzwilliam Jope at Woodbeer Court in 1739, it was specifically added to her indenture that 'She shall have liberty to attend Langford Fair'.

Cullompton held its fair in the Spring, on the first Wednesday in May every year which, judging by the early Plymtree School log-books, attracted most of the children from every village within walking distance.

It would appear from a piece in the *Exeter Flying Post* in 1849 that an annual 'pleasure fair' used to be held in the village each Easter Monday:

The dance has always been a great attraction, and we had (though much lesser number than hereto-fore) a fair sprinkling of lads and lassies, who kept up the merry dance until a late hour, and one would fancy they all thought the good time come.'

Queen Victoria's Golden Jubilee was celebrated in Plymtree on Thursday 24th June 1897. 'The bell ringers not only ushered in the day at 6am, but also rang at intervals throughout the day. After a short service the rest of the day was spent in a field lent by John Sanders, decorated with flags and bunting. A 'capital dinner' for 140 men and lads over 15 at 1.30pm was provided by Mr Jarvis, with joints being carved by members of the organising committee and several farmers. After the dinner the Loyal Toast was proposed by Mr T.H. Baxter, and the Cullompton Volunteer Band did the musical honours. An extensive sports programme was arranged (100 and 200 yards races for girls and boys under 14 and for women; half-mile for men; egg-and-spoon, sack and hurdle races; bicycle races; and a race 'for little boys') lasting in all until nearly 9 o'clock. Tea for about 280 women and children was served at 4pm, also supplied by Mr Jarvis, baker, of Plymtree.'

In May 1902 a meeting of the Parish Vestry discussed appropriate celebrations for King Edward VII's Coronation. Richard Sanders, churchwarden, William Franklin and George Pine were appointed a committee to manage, with instructions to invite the Plymtree congregationalists along.

The ceremony was delayed until 9th August (the King had appendicitis), but in Plymtree the festivities were put off for a further five days in order to secure the Cullompton Volunteers Band, though services were held on the 9th. 'The organising committee, plus James Cligg and Henry Wheaton from the Congregationalists, ensured everything was most successful. Mr J. N. Franklin lent the big meadow opposite Greenend Cottages, and the large club tent was hired from Payhembury. Dinner was served to 155 men and lads over 15 years, and tea to 425 women and children. The weather was perfect, and the afternoon passed quickly in sports and performances by the Cullompton Maypole Dancers (63 in number), and the evening closed with dancing, evidently enjoyed not only by Plymtree, but by the hundreds who

Plymtree's men celebrate the Coronation of King George V, June 1911, with a dinner.

Celebrations for the Coronation of King George V, June 1911.

*Cullompton Volunteers Band entertains outside the New Inn, probably before the
Club Walk at Whitsun, 1909.*

A charabanc outing leaves from the New Inn, c.1920.

The Plymtree Club Walk, Whitsun 1909.

came from villages around. The catering was very efficiently done by Mr Eli James, and the day's expenses were £39-11s.-1d. Mr Cligg gave a hogshead of cider as his donation.'

In 1909 the first United Friendly Societies Festival (known as the Plymtree Revel) was held on Whit Tuesday. After a church service, every resident who was a member of any Friendly Society paraded around the village, led by the Cullompton Territorial's Band; there was a dinner in the schoolroom, sports in a large meadow at Fordmore, and a dance in the evening. This event later developed into an annual 'Club Walk', an event which attracted large crowds.

The successful arrangements of 1902 were repeated on 29th July 1911, when King George V was crowned. The tents, plus swing-boats and other fairground attractions, were erected in one of John Hussey's fields at Pencepool; 125 dinners (with cider) were served for the men and lads by the publican, A. W. Marshall, and 200 teas for the women and children by F. W. Minifie, the baker; many and various sports were enjoyed; and the Cullompton Territorial's Band played throughout. Later on there was a bonfire at the highest point in the parish, on Norman Wheaton's Fordmore farm.

The failure of Guy Fawkes' efforts were celebrated from shortly after the actual event in 1605, in Plymtree as elsewhere, by the ringing of bells. Each year until 1837, when the practice ceased,

the churchwardens' accounts included an item, 'To the Ringers, as usual, on 5th November'; in the 18th century the ringers were paid 7s. which, given that there were only four bells, indicates that they rang for most of the day. The following entry in the *Parish Magazine* showed that the 5th was enjoyed in its modern form by 1903: 'Guy Fawkes Day: It is a distinct loss when the old-fashioned customs, which relieve the monotony of village life, are allowed to die out, and we are glad to report that Plymtree kept up 'the Fifth' with great spirit. The offer of two prizes for costumes brought out quite a crowd of 'Guys', and a large torch-light procession, headed by the Band, marched to the large bonfire on Ridgeway, which burnt for several hours. There was a pretty display of fireworks, and everything passed off in a most orderly manner.'

Meets of the East Devon Hunt outside the Blacksmith's Arms are another long-standing tradition which also bring a touch of colour to the village, though they are now somewhat controversial. The hunt has always attracted 'followers' who, while not mounted, could watch the progress of the huntsman, his pack and the rest of the hunters: nowadays they tend to follow in vehicles which, in the narrow lanes around the parish, cause blockages and therefore antipathy towards them, taking some of the pleasure from this traditional spectacle.

The East Devon Hunt meets at the New Inn during the late 1950s.

In March 1973 Rob Hussey suggested at a meeting of the Hall Committee that all users be invited to assist with a Summer Fête, to help in raising funds for the Hall Improvement Scheme (which was to add the kitchen and committee room). A public meeting held two weeks later decided to set up a special committee to organise the event, to be held on August Bank Holiday Monday and to take the form of a 'Country Fayre'.

This first Country Fayre proved to be an outstanding success, raising a profit of over £541, and was so much enjoyed by everyone that it became *the* annual event for the village. The Fayre was soon extended to include a horse and pony show, which has proved to be enduringly popular. The organisation was and is still left to an independent committee, elected at the annual parish meeting, and though the income from this superb co-operative effort has been the main support of hall finances ever since, other local organisations also benefit, as well as the national charity, Riding for the Disabled.

2nd June 1977 was the H.M. the Queen's Silver Jubilee, and Plymtree marked this with a big party in the parish hall, complete with a celebratory cake, cut jointly by the rector and the congregational minister to mark the unity with which the villagers gathered to give thanks for her reign. The following year the village entered the 'Best Kept Village' competition, and was declared to be the best-kept of villages of its size. A plaque was presented, together with a tree which was planted (by Carolyn Auton and Brice Vellacott) on the

bank at the foot of Ridgeway (now part of the garden of 1 Farthings Rise).

In early 1991, Ian Wilson and Hugh Eaglestone proposed to the committee of Plymtree Cricket Club that a 'Street Party' be held to raise funds for the Club. Since no-one knew what such an event would be, it was agreed. On a Wednesday in July, a farm wagon became a temporary stage beside the Blacksmiths Arms, and in the evening the road was closed off for all manner of enjoyable events, including games for the children, food and drink for the adults, and lots of music and dancing for all. The Club still runs the party every other year.

The church arranges a 'Village Day' or street market on the alternate years, with stalls selling a variety of produce and other items in the churchyard and/ or the street, open gardens, a teddy-bears picnic, and other attractions.

Carolyn Auton and Brice Vellacott plant the copper beech tree awarded for the 'Best Kept Village' in 1978.

Above: 'Village Day' street market as seen from the church tower.

Right: Rev. R.I.N. Edwards (with Rev. Gladys Smith) cuts the cake for Queen Elizabeth's Silver Jubilee, 1977.

Plymtree Country Fayre

Above: The first Country Fayre in 1973. Brice Vellacott, Country Fayre Chairman with guest of honour and Michael Hussey and Helen Reed, the Fayre Prince and Princess.

Top right: George Knight giving rides in the old farm waggon, 1975.

Right: Punch and Judy draw a crowd while the plate-smashing continues next door.

Above: The Tudor dancers entertain, while the various stalls in the background do good business, 1995.

Right: The horse show has always been a part of the Country Fayre. Nichola Reed and her pony take part in one of the showjumping classes.

Plymtree Country Fayre

Above: The Fayre in 1983. Everyone always works hard to raise money for local charities.

Right: The 'greasy pole' – a traditional favourite.

Left: St Georges and dragons compete in the fancy dress contest at the Country Fayre, 1977.

Below: Percy Batten and Jack Turner supervise the Fayre ram roast in 1975.

Bottom left: Helen Purves demonstrates spinning, 1983.

Beating the Bounds

The tradition of 'beating the bounds' of a parish began when parishes became the basis of local government, providing support and protection for inhabitants, and it was vitally important to all to keep out vagrants and others who might pose a threat to the peace or economy of the area. At least every four years the whole population was supposed to walk around the boundaries of the parish, stopping to 'beat' at points where the line changed direction, so as to impress on the people the exact extent of their parish. There is some controversy about exactly what was 'beaten'; some say that the children were beaten, others that it was marker stones or trees. Whatever the truth, the practice was renewed by a group of villagers on 2nd May 1988, when they struggled their way across fields and over streams and hedgerows, following the 19 miles of parish boundary (well, most of it!). The weather was perfect, but they were delighted to have a lunch break in a barn at Hearn Farm, and a few other rests were necessary. No children were beaten!

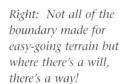

Right: Not all of the boundary made for easy-going terrain but where there's a will, there's a way!

Above: At lunch time, all involved enjoy a well-earned break at Hearn Farm.

Right: Crossing one of the many small streams.

Chapter 15: Village Pastimes and Groups

Skittles were certainly played at the 'New Inn' from the time of its opening in 1851, the 'covered skittle alley' being an advertised feature. Old reports of village celebrations, such as the re-dedication of the church bells in 1936, show that skittles contests have regularly been one of the highlights. Four teams currently have the Blacksmiths Arms as their home alley.

Before television, computers and other high-tech amusements became common, dances were a regular part of village life. As the *Parish Magazine* reported in 1908:

Plymtree dances have a very good reputation, and the schoolroom was somewhat overcrowded on the 25th November, over a hundred dancers attending. Mr Pilkington's spirited piano playing was a great attraction. Tickets were, for gentlemen 1s.-6d., and for ladies, 1s. Small practice dances have been held once a fortnight this winter, and the opportunity of learning thus given has been much appreciated.

In the 1920s the young people of the village became interested in tennis, and the rector created two large tennis courts at the end of the Rectory gardens (at the foot of the lane beside the Rectory building). Two further tennis courts were laid at Normans Green and often teams from both 'clubs' played each other. Bowls was also popular among older villagers, and a green was laid near the tennis Courts at Normans Green.

These activities were very much enjoyed for a time, and although the bowling green gradually fell into disuse, the piece of ground was called the 'Bowling Green' for some time afterwards. The tennis club at the Rectory continued for a while after the war, but eventually ceased to operate; Tandem Cottage was built on the old courts and bowls ground at Normans Green around 1963.

During the 1920s an effort was made to start a Scout Troop in Plymtree, under the guidance of Miss E. Huyshe, scout-leader of Clyst Hydon. Unfortunately, this did not take root, but the girls were more persistent, and their Girl Guides group continued until well after the Second World War. That has now closed, but the Brownies are still a thriving group under their leaders, Janet Barnett and Margaret Draper.

The W.I. Pancake Races, 1979. Doreen Gibbins cheers the little ones, while Alan Lock comforts and encourages an unwilling participant. (Kevin Clarke, on the left, decided he would do better without a frying pan.).

Above: The Friends of Plymtree School won the 'Village Ventures' competition in 1984 for their tremendous efforts in saving the school.

Above right: Some games are not gripping enough for the Cricket Club President, Richard Wisdom.

Above: Bowls at Normans Green late one evening during the 1930s.

Left: Plymtree Girl Guides camping at Knightshayes; and Lady Amory pays a visit.

Bingo became popular for a time in the 1960s and games were organised regularly in the parish hall, but unfortunately Plymtree could not compete with the large prizes being offered by commercial bingo halls and by larger parishes. A 'bingo bus' began to operate, calling at various villages to take players to Willand; for a time it called at Plymtree but, as the number of people using it dwindled, the service was discontinued.

The fight to prevent the closure of the School in the 1980s led to the creation of 'FOPS' – the Friends of Plymtree School – the members of which have since run many fund-raising events enjoyed by villagers, and the money thus raised has done a great deal to improve the facilities of the school.

Plymtree Cricket Clubs

On 15th June 1893 the rector noted that 'the first practice of cricket was held in the field called 'Pidgeons' kindly lent by Mr Richard Sanders, Churchwarden, & it was subsequently decided to hold a committee meeting at the Rectory on the following Monday, June 19th at 8pm in order to draw up rules & form a Club.'

This incarnation of the Cricket Club apparently didn't last long, for by 1905 the balance of funds (£2-10s.) was donated to the church. The Club was revived in the 1930s, but failed again soon after.

From 1954 when Rev. Steele became Rector, he encouraged the boys of the parish to play cricket, which became very popular, with a Cricket Dance held every year. At first games were played on a field at Pencepool, but then moved to another on Frank Clarke's land at Clyst William Cross, with use of a barn as a pavilion. Unfortunately, when Rev. Steele left in 1963, interest died out again, and it was not until 1984 that the present Club was formed.

A Plymtree v Plymtree game in August 1986 saw a good turnout. Present were: Terry Ayres, Willy Bull, Michael Clarke, Malcolm Coombes, Peter Cox, Hugh Eaglestone, Chris Elliot, Henry Franks, Peter Gimber, Norman Grundy, Phil Horsefield, Alan Lock, Tony Miller, Steve Pettitt, Richard Pratt, James Robertson, Steve Sinclair, Brian Smith, Dave Swallow, Jonathan Tancock, Chris Thornhill, and Chris and Robert Webster.

Cricket Club members have been a positive force in the village since their re-founding. During the past ten years they have worked hard to help with the creation and maintenance of the village recreation ground (firstly by Tony Miller, and latterly by Malcolm Coombes and Alec Robson), establishing one of the best and most attractive cricket grounds in the county; building the pavilion there; initiating the unique bi-annual Street Party and annual Supper Quiz.

Plymtree Cricket Club, first overseas tour (to the Isles of Scilly, 1989)
From left to right – standing: Steve Pettitt, Ed Derham, Brian Smith, David Gibbins, Tony Clarke,
Hugh Eaglestone, Bernard Wisdom, Derek Mason, Tony Blount, Peter Gimber;
Front: Tony Miller, Andy Stevens, Martin Miller, Ian Wilson.

Plymtree Cricket Club, first 'President's Day' on the new field, Monday 6th May, 1991.
From left to right – at the back: Grant Davison, unknown, Brian Smith, Jim Barrett, John Caller,
Peter Gimber, Ian Wilson;
Standing: 'Alf', John Akers (behind), Roger Persey, Phil Horsfield, Brian Mackley, Tony Blount, Alan Holder,
Derek Mason, Richard Owen, Will Roberts, Alistair Davison, Peter Labdon, Ed Derham;
Sitting: 'Jinksy' Hutchinson, Tony Miller, Ken Edwards, Bernard Wisdom, Hugh Eaglestone, Peter Cox;
Kneeling: 'Akers', Tim Mason, Alex Mason.

Above: Les Hood is out, Steve Granger walks in to
bat – a typical match.

Plymtree Women's Institute

A meeting was called in the vestry room on 17th March 1926 by Mrs Alyse Lee-Norman of Hayne House, 'for ladies wishing to have the chance to learn various crafts and have talks on a variety of subjects'. At this meeting it was decided to form a group of the Women's Institute. The original idea had come from Canada, but it migrated very well to England, and by the end of 1926 the Plymtree group had 48 members. Many of the meetings were held in members' homes, with demonstrations on topics as varied as raffia hat-making, bee-keeping, first aid, making soft toys and poultry-keeping. One of their early successes in working for the community was to lobby for, and obtain, the services of a District Nurse for the parish.

The W.I. purchased a piano for the use of the village in 1927, which was a good buy, as it was still in use in 1986. In 1928 a proposal to build a parish hall was enthusiastically supported by the W.I., whose members assisted with fund-raising, and the group donated the piano, crockery and some chairs when the hall was opened in June 1929. Henceforth, monthly W.I. meetings were held in the hall.

During the Second World War the members did their bit, not only knitting comforts for the troops, but also by such work as gathering foxglove leaves, and a hundredweight and a half of rose-hips, at the request of the Ministry of Health, and by donating their aluminium pots and pans to help make aeroplanes.

In March 1947 the W.I. held a large 21st birthday party at the hall, with a tiered cake and much fun and games. Other parties have been held to mark important milestones in the history of the group; 1965 was national Jubilee year for the Institute, and The Queen hosted a garden party at Buckingham Palace, Plymtree being represented by Mrs Churchill. Two years later Plymtree W.I. decided to open its annual Flower Show to all residents of the village, since when the Show has been one of the parish's red-letter days, not only displaying high-quality garden produce, but also excellent handicrafts made in the village.

Another innovation, in 1974, was a Pancake Race at Greenend farm. It was so popular that it is still held every year, with races for children of various ages, and for mums and dads, along the drive, while the more mature villagers (known for the day as the 'Ancient Britons') take part by tossing pancakes over a high rope for their partners to catch – great fun!

Plymtree W.I. celebrated its Golden Jubilee in 1976 by holding a big party – with food, fun and games for 57 members and friends from neighbouring Institutes. Further useful items were donated to the parish hall, and a tree was planted in front of the bungalows recently built for the elderly residents at Greenend Close. Fund-raising events were and are held annually, including fashion shows, coffee mornings, whist drives, garden parties, dances and jumble sales. For their own enjoyment, and that of other local Institutes, a number of plays and other costume entertainments have been put on from time to time.

The Diamond Jubilee of the group, in 1986, was marked by a four-course dinner prepared by members for themselves, their husbands and guests, with entertainment from young farmers and the Hembury Choir. Later a very successful three-day exhibition, covering aspects of the history of the parish, was held in the hall.

In 1995 the Devon Federation of Women's Institutes created a banner to celebrate 75 years of constructive existence (*above*), and this was transported to each village in the county having a branch, using various forms of transport. It was delivered to Plymtree from Clyst Hydon by pony and trap, and taken on to Kentisbeare in Phil Bearne's old Rover saloon.

The entertainment and instruction offered to members has changed little over the years. As well as talks on innumerable subjects, classes have been held from time to time on dressmaking, folk and ballroom dancing, lace and rug-making. Every month there is a little competition for members to enter to show off their skills: perhaps one of the most unusual was one in 1944 for 'The neatest head of hair' – but then, materials of all sorts were difficult to obtain in those war years.

Plymtree W.I. celebrate their 21st birthday in 1947.

The 40th anniversary of the W.I., 1966.

Golden Jubilee of the W.I., 1976.

Plymtree W.I., c.1970.

W.I. Pancake Races

The finish at Greenend Farm, 1996 with Rachel and Matthew Tidball holding the tape.

The mums' race, 1996.

W.I. Pancake Races

Waiting to receive their pancakes are (left to right): Ryth Clarke, Tessa Barrett, Maureen Edwards, Bernard Wisdom and Les Hitch (far right).

The 'Ancient Britons' pancake tossing contest – the culmination of the annual races.

Plymtree and District Gardening Club

Gardening has always been a popular (and sometimes essential) part of village life, and between the wars the Plymtree Cottage Garden Society organised an annual Show, held in July 'in a field near the village'. To widen its appeal, sports were held in the same field, and various 'amusements' were laid on, followed in the evening by a dance.

During the Second World War every bit of spare land was used to grow vegetables and raise livestock.

The Gardening Club was re-formed in 1986 and has thrived ever since. Not only does it put on talks on various topics by experts, but arranges visits to large gardens, and also has an annual dinner at the hall, always enlivened by excellent entertainment.

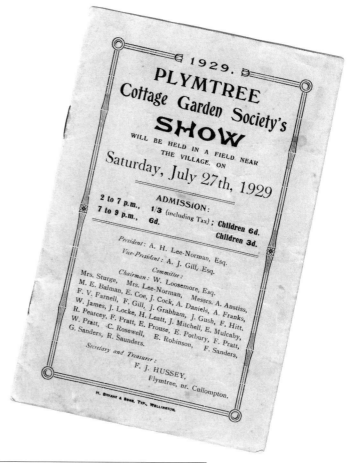

Plymtree Cottage Garden Society Show schedule, 1929.

Plymtree Junior Football Team. The boys and the girls happy with their new strips which were kindly donated by Graham Bere.

Plymtree Football Club

The 'national winter game' has been played on various fields in the parish for many years. In April 1923 the *Parish Magazine* reported on the first (not very successful) season for the village Club in the Ottery St Mary District League. Of the 22 league games played, 2 were won, 5 drawn and 15 lost; there were 22 goals scored for, but 91 against. John White Hussey provided 'an excellent playing field' at Pencepool, and the New Inn was used as the changing room.

Today John Bewick, Graham Bere and others run both a youngsters' and an adult team on the Recreation Ground – where they regularly beat local rivals Clyst Hydon – and much fun is had without joining a league.

Chapter 16: Plymtree Parish Hall

A parish meeting held in the schoolroom on 12th March 1928 was not well-attended, there being only 12 voters (i.e. ratepayers) and five others present. Nonetheless, a new Parish Council was elected, and Frederick Minifie (the baker and shopkeeper) immediately proposed that a public meeting should be called to consider raising funds for a parish hall to be built. Two weeks later another parish meeting agreed unanimously that a non-political and non-denominational parish hall should be built; a committee of 'ways and means' was formed, and Mr A. H. Lee-Norman, (of Hayne House), Chairman, promised £250 towards the cost.

Collectors were nominated, and by 4th April they had gathered £204-1s., plus Mr Lee-Norman's £250. A site at Knight's Cottage was offered, but a decision put off until the hall at Talaton had been inspected for comparison of site requirements. By 16th April £470-18s.-6d. had been promised, and four further sites offered. Since £500 had not been achieved, further effort was required and it was agreed that extra time should be allowed to try to achieve that target. It was also agreed that all subscribers should be invited to vote on the final site.

At a meeting on 7th May, a total of £502-8s. had been attained, and it was agreed that plans should be prepared for the hall. A full parish meeting a week later voted that the hall project should proceed, and the site offered by Robert Lear was unanimously accepted by the meeting. Three days later Robert Lear conveyed the freehold of the site to the chosen trustees, i.e. Alexander and Miss Emily Lee-Norman, Gordon Lear, Arthur and Frank Sanders, Ernest Prouse, Alfred Gill and Harry Churchill. In view of their generous donation, Mr Lee-Norman was proposed and confirmed as permanent President of the hall, and his wife as Vice-President.

At 'The Manor' (Hayne House) on 8th June the Building Committee met to consider plans prepared by Captain Coe, which they agreed. Applications for tenders were advertised in the press following a meeting on 14th August, and on 4th September the Committee considered those received. They were disconcerted by the high level of tenders (the highest being over £1,028) but, after another meeting when they agreed that the specification should not be reduced, they agreed to accept that from Streats of Ottery for £668-10s. The contract was signed forthwith.

By January 1929 all bar 10s. of the promised money had been collected, and a further £10 had been raised by a 'Sale of

The opening of the Parish Hall by Lady Sidmouth on 20th June 1929.

work & social', organised by Mrs Lee-Norman and the Women's Institute. The money needed was reduced by £3-10s. by John Baker ('assisted' by his young son, Reg) digging the foundations, after young Bill Lovering and his father had spent many weeks levelling the site by hand. The iron railings around the back and sides of the hall were made by Mr Sanders at Normans Green, at a cost of £14-15s.

When building work was completed, it was decided to purchase 50 chairs, and Mrs Lee-Norman donated curtains for the windows. The W.I. took more chairs, china, and a piano (which they had bought) to the hall and from that time held their meetings there. The opening date was set for Thursday June 20th 1929, and Lady Sidmouth performed the opening ceremony, (Wolf-Cub Reg Baker presented her with a bouquet), and there was then a fête at Hayne House.

The first regular users of the hall were the Women's Institute, Scouts, and Guides, but from

November there was also a Men's Club held on Wednesdays from 7 to 9.30pm (subscription 2d. per night), the rules of which included 'No bad language' and 'No games to be played for money'. The Club apparently met a need, since a month later two meetings per week were available, and the hours extended to 10pm.

The Hall Committee arranged the celebrations for King George V's Silver Jubilee, held on Monday May 6th 1935. They decided to pay for dinner ('cold beef, pickles, bread & beer') for 120 men, at a cost of 2s.-6d. per head, and tea for 120 women, at 1s. per head, all provided by Mr Mulcahy, the publican; some of the money was to come from the funds of the defunct Plymtree Cottage Garden Society. There was a programme of sports, including egg and spoon and potato races for the ladies, and a slow bicycle race. One thing that hasn't changed was that it was the members of the Committee who had to do all the setting-up!

In July 1949 an Entertainments Committee was set up both to provide evening activities for villagers and to raise money for improvements to the hall. Their first target was £145 to provide an electric plant and lighting to replace the old oil lamps which still lit the building.

An ambitious programme was planned, consisting of dances (to live music) every fortnight, and other entertainment on the alternate Fridays. Jan Stewer, the well-known dialect story-teller was one of the first attractions, but there were also choirs, poultry whist drives and concert parties. They also began the tradition of holding a dance to celebrate the end of the harvest, which is continued as a supper and entertainment. By April 1950 they had almost reached their target, but this had to be increased because the cost had risen to £226 for a 'plant' consisting of a 3-hp, water-cooled Lister engine, driving a 27-amp generator, which charged a 25-volt battery system. Mr Baker agreed to run it whenever light was

needed at the hall, for a salary of £3 per year! When mains electricity reached this part of the village, in mid-1954, the hall was rewired and connected. Electric heating replaced the previous solid fuel stoves in October 1957.

Mains water was laid on at about the same time, and at last Mr and Mrs Baker were spared the task of using a yoke to carry large cans of water from their home at Hayne Cottage whenever it was needed for a function. Mrs Baker retired from the post of caretaker at the end of 1960, after 32 years hard work, and a comfortable armchair was presented to her by a grateful Hall Committee.

In 1973 proposals were made to extend the hall by creating a committee room and new kitchen, but it was not until 1976 that they actually came to be built with great assistance from the Community Council of Devon. That marvellous body was, with East Devon District Council, also responsible for helping with grants to install up-to-date toilet facilities, and a disabled toilet, as well as turning the porch into an enclosed hall, in 1994.

Also in 1994 the Committee agreed that the original fixed stage took up too much room in the hall, and restricted its use. A mechanical miracle of a folding stage replaced it temporarily but that, as well as being extremely heavy and difficult to move around, was also somewhat inflexible and, when a National Lotteries Charity Board grant became available in 1997 it was sold to Weare Gifford Village Hall, being replaced by a wonderful modular staging system.

Central heating was next on the agenda, and the new oil-fired system with radiators has transformed the building, making it welcoming in the most inhospitable weathers. An old hi-fi system was bequeathed to the hall by the departing Sir John Hannam and, thanks to David Estcourt, this now forms the basis of a built-in amplificatiom system.

Chapter 17: Recreation Ground and Pavilion

Until the creation of a dedicated recreation ground, village events were held on whatever field was offered by one of the generous local farmers. But in 1987 the prospect of creating such a village asset was put to the Parish Council: the Parish Hall Committee thought it to be a good idea, and a public meeting on 9th November supported it. A lease of Crossway Meadow was offered by Herbert Persey of Fordmore and, after lots of fund-raising, a lease for 21 years was signed in September 1989; Richard Batten immediately launched his JCBs on the huge task of levelling and laying drains in the field, and he and his friends finished the work amazingly quickly.

The result is a superb flat field, used for the annual Country Fayre, as the school's sports ground, and by the village football and cricket clubs, as well as informally by most villagers. In 1990 it was 'highly commended', and won a prize of £500 in a Village Ventures competition funded by the Shell Oil Company.

Plymtree Cricket Club spent a £10,000 loan from the District Council on creating a cricket square and an all-weather track, and its honorary 'groundsmen', Tony Miller and then Malcolm Coombes, have kept the field in beautiful condition since its creation.

Sue Tidball conceived the idea of a play area for younger children in a corner of the field, and made some enquiries about fund-raising and equipment suppliers before bringing it to the Hall and Field Committee. Since everyone supported the idea, work towards it began immediately and, through Sue's charm and persistence, it was opened on 12th September 1992 by the late Brice Vellacott. Brice was by that time well over 80 years old but was always in touch with youth – he wore a badge declaring himself to be a

'Re-cycled Teenager', he had been Chairman of the Hall Committee for over 30 years, and was much-loved by all.

The most recent addition to the recreation field is the pavilion. This sectional, wooden building began its life as a day ward at Exmouth Hospital, but was declared redundant and was due to be destroyed. Richard Batten who was working on the site realised its potential and, after a few words, the site foreman agreed that if Plymtree wanted to take it down, Plymtree could have it. The late Alistair Davison organised members of the Cricket Club to do the work and they, very well assisted by Ian Walkley and 'Jinxy' Hutchinson, stripped the felt from the roof, demolished the internal walls and then disassembled the building. Every last bit was then transported to Fordmore, where Herbert Persey made an old barn and an open space available to store 'the kit of parts'.

With new grass and a new pavilion, the recreation ground is a source of pride for the villagers.

It took nearly three years to raise the money to lay a new concrete base, but the building was re-erected with the help of many hands in three hectic days before the Country Fayre in 1994, when the 'Bat & Hammer' bar replaced the usual beer tent.

The Cricket Club raised more money to have the roof properly slated; donated metal windows were fitted to let in more light; internal partitions were fitted by Ernie Dolloway and Derek Mason to create a kitchen, changing rooms, space for toilets and a store; and a gift of paint for the outside was secured from the Dulux Challenge. Then, in 1997, grant money helped pay for the installation of toilets, and a sealed tank was obtained, sunk and plumbed-in by Richard Batten.

It is hoped to have electricity in the pavilion by the millennium.

PLYMTREE PARISH COUNCIL
invites you to

AN OPEN PARISH MEETING

PLYMTREE PARISH HALL
ON
MONDAY 9TH NOVEMBER
AT
8 P.M.

THE PLYMTREE PLAYING FIELD + RECREATION AREA

DO YOU OR YOUR FAMILY THINK THAT WE NEED A PLAYING FIELD? WHERE COULD IT BE?

HOW COULD IT BE USED?

TENNIS? FOOTBALL? ROUNDERS? BMX? BOWLS? CRICKET? NETBALL? CONSERVATION? PLAYGROUND?

PLEASE COME ALONG AND EXPRESS YOUR VIEWS. WHERE COULD WE FIND THE MONEY? HOW COULD IT BE ORGANISED?
YOUNG OR OLD - ALL ARE WELCOME.

From Field to Recreation Ground

The beginnings of Plymtree's recreation ground. Richard Batten and his JCB make short work of levelling Cross Way Meadow in October 1989. In the background is the Parish Hall with the new drainage pipes to the right.

Right: Tonnes of earth had to be moved from one end of the field to level it out but all the hard work paid off: the result: a nice, flat, drained field.

District Councillor Bill Thorne declares the recreation ground officially open, 1990.

The first (and last) game of croquet on the recreation ground.

Building the Pavilion

Above: The 'kit of parts' for the pavilion laid out on the new concrete base, spring 1994.

Right: The workforce consider what to do next. From left to right: Tony Eames, Jim Barrett (behind), Les Hitch, Chris Barrett, Jason Eames.

Left: Dennis Cooper-Jones inspects the first day's work.

The Completed Project

Above: The pavilion, 12th June 1994. The building remains un-painted, and with the roof felted and battened, but it is ready for use for the Cricket Club's President's Day.

Right: The first bar, nicknamed the 'Bat & Hammer'; barmen Tony Eames and Brian Smith try to work out whether they can supply Ken Edwards and Derek Pinn with what they want.

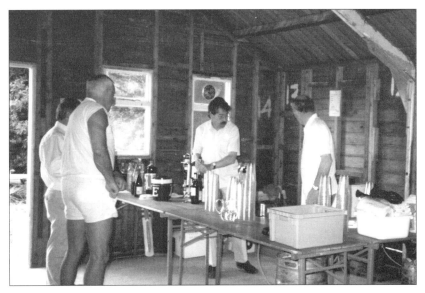

Left: The new childrens' play area. The late Brice Vellacott, who had been connected with the Parish Hall Committee for over 25 years, opened the area in 1992. He loved children and they loved him. The play area's driving force was, and remains, Sue Tidball, to whom the village owes a great deal.

Hester Blackmore outside Nos 1 and 2 Moor (Fordmore) Cottages, after the thatched roofs had been replaced with corrugated iron.

Chapter 18: Growing Up in Plymtree after the War

by Hester Blackmore (now Hester Joy)

I was born in September 1943 at Fordmore Cottages, the youngest child of Len and Nell Blackmore. My father worked at Fordmore Farm for over 45 years, and the cottage in which we lived was part of the farm. The cottage was built of stone, though I believe the one adjoining ours was at least part cob, and both were thatched. Each originally consisted of just four rooms – two up and two down. There was no bathroom, no electricity, nor even a water supply – that had to be pumped by hand from a well out in the garden – and the only other 'room' we had was the toilet, at the end of a very long garden path!

Lighting was by oil lamps and candles, and washing was undertaken in an old tin bath. Heating the water for this, and cooking, was done on an old kitchen range, which had to be polished regularly with 'black lead'. There was also a tin oven of some kind, which sat on a paraffin heater.

Over time the interior of the cottage changed. One bedroom was divided into two as there were two girls (my sister, Gladys, and I) and one boy (Kenneth) in the family. An indoor pump was installed in the kitchen, still worked by hand, but this time from side to side instead of up and down. A wash-house was built on the side of the house, which contained not only the 'furnace' and copper for boiling the wash, but – joy of joys! – an indoor toilet. It also housed the mangle and tin baths for rinsing the clothes in 'blue' water.

When the wooden lintel (the old people called it a 'clavill') above the fireplace was found to be smouldering – which it had probably been doing for some time – the whole fireplace was demolished, uncovering an old bread oven, complete with its wooden door, built into the side. When a new fireplace was installed the bread oven was just filled with rubble and covered up again, though I believe the wooden oven door was taken

Hester (third from the left, front) visits London c.1953 with other members of Plymtree School and their teacher, Miss Millett.

away by Mr William Persey of Fordmore Farm.

I think it was also about this time (around 1960) that the thatched roof was replaced by corrugated sheets. Since the new fireplace also heated water, and my brother and sister had left home, a bathroom was installed in one of the divided bedrooms – super luxury!

I can recall electricity coming to Plymtree. The school seemed to have been one of the first places to connected.

The large classroom at the school was heated by a coke-burning stove, surrounded by a railing and it was the job of the older boys to fill the coal scuttles every day. On rainy days wet coats were draped over the railing to dry. The small classroom was only used for school dinners (brought in metal containers from Cullompton Secondary Modern School), and by the school dentist, doctor and 'nit nurse'. The dreadful toilets around the back of the school still stick in my memory.

We had only one teacher, Miss Millett, who somehow managed to teach 5 to 11-year-olds all in the same room. Every day ended with Miss Millett reading a story to the whole school for the last fifteen minutes of the day and it was through this that my love affair with Winnie the Pooh began. There were two playgrounds – a tarmac one between the school and the road, and a grass one on the lower side of the school. Rounders was played frequently, as were games such as 'who's afraid of the big bad wolf' and skipping.

Each spring-time the children brought bunches of primroses to school, which were packed into boxes padded out with damp moss and sent to a school in Oldham, Lancashire. In return we received 'thank you' letters from the children there, and small baskets made from thin card containing tiny Easter eggs. Primroses were also stripped from the hedgerows by people who sold bunches of them (50 flowers and 5 leaves) to the paper mills at Hele for 3d. a bunch; I wonder what they did with them?

On Ascension Day we took bunches of wild flowers, such as bluebells, forget-me-nots or 'snap-jacks' to school; these were put into small jars with letters tied to them making up the words 'ASCENSION DAY'; then the whole school walked down to the church for a short service, after which the pots of flowers were placed at the foot of the cross outside the church door. In return, we were all given lilies of the valley, being told that the flowers growing up the stem represented the steps of the ladder leading up to heaven.

At Christmas we made paper chains by gluing strips of coloured paper into joined rings; rolled up silver paper was threaded on to cotton; and paper was folded and cut in various ways to make lantern or bell shapes. We each had a small branch from a fir tree, pushed into a soil-filled cocoa tin, which we decorated to make our own, individual Christmas trees. Another Christmas favourite was a shoe-box with windows cut in the sides and ends, and with coloured cellophane stuck over the windows at one end and on both sides. Inside the box we placed plasticine models of Mary, Joseph, baby Jesus and the shepherds, all dressed in coloured crêpe paper. The lid was replaced, and the nativity scene was viewed through the uncovered window.

Although we never saw him, Miss Millett ensured that Father Christmas always left a box of presents, with something for every child; I think she paid for them herself. At the end of term we struggled home carrying all the things we had made, leaving a tell-tale trail of paper decorations in our wake. Miss Millett lived in the School House next door, with her brother who taught at Cullompton Secondary Modern School: he owned a car long before most people in the village.

My memories of the war are very hazy, but I remember the feeling of apprehension every time I heard an aeroplane at night. My father was exempted from military service during the war because of his job at Devon Growers in Cullompton, but he used to tell us about his journey to work on his old motorcycle, with the lights almost blacked out. He was stopped by the police on several occasions because he had rubbed off some of the black paint to see where he was going. My mother told me that we housed a family of evacuees for a time, but I was too young to remember that. I do recall going to the village hall to collect new ration books; and being given toys and plastic belts by some of the German prisoners of war working on the farm.

After the war, although we had no televisions, videos, computers, or other modern playthings, I don't recall having time to be bored. We could disappear for hours across the fields without any-one being concerned. A stream ran along the side of our garden, and that entertained me for hours; with a farm almost on the doorstep there was always something to watch or to do – cows being milked, calves being fed from buckets, or grandad collecting eggs in large baskets from the hen houses dotted around the fields. (My grandparents lived at No. 4 Hillside, one of the original council houses near the Congregational Church at Normans Green. When other houses were built in between the existing ones, my grandparents' address changed to No. 6 Little Normans, without them moving house!).

Haymaking provided plenty of interest, with mowers, hay turners and hay-rakes; waggons took the hay to the elevators, and men stood on the pile, building it into a hay-rick. Harvest brought the binders into the cornfields where we watched for rabbits running for cover as the corn in the centre of the field gradually diminished in size. We played hide-and-seek among the stooks made from the sheaves: but oh! how sore were our bare arms and legs in the evening from the short, sharp stubble.

At this time of year the men often worked very long hours. When my father was working in the fields, ploughing, hedging, hay-making or whatever, he would stop at about 9.30am for his 'fore-noons', which always seemed to consist of a chunk of bread and a piece of cheese, washed down with a bottle of cold tea. It always fascinated me to watch him take out an old pocket-knife, which he seemed to use for many jobs, and proceed to cut the corners from his bread and cheese; no matter how many pieces he cut off, each piece seemed to be a prism.

On Sunday evenings in summer the whole family went for long walks through places such as Clyst William or Woodbere, and we knew all the best places to find wild strawberries. Winter evenings were spent playing cards, ludo, snakes and ladders, etc. and listening to the radio; mother had the radio on most of the day. I can recall programmes such as *Housewives' Choice*, *The Morning Service*, *Workers' Play-time*, *Mrs Dale's Diary*, *Ray's a Laugh*, *Educating Archie*, *In Town Tonight*, *Friday Night is Music Night*, *Paul Templar*, and many others. The radio was powered by accumulators (which were 'wet batteries', made of glass and filled with acid, a bit like car batteries), brought from Cullompton and delivered to our door, as were bread, milk, coal and fish.

Our only visit to the seaside was the annual Sunday School outing, usually to Sidmouth or Exmouth. Each November the whole family walked to Cullompton for the annual Carnival, an evening procession lit by burning torches carried by local youths. Occasionally, 'social evenings' were held in the village hall, usually consisting of short sketches performed by local people, sometimes a song or two by the school children – I can still remember singing 'Tip-toe Through the Tulips' while walking in and out of small, green cardboard boxes with paper tulips sticking out of them. Mrs Blanchford, one time Postmistress who farmed at Weaver, always sang 'Bless this House'. On one occasion I recall the postman playing his cello, but the room was so hot that the strings stretched and he had to stop to re-tune them. Sometimes the evenings would include dances or party games.

Proper dances were occasionally held in the hall, and my brother and sister would cycle with a group of friends to other dances held in the surrounding villages. There were also whist drives – particularly poultry drives at Christmas – in the hall at Plymtree, and my father and uncle would cycle to other villages for whist drives. My mother, who was quite a shy person, was persuaded to join the Women's Institute, and she also went to bingo sessions when they became popular.

Mrs Persey of Fordmore and Mrs Rudd from Weaver ran a guide troop and brownie pack, to which my sister and I belonged. My brother played cricket for the Plymtree team, their ground being a field at Clyst William Barton: he still treasures the Plymtree C.C. cap which he got at that time, and it has accompanied him everywhere during his long career in the army.

I left Plymtree in 1962, but my parents remained in the village. After my mother died, at the age of 57, my father continued to live at Fordmore for a few more years before moving to Church House (then 'the Almshouses'). At that time the building consisted of five small flats and the vestry room, and my father lived in the upstairs flat nearest the shop; it had a bedroom, sitting room, sink and toilet, and each flat had its own strip of garden between the building and the road. When work was carried out to modernise these flats, the original five were transformed into three very pleasant modern homes, and my father moved into the one below the vestry room.

Moor (formerly Fordmore) Cottages, 1998.

Chapter 19: Some Plants in Plymtree Parish

by Barbara Benfield

As Plymtree parish consists mainly of rich farmland, most of the interesting plants are isolated on islands of old hedgebanks and even rarer undrained meadows. The true wild daffodils can still be seen in the river meadows at Lower Weaver, and have survived in some hedges. In the same area, monkshood, another plant of alluvial soils, now only grows beside the road and has become scarce throughout the country, though it was once abundant along the river banks according to Mrs Barbara Batten. Marsh marigold, also a plant of wet ditches and ponds in heavy clay, can be found in the small pond beside the lane near the River Weaver, and great hairy willowherb in the wet verges nearby.

At the east end of the parish the boggy ground on the Plymtree side of the stream is, unfortunately, not as botanically-rich as Colliton Moor, which is adjacent but just the other side of our boundary. However, the fact that intensive farming does not reach the edge of the Moor will partly contribute to the diversity of plants, insects, amphibians and birds there. Drainage of a field alters the water table of an area beyond the field: disturbance, fertiliser and spray-drift affect both plants and animals because of their inter-relationships. Here the soil is acid, in contrast to the rich alluvial soil of the Weaver Meadows. Centuries of adaptation have developed a rich flora able to cope with low fertility, though on the Plymtree side of the stream the soil is more base-rich, indicated by the plant communities: sneezewort, marsh woundwort, cuckoo flower, hemp nettle, bog violet, meadowsweet, southern marsh orchid, lesser spearwort, fleabane, common valarian, greater birdsfoot trefoil and meadow or marsh plume thistle (not a common plant, but well-loved by butterflies and other insects), to mention a few. Moscatel, dog's mercury and guelder rose can be found in the small wood beside the road, where alder buckthorn supplies food for the caterpillar of the brimstone butterfly.

That the east of the parish has been less disturbed is indicated by the diversity of plants in the hedges near Stockland Cross. Early purple orchids are still comparatively abundant, violets, primroses, shining cranesbill, forget-me-not, wood spurge, ox-eye daisy, betony, black knapweed, strawberry, foxglove and orpine (a showy plant), can be found with bluebells as a reminder that this area was probably woodland for a longer period than some other parts of the parish.

Common, striking flowers throughout the parish are greater stitchwort and red campion, while in winter the ferns common polybody and hartstongue catch the eye. Primroses can still be seen in many hedge bottoms, but are less frequent than formerly, owing, in large part, to the detrimental, modern methods of maintaining hedges and verges.

The other area of wetland we can be proud to have in our parish is at Danes Mill. Here southern marsh orchid is comparatively abundant, with ragged robin, yellow flag and one clump of the handsome, uncommon, wood clubrush. On drier hedgebanks towards Cullompton, toadflax, tufted vetch, yarrow and the occasional plant of musk mallow are a few of the more showy plants.

Two flowers which appeared in the village in 1978, orange hawkweed and sulphur cinquefoil, neither common, were unfortunately removed by the Council. Part of the cinquefoil was saved and now grows at Pencepool. Other wild flowers growing by the stream at Pencepool, but not found in other parts of the parish, are dusky and meadow cranesbill and stinking iris. Trifid (or tripartite) bur marigold made an appearance in Reeves Meadow in 1985 where the diverse wetland flora was lost when the land was ploughed in 1984.

The Rectory field and orchard were one of the last remaining large nectar-producing areas. There, apart from the dominance of buttercups, grew the saprophitic eyebright, bluebell, primrose, cuckoo flower, birdsfoot trefoil, black knapweed, selfheal, betony and, least common, bistort (snakeweed).

The last of our large elms has gone, but it is very encouraging to see so many ash saplings being left to grow up in the hedges of our parish.

Two of the most interesting lichens found in Plymtree were on ash – unfortunately 'were' because one tree blew down and the other was felled. One lichen common in Plymtree but not elsewhere owes its abundance to the former long-standing importance of orchards in the parish.

Since 1984

The slow decline of existing wildlife habitats has continued, but some small new ones have been created in different areas. Major habitat losses have been due to degraded road verges, building sites and gardens, hedge removal, more intensive cultivation of land and a reduction in the width of land left around the edges of cultivated fields. Though the practice of ploughing close to the base of hedges could change in one season and the benefits to wildlife quickly become apparent, the land which has been lost to building is lost forever.

Grass snakes, slow worms, lizards, and bats have suffered a marked decline, and glow worms have not been seen in the village for some 20 years. Some plants, such as the early purple orchids in the bank at Higher Weaver have been lost through a natural succession from herbs to woody hedge shrubs; orchids cannot thrive where competition from shrubs causes a closed, shaded environment. On other banks the number of early purple orchids has increased, and the perennial pea still thrives in the hedge near Weaver Cross. The quantity of wild daffodils at Lower Weaver continues to fall, but the monkshood (*see page 18*) in the hedge beside the road remain as spectacular as it has done for many years. Monkshood is on the list of nationally scarce plants and grows naturally at only two other sites in Devon. Fortunately it is well out of the way of any vehicle, because another major cause of habitat loss is the increased traffic on the lanes. Many vehicles drive on to verges rather than pass at wider parts of the road and sections of formerly wild-flower-rich roadside edges in the parish have been destroyed, especially between Stockland Cross and Dulford. Elsewhere, large lorries, struggling with the sharp corners, have scraped off layers of vegetation, producing vertical banks of bare earth, making succession and re-colonisation difficult.

The richest wildlife areas in the parish are still the rough, wet meadows of permanent pasture and alder carr at Stockland and Danes Mill, which have remained relatively unchanged in the last decade, though over grazing at Danes Mill could degrade that site.

For lichens the last decade has not been a success, despite two new county records having been found here - one in the churchyard and one on an old fence post by the footpath to Sanguishays. Lichens are very sensitive to pollution and there have been dramatic losses in the number of species in the parish, due to a decline in air quality – mainly caused by nutrient enrichment.

On the positive side, many farmers have planted small areas of trees as new copses and along hedges. Some old marl pits have become sheltered hollows where roe deer return year after year to have their young, and in all parts of the parish small and large new ponds have been dug.

The centre of the village in about 1996, showing Lear Park (centre front) and to the right of that, Tyes Orchard, as well as the beginnings of the Pencepool Orchard estate (top right).

Chapter 20: 100 Years of Change

In 1901 Plymtree contained about 84 dwellings, housing 359 people, most of whom were connected with the land, either working it themselves, or serving those who did so. Village-based tradesmen and shopkeepers made Plymtree virtually self-sufficient; all types of food and clothing, shoes, furniture and ironmongery were produced locally, and all other necessities were brought in by hawkers, or by carter delivery to the shop. Only a handful of houses had been built in the previous 50 years, and very few more were constructed during the following half-century – though six houses were built at Normans Green by Honiton Rural District Council in the 1920s.

Over the decades, technology saw more mechanisation in agriculture, with fewer people working on the farms, and hence less need for housing. This caused hardship for some local people, and six further council houses were built between, and to the west of, the original ones at Little Normans. Transport improved, enabling bread-winners to travel the whole country to find work. As a result the population of the village began a steep decline.

It was only in the late 1960s, with general car ownership and greatly-improved roads allowing easy commuting to places many miles away, that the population began to increase again. Bungalows were built down Greenend Lane; then more on the north-west side of the lane from the village to Normans Green, firstly above Penspool Cottage, and then between Old Forge and Fingle Cottages at Normans Green. When the old stone and cob houses at Colliers Court became dangerous, in the mid-1960s, they were replaced by bungalows. A new estate of bungalows was built at Tyes Orchard, followed by the houses at Lear Park, both in the former orchards of Tyes Farm.

In 1978 the former M.S.T. site, owned and used by Ken Edwards as a motor vehicle repair facility, began to be developed into the Sandersfield estate. The small 'courtyard estate' at

Plymtree, c.1900, taken from the Ridgeway.

Rusper Close followed, fitted in between Normans House (formerly Cooks Farm) and the two new bungalows down the hill, opposite the houses at Little Normans. And in 1988 four executive homes at Farthings Rise were erected opposite the 'Town' cottages.

The newest estate, Pencepool Orchard, was originally intended to be for 'self-build' houses, but the housing market collapsed just as the project was about to start, and it took nearly ten years for the estate to be completed.

Individual houses have been built opposite the Blacksmiths Arms, in the grounds of the old Rectory, between Clyst William Barton and Brewers Cottage, at Perhams Green, and along Tyes Lane. Many old farmhouses have been modernised and sold off, with their farmer-owners moving into more convenient bungalows, and some of the out-buildings at Woodbeer Court have been rebuilt as homes.

As we approach the millennium the population is at an all-time high, made up of a good mixture of people, some involved in farming, many who commute to work in Exeter or elsewhere, some who have retired, and others running businesses in the village.

There are now some 235 dwellings for the approximately 540 men, women and children who comprise the inhabitants of Plymtree – a large demographic shift over the past century. The most obvious visual change (apart from the unsympathetic design of some new houses) is the plethora of overhead cables in and around the village.

Despite these dramatic changes, however, Plymtree has remained – and we hope will for ever more remain – a real village, with people who care about one another, where strangers are made to feel welcome, where a cheery greeting is exchanged whenever neighbours meet, where courtesy prevails, and where many of the ills of the present day are nowhere to be found.

From the tower, 1998, looking N.N.E. The end of Redgate Cottages are to the left, with Stuan House behind, then Pencepool Farm and the new estate, Pencepool Orchard. In the foreground is the garden and orchard of Rose Cottage, with the Blackdown Hills in the far distance.

From the tower, 1998, looking E.S.E. In the right foreground is the Church House, with the taller roof of the Post Office Stores to its left, then the Blacksmiths Arms. The pair of cottages with the light-coloured roof are Tyes Cottages with the houses of Lear Park behind them.

THE
HISTORY OF
PLYMTREE'S OLDER
HOUSES AND FARMS

Sanders' Post Office and Stores at Normans Green, c.1920 (with the forge on the left).

Included in the House Histories:

Beech Cottage (photograph, 1998)

Blacksmiths Arms (New Inn) (from a postcard, 1910)

Bowling Green & Leat Cottage

Brewers Cottage

Bridge Cottages & Bridge House (seen from Great Pit Park)

Buckhurst Cottage (photographed in the 1940s)

Clyst William Barton (from the rear)

Clyst William Cross

Middle Clyst William

Little Clyst William (from the air, c.1967)

Colliers Court & Cottages (Mary Widgery, c.1912, holding Ted, with Alma and Ivy)

Danes Mill (from the bridge)

Raymonds Cottage

Fordmore (photograph, c.1910)

Fordmore Cottages (photographed in the 1950s)

Greenend Farm (photograph, 1917)

Greenend Cottages

Hayne House (Plymtree Manor) (photograph, 1917)

Hayne Farm

Hayne Cottages (photograph, c.1926)

Herne Farm (photograph, 1980)

Knights Cottage (photograph, 1998)

Motts Lane Cottage

Normans Green House (photograph, 1998)

Normans Green Cottage (photograph, 1998)

Normans House (Cooks Farm) (photograph,1980)

Fingle & Fox Cottages (photograph, 1998)

Old Forge Cottage (photograph, 1980)

Orchard House (Fordmore Dairy) (from a postcard, c.1910)

Pencepool Farm

Pencepool Cottages

Pens Pool Cottage (photograph, 1980)

Perhams Green Farm (seen from the chimney of Perhams Green Cottage)

Perhams Green Cottage (photograph, 1980)

The Post Office-Stores (the shop, New Inn and Clarkes Cottages, c.1920)

Plymtree Rectories (top: the old rectory, c.1905)

Redgate tenement and cottages (p.22, right to left: end of Rose cottage, Carriers Cottage, Richards Cottage, Horseshoe Cottage, Stones Cottage and The Old Bakery):

Rose Cottage (photograph, 1998)

Redgate Cottages

Carriers Cottage

Old Bakery Cottage

Richards, Horseshoe & Stores Cottages

Sanguishayes Farm (photograph, 1980)

Stockland Head Farm

Tyes Farmhouse (from the air in 1967)

Tyes (Clarkes) Cottages

Weaver House Farm(photograph, 1980)

Lower Weaver Farm

Middle Weaver Farmhouse (photograph, 1980)

Lower Weaver (The Long House)

Woodbeer Court (front of the court, 1980)

Middle Woodbeer Farm (photograph, 1998)

Lower Woodbeare Farm

Woodbeare House Farm (photograph, 1980)

Chowns Pool

Sewards Farm

Plymtree, c.1920. Clarke's (Tyes) Cottages to the left, then the inn and shop, and Knights Cottages on the right.

The History of Plymtree's Older Houses and Farms

In these days at the end of the second millennium, with a mobile and somewhat fragmented population, many people want to know more about the history of the house they now call home or grew up in. Perhaps this helps to give them a sense of stability, making them feel 'rooted' in the same way as a known family history can. Buildings, by their very nature, suggest permanence and indeed, many Plymtree residents who do not themselves live in an older house gain satisfaction by the fact simply that such buildings are there, speaking of the antiquity of their village. It is also hoped that many readers, whose forebears once lived in Plymtree, will be able to refer to this section to find out exactly where their ancestors were living at a given period.

The Wheaton ladies playing chess in the kitchen at Fordmore, c.1910.

Beech Cottage Details of the occupants of this perfect thatched cottage (probably built in the 17th century) are, as with its neighbour Knights Cottage, impossible to discover before 1836 due to a lack of records about cottages as opposed to land. It seems likely that it was purchased in about 1810 by the rector, Rev. Daniel Veysie, as a home for himself and his family in preparation for his retirement, or perhaps as a more convenient house than the huge old Rectory: sadly he died at the age of 62, in 1817.

At the time of the Census in 1841 its occupants were the Rector's widow, Anne Veysie, then in her 70s, and her unmarried daughters, Mary and Gertrude, together with two servants, Charlotte Richards (25) and Susan Elmsleigh (20). Anne senior died in 1847, and her spinster daughter, also Anne Veysie, was living there in 1851 with her sister Gertrude, her young niece Charlotte, and two girl servants.

From about 1857 until his death in 1883 the occupant was Lt. Col. William Veysie, son of Rev. Daniel Veysie, who had been born in Plymtree in 1801 and was retired from the Bengal Army: he must have had long chats with the then rector, Rev. Fowler Barrington Blogg, who had been born in Madras. After the Colonel's death the

cottage was purchased by Ellen Blake, and rented to a Miss Kemp, but some time later it was bought by William Salter for his own use, and he and his family remained at the cottage well into the present century. Capt. and Mrs MacPherson then became the owners of Beech Cottage until 1926/7, when Miss McLelland purchased it; when the weather was kind she opened the large gardens for Women's Institute meetings.

Mr and Mrs Scholey retired from running a public house in the south of Yorkshire to live in the cottage in the 1970s, and visits by friends from the South Yorkshire Police are remembered with pleasure by some villagers: Mrs Scholey still lives at Beech Cottage.

The 'Blacksmiths Arms' (formerly the 'New Inn') Plymtree's first and only public house was created in 1850 by Thomas Govier by extending an original cottage (until then occupied by John Ireland and his family), the new walls (forward from the back of the bar) being built of brick – the original house was a much narrower building, with thick stone walls. Above the new bar area a single room was built, possibly as a function room for the village, but now partitioned into bedrooms. A new staircase was added to the outside of the old building, within an attractive, rounded brick wall. With these alterations, access to the rear garden and outbuildings of the 'New Inn' was through carriage doors built into the front of the building at the west end, the huge jambs and hinge-pins of which can still be seen inside the pub.

The first licensee was Samuel Bearn, a master tailor, and the house was home not only to his own large family but also to his assistant and an apprentice. When his 15-year tenancy expired he decided not to carry on, and in February 1866 an advertisement appeared in the *Exeter Flying Post* for the lease of 'All that old-established Inn known as the 'New Inn', Plymtree,

together with three cottages, walled garden, covered skittle alley, stable, outhouses, etc.' The freehold was also sold, to William Furze.

James William Webber took over the tenancy of the inn, and he supplemented his income by dealing in coal. His son helped to run the pub until the turn of the century, when first William Edward Pearcy and then Arthur Wyndham Marshall, took over. A butcher, Mr Marshall, opened an abattoir at the rear of the inn, selling his meat from a small shop beside it, now used as the beer cellar.

The next licensee, from 1931, was Maurice Mulcahy, whose parents had been brought to Plymtree from Ireland by Mr and Mrs Lee-Norman in 1921, when the predations of the IRA threatened their lives there. Both Maurice and his wife were very active in village life and, when the war came in 1939, he joined the Local Defence Volunteers (Home Guard).

After the war there were a number of changes of licensees, including a Mr Marshall, who had allegedly been game-keeper at The Grange in Broadhembury and who would tell the story of how, while going about his duties he had come across a well-known, one-armed poacher, who shot him. Believing he was going to die, he wrote on a cigarette packet, 'Jimmy Main did this.' He didn't die, and Jimmy Main went to prison. Bill Bray – very much a local man – also ran the pub for a short time from 1951.

In the 1970s the garden of the Post Office/Stores still extended to the wall of the inn, the only access to the rear of which was via the carriage doors. Mike Hutchings, the then licensee, purchased the shop from Bill Jones, and put up a wall on part of the shop's land to give himself a separate side entrance. This permitted

the removal of the old carriage doors and a large extension to the area in which Iris Hutchings served excellent food to her customers. With the alterations came a competition to find a new name for the pub, it being thought that after 120 years it was no longer a 'new' inn, and the present name of 'The Blacksmiths Arms' was chosen – harking back to 1850 when the inn was built, and Edward Quick ran his smithy in 'Mayors Alley' behind it.

These alterations did not change the small bar area, which remained at the rear of the room, on the right-hand side.

Robin and Sue Rolfe purchased the Blacksmiths Arms in the 1980s, and completely remodelled the interior, creating the present layout. Les and Ann Hood were licensees for a couple of years after the Rolfes left, and since 1997 Martin and Sue Hopper have been the pub's popular hosts.

Bowling Green Cottages This pair of workmen's cottages were known as Venn's Cottages in 1741, when they were the only such accommodation owned by John Harward of Hayne.

In 1842, John Richards senior, his wife Grace and their children occupied one, while John and Sarah Ireland's family were in the other. John Richards was a labourer and John Ireland was a carpenter, both probably employed by Rev. Harward at Hayne. John Ireland's sons were self-employed, William working as a shoemaker and Henry as a tailor. The following year the Richards and Ireland families opened shops in both cottages. By 1847 John Ireland's son, John junior (a carpenter), had moved into the other cottage with his wife, Rebecca, and their children. When John senior died, his son changed cottages and William and Mary Brice took over his cottage for some years, being followed by James, and then John, Salter.

John Ireland was still working in 1881, Bowling Green having become a centre for carpentry in the village, as two of his younger sons were engaged in the trade, and

the other cottage was occupied by another carpenter, John Quick, a widower.

The Ireland family had left by 1896, and until early this century the occupants were William Farnell and the Franks family – the Farnell family still being in occupation until the 1940s, and the Franks family until 1951.

Bowling Green Cottages are now home to Malcolm and Chris Minifie and their sons, and Rupert and Peta-Jane Wise and their daughter.

Leat Cottage Why 'Leat' Cottage? No person named Leat appears in surviving records, and there is no history of a mill nearby; however there is evidence of a stone-lined stream running around the property towards Fordmore, so perhaps there was some kind of mill there. Built from similar stone as Hayne Cottages, it was not constructed to the same high standard as that building, though it had a high-quality front added in Georgian times (when the side facing the road was also re-faced).

The cottage appears always to have been connected with Fordmore, and one expert believes it may have been built as a hunting lodge for the estate.

In 1780 its occupant was John Leaman, but we have no record of other occupants until the census of June 1841, when the building had been split into two cottages (each having its own inglenook), and John Salter and his family lived in one.

The following year James Stamp, a shoemaker, occupied the other with his new wife Ann (Peters). In the late 1860s John Salter moved to Moor Cottages, and the family of Thomas Clarke arrived; they stayed for ten years.

From 1871 to 1874 James Vinnicombe replaced James Stamp, though the Stamps then returned. In about 1877 a large part of the garden belonging to the cottages was removed, presumably to increase the size of the fields on to which they backed, i.e. Moor Close and Boar Park Meadow. The recently-widowed Elizabeth Burnell and her large family moved in in 1881, though they removed to Bowling Green after some years.

Brewers Cottage This 18th century cob and thatch cottage was probably built by Mr William Brewer, who appears in Plymtree records from the 1730s, when the Brewer family owned a small tenement called Pyles. It remained in their ownership until 1793, when Robert Gould purchased it. In 1816 Thomas Richards bought the property, followed by Richard Richards, and in 1825

it became part of the Hayne estate when Rev. Charles Harward bought the tenement, including Brewers Cottage.

In 1841 the cottage was still owned by the Harward Trust, and Robert and Lucy Eveleigh were living there with their family: Robert was an agricultural labourer, presumably for the Hayne estate, and the family was

still there in 1851. Later that year the property was purchased by J. F. Pearce, and Robert Stiling and his family became the tenants for a time before Edward Bastin moved in. In the late 1860s, ownership again changed when Capt. D. B. Davey (of Clyst William Barton) bought the cottage: his tenant was John Wheaton, the retired farmer of Fordmore.

Edward Bastin was back there from 1875 until 1885, when James Tucker moved in. Thereafter the cottage was home to men working for the Prouse brothers at Clyst William Barton, but whose names are, unfortunately, unrecorded.

Until the middle of the last war the Garnsworthy family were living at Brewers Cottage, and they were followed by the Lowmans. The French family lived there after the war, before they moved to Raymonds Cottages.

The cottage is now the cherished home of David and Denise Mitchell, who run a small gardening business supplying shrubs, gates, etc.

Bridge Cottages and Bridge House This group of cottages (originally four) was built in the 18th century beside Bonds Bridge, which carries Fordmore Lane over the stream there; hence they were known as Bondsbridge Cottages. The puzzle is why the bridge was called 'Bonds'; no-one of that name appears in the records of the parish, and it is possible that it was paid for by the interest on loans made to farmers by the churchwardens and overseers, which were secured by contracts known as bonds.

In 1841 William Brice owned a pair of these cottages; in one lived a thatcher, Richard Knight (27) with his widowed mother, Ann, and two younger siblings, while the other housed Henry Farley, an agricultural labourer, and his family. Ten years later Henry was still there, though his children had all left home, and his wife was a living-in nurse in Bradninch. His neighbours were William and Jane Lake, both agricultural labourers, and their two young daughters. The other two cottages were part of the Fordmore estate, and while the occupants at this period cannot be identified, they would undoubtedly have been farm workers. These two cottages were purchased by the Brice brothers in about 1860.

Thomas Brice was the owner of four cottages in 1878, though the following year he sold three of them to George Ware, followed by the fourth in about 1884. One of these cottages was still standing, but was uninhabited or uninhabitable for the following decade.

At the turn of the century George's widow, Meriah Ware, owned the four cottages which were let to old Henry Farley, Elizabeth Burnell, John Vales and John Vinnicombe; it seems likely that one of these cottage was demolished in the early years of this century.

After some years the two properties known as Bridge Cottages were bought back for the Fordmore estate, though the third has remained privately owned; now known as Bridge House, it is home to Hayden and Jackie Webb.

Buckhurst Cottage (formerly The Rest, and afterwards Shell Cottage)

This beautiful small cob and stone, thatched cottage, with its spacious garden, was probably built in the 17th century.

By the beginning of the 19th century it was part of the Fordmore estate, and when cottages began to be rated in the 1830s its occupant was John Peters, a carpenter for the estate, and his family. The census of 1851 shows that 71-year-old John Peters and his wife, Ann, were still there.

After the deaths of first John, and then Ann Peters, John Salter took over the cottage, and John Salter junior was there by 1869. He remained in the property until this century.

In the 1920s it was called 'The Rest', and that name was then changed to 'Shell Cottage'.

Bryan and Jane Franklin purchased the cottage from its previous owner, a Mr Ackerman, who had re-named it 'Buckhurst' after the area he had come from hundreds of miles away in Essex.

Clyst William Farms

The land at Clyst William (or much of it) was owned by St Katherine's Priory at Polsloe before the dissolution of the monasteries. By an indenture dated 1 April 1529, the Prioress, Cecilia Mylyton, leased 'to John Salter, his wife Thoma: and John their son, the reversion for 98 years of messuages, lands and tenements in Clyst William, with three virgates of land there lying in a certain close of John Goodwyn, called Cross Park. Also a cottage, with common of pasture throughout the whole land late of Robert Swythynge. Which all, William Salter and Margery his wife hold for his life. Annual rent 35s.-4d.' However, in August 1543 Thomas Goodwyn, 'of Plymtree and London, Gent' purchased all the confiscated lands of the Polsloe Priory, including that at Clyst William.

Clyst William Barton The name 'barton' indicates an ancient farm, and it is almost certain that part of the foundations of this house are those of the Domesday manor house of Clyst. The present building of stone, cob and thatch was built in about the 15th century and, as well as its front garden, it also has a large enclosed farmyard at the rear. The house has some unique features, including a cake oven in addition to the more common bread oven.

In the 1620s the Barton was owned by Bernard Wright, and in the 1640s by his son, John, who paid the third highest rates in the parish, so their land-holding must have been considerable. For the next century, and until 1818, it was owned and farmed by John Fortescue and his family.

At the time of the Tithe Apportionment (1842), John Fortescue Pierce owned the 163-acre farm (including Clyst William Cross), the farmer being William Bickley. William Prouse was tenant there in 1851 (with Robert Davey as his landlord), and Philip Prouse farmed the land 30 years later.

The 102-acre farm was put up for auction in May 1914, but attracted no bidders. It was sold in 1917 to

Capt. D. B. Davey; it was then occupied by Miss W. Prouse, and the Prouse family was still in occupation in 1948.

Roger and Ruth Clarke were the last farmers to occupy the Barton and they, like others in the same position, built a bungalow on their land where they could be more comfortable than in the huge old house, which was later sold to Geraldine Holt (the well-known cookery writer) and is currently the home of John and Caroline Corringham.

Clyst William Cross The 'Clistwilliam Tenement' was (together with Danes Mill) owned by John Tilley from at least 1678 (although since he had been churchwarden in 1651 it is likely that he and his family had owned the land for many years prior to that date). When John died in January 1712/13, his wife Mary took over the property, but she sold it three years later to William Richards, whose daughter, Mary, ran the farm (and kept Danes Mill) from 1725 until 1760. A Mr Bartrum then became owner of both properties until 1778, when he was succeeded by a Mr Gore. The farmer at this time was a John Ebdon, and he continued as such in 1787 when Clyst William Cross was added to John Fortescue's land-holding at Clyst William Barton.

Together with the Barton, the property was sold to a Mrs Pierce in 1822 by John Fortescue's executors, when the farmer of both properties was William Webber: William Bickley had become the tenant by 1834.

The present house was built of brick in early Victorian times to serve as the dairy for Clyst William Barton, and in 1851 William and Sarah Hussey were running it.

They were followed by John and Mary Blackmore and their family, who were there in 1881.

During the First World War it was farmed by Mrs W. Prouse, having been sold as a freehold farm of 49¾ acres in May 1914, for £1,920; the Rounsevell family were the owners during and after the Second World War.

Having been occupied for some years by Fred Baker and his authoress wife, Sylvia, the present owners are Robert and Christine Crisford, the outbuildings being used for Robert's joinery business.

Middle Clyst William The construction of this beautiful Devon long-house, and its situation near the spring which is the source of the River Clyst, make it likely that the present 15th century building was the 'home farm' of the original manor house of Clyst.

The Salter family owned the property for many centuries, but by 1740 it was part of the Harward estate, the farmer in 1780 being Henry Pratt.

At the time of the 1842 Tithe Apportionment it was farmed by William Brice junior: William Gay was the Harwards' bailiff in 1851, running the 168 acre farm

with only four full-time labourers. By 1881 the building was occupied by George and Maria Ware and their six children, but the land he farmed had by then shrunk to 100 acres.

The Daniel family took over later in the 1880s, and when it was sold as part of the 'Plymtree Estate' in 1917, Arthur Daniel continued as the tenant. In 1959 there was a row of thatched outbuildings (used for stock and fodder) beside the road which, on a dry and windy 23rd May, caught fire. Arthur Daniel was at home with his wife and sons, Cyril (always known as 'Ike') and Gilbert, and visiting son, Fred. They got the stock to safety, but sparks carried the fire to the house. Fire engines from Honiton, Cullompton and Ottery arrived quickly and pulled 100 feet of burning thatch from the house, thus saving the building.

The present occupants, Bernard Wisdom, JP, and his wife Isabella, had a lucky escape in the summer of 1996, when the great chimney at the front of the house suddenly collapsed inwards, destroying their bedroom.

Little Clyst William This tenement of 56 acres, with its 16th century stone and cob farmhouse, was part of the Salter family's Clyst William estate for many centuries, but in 1720 John Salter sold off this 'part of Clistwilliam' to Ellis Button, whose tenant farmer was Samuel Pyle. From the 1750s the land was let to other land-owners until John Fortescue bought the farm in 1787. In 1816 a Mr Bath took it over, and he remained the owner until 1830.

John Dimond senior then purchased Little Clyst William, and his son, John junior, was the farmer there until he married and moved to Crediton in about 1850. Thomas Hussey, a bachelor who lived in the farmhouse alone, save for his 12-year-old servant (a relative), then became the tenant. When John Dimond brought his large family back to the house in 1868, they must have enlivened it considerably.

At some time before 1896 the farm became part of Thomas Henry Baxter's Greenend estate, with James

Cligg as tenant, followed in 1900 by William Cligg when James moved to Woodbeer Court. An advertisement appeared in 1902: 'To be let by Tender from Michaelmas 1902, that desirable and attractive farm at Plymtree, known as LITTLE CLYST WILLIAM, containing about 61 acres of rich pasture, meadow and arable land, together with a comfortable Farmhouse and commodious outbuildings, now in the occupation of Messrs. F. J. & J. Cligg. To view, apply to T. H. Baxter, Esq, Hayne House, who will send a man to assist.' When the estate was sold in 1917 the farm was still of 61 acres. Frank Daniel farmed the land there from 1915 to 1948, and during that period the thatched roof away from the road was replaced with tin. They were followed by the Tidball family, and the house is now occupied by Mrs Gwendoline Tidball, whose late husband Miles demolished the old out-buildings on the western side of the yard to create a longer and safer entrance and driveway.

Colliers Court and Colliers Cottages This now-vanished group of cob-walled and thatched cottages were sited on the left-hand side of the road from Normans Green to Woodbeer, just prior to the 'dog-leg' before the entrance to Woodbeer Court. They had all disappeared by 1961, when the cob walls had become so unstable that demolition became inevitable, and the land was sold off. The bungalow named 'Meadow View' now occupies part of the site.

Colliers Cottages were built beside the road, with Colliers Court behind them. Surviving photographs of the buildings show them to have been a pair of typical Devon long-houses, built side by side in an open 'V' plan, which could have been erected at any time

between the 13th and 17th centuries. The earliest record we have shows that John Collier paid fourpence in church rates in 1613 for his tenement in Plymtree, which sum shows that his land probably amounted to less than 12 acres - at that time a 'farm' sufficient to support a family. In 1674, Charles 'Colyar' had to pay hearth tax for one hearth, or what we would now call an inglenook, where all food would have been cooked.

By 1691 the land and buildings were in the hands of the Fortescue family, yeomen of Clyst William. They let it to William Potter from 1722 to 1738, after which the Fortescues took the land, while the houses were sold to John Crago and his wife Rebecca; John and his sons were carpenters. John died in 1749, but Rebecca continued to live at Colliers, though clearly in reducing circumstances. She began to take in lodgers, including paupers whose rent was paid by the parish, and by 1770 Rebecca was herself 'on the parish', receiving monthly 'pay' from the overseers of the poor, and her son William became the ratepayer for Colliers. The Land Tax return for 1780 shows that Grace Fortescue, who still owned the land formerly attached to the buildings, was herself Collier's tenant.

George Beacroft took over the buildings for ten years from 1808, after which William Veysie bought them; he

lived there until 1850, being followed by Benjamin Parris. Benjamin Parris left the three cottages (and the fields then known as Pearces) to his three daughters 'as long as they remain unmarried' when he died in 1858, and eventually the property passed to his grandson, William Macartney Reed, who in 1907

sold all of it to John Sanders of Normans Green. At that time Colliers were let to Henry Disney and Fanny White.

The 1881 census recorded John and Fanny White in one household; Elizabeth Salter and her sons Thomas and William, all retired farmers, in a second; and John and Mary Anning, with Mary's mother, Elizabeth Farley, in a third.

By 1948, the two houses contained five dwellings, the occupants being Frank Salter and his son, and the Widgery family in the Court (*left*), the Churchill and Robinson families being in the Cottages. The Smith family purchased the buildings in 1953, living in one of them while the other was let.

Dinah Smith was 12 at the time, and she recalls that the house was very cold, with a stove at each end and extra heat being provided by paraffin heaters. There was no electricity supply to Plymtree at the time, so the evenings were lit by oil lamps, and cooking was done in a paraffin oven and on a small, cast-iron range. The usual tin bath was filled by using a Primus stove to heat an old copper water-cylinder, while a smaller copper provided hot water for washing and washing-up.

The village had the post office and Mr Minifie's shop, and fuel oil came from Medland Sanders & Twose (where Sandersfield now stands). In addition there was Mr Batten's travelling shop, and a van that delivered accumulator batteries to power the radio.

Danes Mill Why 'Danes' Mill? Nobody knows, though it is possible that some event occurred here while the Danes were ravaging east Devon after their victory over the English 'fyrd' at Pinhoe in AD1001, or possibly one of the raiders settled on the banks of the River Tale here.

Bread is the 'staff of life', so it is said, and a mill of some sort is essential to grind grain to make it: when there were very few people in the village, perhaps most could make do with hand-mills, but the lords of the manors would have needed larger capacity. Certainly there was a mill on the site from about 1580, the miller being Edward Tye, and the original house dates from about this time. A leat was created by cutting a banked ditch to bring water from upstream on the River Tale, along the back of the mill-house, to work the mill-wheel.

Peter Fursdon was the miller in 1613, but by 1624 the mill became part of the Woodbeer Court estate owned by the Land family, and the names of the millers ceased to appear in parish records.

The Jope family paid the rate for the mill from 1703 to 1774, the Young family took over until 1864, followed by Samuel Ford and, from 1885, Frederick Burrow: however, from 1835-1900 we again have the names of millers recorded. They were Peter Sparks in 1835, William Bickley (1844), Robert Brewer (1866), Thomas Ford (1869), John Marks (1871), John Baker (1878) and John Norrish (1896). The freehold of the mill was sold in 1902, when Mr Norrish was still the miller, paying £30 per annum in rent.

At some time when the Young family owned the Mill they installed a double-wheel system, with both 'over-shot' and 'undershot' wheels – the first being driven by water directed to the top of the wheel, its weight (in the buckets built into the wheel) driving it around; and the second being turned by water running underneath, pushing against vanes on the wheel: all the water then passed down a cobbled run-off back into the River Tale. The shafts of both wheels ran a complicated system of gears (inside a new building attached to the original one), which turned the mill-wheels.

The grain was originally stored in the loft area of the mill-house, but when the new water wheels were installed a new storage area was built over them.

The mill had already ceased to function as such when Sid Pope moved there in about 1953. Bill Persey then bought the Mill, and it was empty when Bill and Marjorie Broom took it over in 1956; Bill removed the operating machinery, and used the property as the base for his agricultural contracting business until his retirement. They still live very happily in their beautiful house by the river.

Raymonds Cottages This pair of cottages, now much modernised, may have been built as the farmhouse for the small tenement described in 1678 as 'what was Mrs Raymonds', but which had by then become part of Mr Land's Woodbeer estate.

The names of the occupants were not recorded in the rates lists until 1866, but the census of 1851 shows there were then two separate dwellings, one the home of John and Ann Vinnicombe and their two children, while in the other were John and Susan Lane and their daughter; all the adults were agricultural labourers.

The Lane family left in about 1880 (possibly because of a fire or other damage, as the cottage remained empty for six or more years), but in the other cottage James and Hermina Vinnicombe and their three children were there by 1881, and lived there until the end of the century.

Meanwhile, when Samuel Ford died in about 1885, the link with Woodbeer Court came to an end, as Frederick Burrow purchased the 11 acres of Raymonds 'farm' and the two cottages, as well as Danes Mill.

In 1948 the cottages were home to the Antel and Clarkson families, and they were later followed by Leonard Glanville and the French family. The owners are now Graham and Nicola Bere, and Ronald and Teresa Chambers.

Fordmore Fordmore nestles in a small valley, beside a stream feeding the River Weaver: it is easy to see why the site was chosen by the original settler. Local tradition is that there has been a farm there 'from time immemorial', and that the Black Prince once stayed there (in the 1350s).

The original building was probably erected in the 13th century as a 'hall-house', i.e. a large, single hall with service rooms built on to it, and the hall itself having 'chambers' and floors gradually created within it as personal privacy became important. In the late 17th century the present front, only one room deep, was built of brick and the buildings to the rear were demolished. The only ornaments now are the wooden 'mullion-and-cross' windows, inserted when this 'new house' was built, and originally there would have been a cornice around the eaves of the roof, which was replaced in the 18th or 19th century.

Rev. Richard Polwhele in his book *The History of Devonshire* (1797) said that Fordmore 'was the seat of an ancient family of the Fords, who have dwelt there from the time of Edward the 1st. They were possesst of great property formerly, and seem to be of the family of de Fortibus, the founder of Ford Abbey in this county, as the manor of Thale or Tale, adjoining to their present estates, was annexed to that monastery. The family became extinct at the death of the last two co-heiresses, and the estate is now in the possession of a Mr Wright of Bath.' He went on to describe the church, including the 'south-aisle, which is supposed to have been built, and was repaired, by the family of the Fords, till the time of the late heiress, who threw it upon the parish.'

The heiress was Mistress Anne Ford, the last of her line, who was ratepayer for Fordmore from the 1740s and died in 1772. Her known predecessors were Richard de la Forde in 1250, Edward & William in the 1540s, Richard in the 1580s, Charles from 1610, Roger in the 1680s, George from the next decade, Anne from 1700, and Elizabeth and Anne in the 1730s. They employed farmers, of course, though the only ones we know of were Ager Gilbert in 1654, and Isaac Westlake in 1733, both of whom took on parish apprentices for Fordmore.

After Anne Ford's death, Henry Wright (of Bath) bought Fordmore, but in 1795 the property passed to the Phillott family, in the persons of Charles from 1795, Johnson from 1831, and Miss Ally (in partnership with Mrs Slater, believed to be her sister, and later with John, and then Thomas Slater) from 1836. From 1842-44, Thomas Slater was recorded as the sole owner, but then Ally Phillott reappears as the proprietor until 1847, and thenceforth until 1900 'Phillott & Slater'.

The men who farmed the land for these owners were John Shiles for Henry Wright, and for the Phillotts, Joseph Salter, then widow Alice Salter and, from 1821, Thomas Griffin. At this time the farm extended to 175 acres, but by the time he retired in 1850, Thomas Griffin had expanded it to take in almost 190 acres. His successor was John Wheaton, but he retired to Brewers Cottage in 1866, and his son Henry took over. Because of its size, the farm needed seven male and two female 'farm servants' to keep it going. Henry Wheaton and his wife Lucy had a large family, with five sons and three daughters, and their household in 1881 included three house servants and one living-in farm servant.

Early in the present century, Col. J. Barry Slater inherited Fordmore, and he became a great benefactor of the village, despite living far away.

For 1918, as a contribution to the the war effort, Ernest N. Wheaton was required by the Devon Agricultural Board to grow corn crops on one-third of his arable land, which amounted to about half of the 191½ acres of Fordmore Farm, for which the government would pay a guaranteed price. The records of the Board show that he was given a quota of 65 acres to thus cultivate, but sadly the entry is noted down as 'Disallowed - bad cultivation'.

From about 1926, Frank Sanders took over Fordmore; William (Bill) Persey purchased the farm in 1943, and his son, Herbert Persey, runs what is today the largest farm in Plymtree with his wife, Sue.

Fordmore (formerly Moor) Cottages

These two cottages were erected to house the farm workers of Fordmore, and have always belonged to the farm. Built of stone and cob, they were thatched until the 1950s.

In 1841, the cottages housed 12 people, including Thomas and Elizabeth Lovering, their four young children, and a lodger; and William and Mary Vinnicombe and their three children. Thomas and William were both agricultural labourers. Ten years later there was another child in William's household, and they had new neighbours, John and Mary Salter with their son and grandson.

For a description of one of the cottages from the 1940s, when the Blackmore family were in one cottage and Ernie Glanville in the other, see 'Growing up in Plymtree after the War'.

The present occupants are David and Natalie Barrow, and Paul and Nicola Holding, and their families.

Greenend

Described by the National Monuments Register as 'a probable medieval manor house', Greenend was very much modernised by William Blake, and his successor Thomas Henry Baxter, in Victorian times. In fact, so many architectural 'improvements' (such as 'modern' windows and a Palladian porch) were imposed on the ancient house as to change its external character completely.

There is no doubt that it has for centuries been one of the most important buildings in the parish, and probably the seat of the lord of the manor of Plymtree: but that is difficult to prove in the absence of any more than the few surviving manorial records. The oldest of the copies of deeds which survive is one dated 4th September 1482, which shows that the lord at that time lived at Clyst Hydon, and that Greenend (or at least part of it) was then called 'Laneyende'. 'Richard Soper and his wife are granted a tenement called Laneyende in Plymtree, the rent to be 6 geese, and doing suit at John Syncler's Court of Clysthydon, and 32 shillings per annum'. The witnesses were William Warryn, James Waryn and Robert Parker.

It would seem that Greenend still had the same family as landlords in 1567, as 'a grant of land and a cottage at Greenend' of that year was made by John Seyntcler who sold 'to John Pratt, Esq., all the land in Plymtree now in the possession of Matilda Warren, widow'. The Pratt family of yeomen then held the estate for 200 years; William was there in 1647 and in 1666 'Wm: Pratt th'elder of Plymtree, clothier, and his sons Wm: and Richard, granted Greene End and 34 acres of land in trust for Wm: junior' as part of a settlement on his marriage to Mary Slade, otherwise James, (who was bringing a dowry of £180). The settlement also included 'a messuage of 15 acres in Plymtree, in possession of Johan Way, widow, who had held the same in trust for Wm: senior and Eliz: his then wife'.

Thomas Blake purchased Greenend in 1763, and the Pratts left the parish (though some other land was still held in Plymtree in 1787 by Edward Pratt of Cullompton). A succession of Thomas and William Blakes then extended the estate until, by 1829, William Blake owned the tenements of Greenend, Crosses, Tyes, Clarkes, Chases, Mays, Mutters, Hawkins, Skinners-Clarks, Willses and part of Weaver, though most of these were farmed by tenants.

From at least 1836 until 1866 John Hole farmed the 240 acres at Greenend, assisted by two of his sons and four labourers (two of whom lived in), while his wife ran the house with the help of three young 'general servants'. There was also, no doubt, at least one gardener to look after the 'large walled fruit and vegetable garden, and heated greenhouse' to the south of the house. The farmer in 1881 was Thomas H. Bayles, a single man aged 76, who claimed that he worked 332 acres – which must have included the land of Tyes Farm. He shared the huge house only with his aged aunt.

Another Thomas Blake sold three tenements to Thomas Baxter (who was also buying up land elsewhere in the parish) in 1866, and the rest of the estate followed in 1897, by which time Thomas's son, Thomas Henry Baxter, was the owner, though he had moved into Hayne House. Thomas Henry had two sons, Thomas Harold and Charles Augustus, to whom he left the estate when he died in 1904. They were obviously not good businessmen/farmers, as by the time the first of their four sisters reached 21 there were insufficient funds to pay her father's legacy. Charles mortgaged half of his half-share in the estate for £850, only to die the next year (aged 23), on the eve of the First World War.

Finally, on 28th September 1917, the 'model grazing farm known as Greenend' made up 214 acres of the 1000 acre 'Plymtree Estate' put up for auction by Thomas Harold Baxter. The farm buildings were described in the sale particulars as being 'in extent, design, construction and general arrangement probably unequalled in the County'. The farm was let at the time to J. N. Franklin, JP (who lived there) and Robert Lear (of Tyes Farm).

It was purchased by a Mr Gent, who let it to Alfred Gill until Humphrey Chattey purchased the farm in the mid-1930s. In 1957 Martin Gibbins bought the property, and he and his son David have farmed there since.

Greenend Cottages The first three of these six-roomed cottages were built of stone in about 1860 by the Blake family to house the families of workmen at Greenend Farm: the largest one, furthest from the farm, was built at the same time as the farm Dairy House. As well as having four bedrooms, this house (now No. 1) boasted a sitting room, kitchen, dairy and wash house, w.c. and a large garden.

Across the road was the dairy yard, surrounded by a separating house, meal house and root house, a shippen for 21 cows and a calves house.

The first occupants were the families of Giles East, James Knight, Joseph Pratt and Simon Vinnicombe. By 1881, Giles East was still there with his wife, Rachel

(both still working though in their 70s), the other three cottages being home to William and Mary Salter and their infant son; Joseph Wilcox (the gardener at Greenend), his wife Elizabeth, their four children, and a lodger; and James and Ann Baker with their five children, plus two nieces as boarders.

At the turn of the century, two of the cottages were empty, the others housed W. Henry Clarke and Richard Pratt. For many years, until the early 1930s, No. 1 was used as the village Police House. Today the cottages are still part of Greenend Farm, the old dairyman's cottage being occupied by Kevin Peters who works on the farm, and his family, while the others are let to villagers not connected with the farm.

Hayne House (now Plymtree Manor) and Hayne Tenement The tenement of Hayne always formed a large part of the manor of Plymtree. In 1250 part of the Woodbeer estate owned by Sir Reynold de Albemarle, lord of the manor, was given to Bido de la Pen de la Ryole (who, from his middle name, was possibly the owner of Pen's Pool), who later sold it to Forde Abbey: they in turn rented that land to John Chamberlain for 22s.-10d. per annum.

From at least the time of Henry VIII the Harward family of yeomen were living at Hayne: indeed, the connection may go back much further, since the Odo who held the manor of Plymtree before the Norman conquest was the brother of Hereward the Wake, and the *Magna Britannica* states that 'it is probable that [the Harward family] descended from a younger son of the ancient family of Hereward'. Harwards took part in one or more of the Crusades: the family coat of arms includes a leopard chained to a cross crosslet, with four drops of water, symbolising the experience of a crusader who retained his faith even after four years in the desert.

The names of Richard Harwode (the spelling is variable) appears in the Lay Subsidies for 1525 and 1545; Charles Horewood was an archer at the Muster of 1569; and George Harwood was taxed on land worth £8 in 1581; 40 years on George Harward gave 31s.-8d. to the

poor, and Richard Harward was a churchwarden. Thomas Harward was churchwarden in 1655, and a Richard served that office in 1658. Christopher Harward was an overseer in 1677. Until his death in 1685 Richard Harward was the ratepayer for Hayne: he held land in eight Devon parishes and two Dorset villages, but he and his wife Rebecca were buried in the family vault at Plymtree. He was succeeded by Mrs Mary Harward.

The design of house lived in by these family members is not clear, though they paid for six hearths when these were taxed in 1674 – more than any other house in the parish. The present grand house was built by John Harward, Esquire, in the late 17th century, possibly by building on to an original farmhouse. The front shows very high-quality carved stonework, including a giant pair of pilasters which divide the frontage into three parts; these pilasters have garlanded capitals, a design imported from Holland and most unusual in England.

In 1698 John Harward was the ratepayer for Hayne, plus (Middle) Clyst William and three other tenements: by 1741 he paid land tax on six farm tenements, plus Venn's Cottages (later renamed Bowling Green): and 40 years later he had added another two tenements. There followed his son, John, and in 1787 John's brother, Rev. Charles Harward, Dean of Chichester from 1770 and Dean of Exeter from 1790 until his death in 1803. It was undoubtedly the Dean who added the family coat of arms, with the religious motto 'Crux Vincit Mundum' ('The cross wins the world'), above the front door of the house: the arms consist of a silver cross, each arm of which also forms a cross, with a blue ring in the centre of each crossing and in the centre, and four teardrops surrounding it, all on a red ground. The original motto was 'Nec Cupias Nec Metuas', meaning 'Neither desire nor fear'.

Dean Charles Harward was a keen farmer, and also a sporting parson; but much of his time was spent at the court of King George III, where he acted as Chaplain to Augusta, Princess of Wales, and tutor to the children of many important courtiers. He was a large drinker, with a particular taste for the excellent local cider. In the 'pound house' he had a cider press and 'apple engine', and five vats to receive the brew; the pound chamber cellar held eight large butts, eight cider pipes and 34 hogsheads for storing cider, plus other barrels for the beer which was made in his fully-equipped brew house.

It is said that the Dean exercised discipline in the Cathedral with a beady eye – 'and by judicious spitting at any choirboy who fell asleep during his services.' His sons having predeceased him, he left his property to his daughter's son, Rev. Charles Blake, who had to change his surname to Harward in 1816 in order to inherit.

Woolmer's Exeter & Plymouth Gazette, in spring 1841, had an article about a ghost at Hayne House: it reported, 'Much confusion, in our hitherto quiet little village of Plymtree, has been occasioned of late by the appearance of a 'ghost'! Most ancient houses are deemed 'troublesome' and such has long been considered the case with Hayne House, about the precincts of which, after many years of absence, the ghost has once again appeared.' A 'gay young shoemaker' had apparently been wandering past the iron gates to the house when he saw the apparition, though he gave no description of what he claimed to have seen. 'A night or so after this,

a certain maiden, tripping it lightly onward, saw this phantom looking on her with pale and ireful glance'. It seems that ghost-watching became a very popular occupation for a while!

There has, in fact, been a long history of ghostly apparitions at Hayne. There are tales of cowled monks walking in the garden, and one family sold the house allegedly 'because of the ghosts'. There were at least two appearances while Gen. Schreiber was in residence. His daughter was woken by the barking of a dog, and saw a young girl standing at the foot of the bed, who then vanished. (Years before, a little girl had died when she fell over the banisters to the floor below; that part of the house had then been remodelled.). The General's son-in-law, who had been invalided back from Italy at the end of the Second World War, was surprised one morning to see someone walking away from him down a passage from the pantry; although his wound had made him lose all sense of smell, he nonetheless smelt a very particular, strong odour and, just before the apparition disappeared through a wall, he realised that it was wearing Tudor doublet and hose. And the spirit of one of the Harward widows from Victorian times has been seen sitting beside the window to the left of the hall, on a pane of which she had used a diamond ring to scratch the words of a poem.

The 1842 Tithe Apportionment shows that Rev. Charles Harward, son of Charles Harward (formerly Blake), owned Hayne House and Farm, Middle Clyst William, Pencepool, Middle Woodbeer, Brewers Cott and Bowling Green, encompassing over 419 acres. However, as this Charles was the English Chaplain in Boulogne at the time, the house was let while he pursued his ecclesiastical career. One of his tenants, in 1851, was John Locke, a 'lead-smelter' from Dalston in the East End of London. When Rev. Charles died in 1859, his widow had his body brought back to Plymtree for burial, and the family land (amounting to 460 acres in various parishes) passed to the Harward trustees.

The House was then let again, to B. J. Marshall, then to Samuel Forde, and later to Frederick Manfield, during whose tenancy (in about 1881) the estate was sold to Thomas Henry Baxter of Greenend. After the Manfields left, in 1885, further tenants lived there, including Col. the Hon. J. S. & Mrs Eva Trefusis until 1911 and then Capt. M. P. R. Oakes to 1916; all the Baxter land in Plymtree was sold in 1917. The sale particulars for Hayne House are as follows - and give an indication of the staff then required to run a large country house:

"Hayne House has a particularly pleasing Facade, is substantially built of Brick and roofed with Slate, is well planned and with all modern conveniences, including an Installation of Ascetylene [sic] Gas. It contains:

"On the top floor - 3 Servants' Bedrooms and Box Room.

"On the first floor - 3 Principal Bedrooms, 2 other good Bedrooms, Day & Night Nurseries, Bathroom and Lavatory (with Hot and Cold Water Supply), Housemaid's Cupboard, &c.

"On the ground floor - Lofty Drawing Room with elegant decoration, imposing Lounge Hall, Panelled Dining Room, Cosy Smoking Room, 3 Bedrooms, Bath Room (Hot & Cold), 2 Servants' Rooms, Housemaid's Pantry (Hot & Cold), Tiled Vestibule &c.

"Ground floor (back) - School Room, Servants' Hall, Butler's Pantry, Kitchen (Hot & Cold), Strong Room, Boot Room (with Man's Room over), Scullery, Dairy, Larder, Servants' W.C., &c.

"At the rear are an Apple Loft and Gas House and a good Garage with Inspection Pit and Paved Yard.

"There is a Capital 4-Stall Stable, Loose Box & Saddle Room, and a convenient 4-Roomed Cottage suitable for Gardener or Married Servant.

"There are other useful buildings.

"The Park-Like Grounds are well laid out, possess some fine Timber and Ornamental Trees, pleasant Lawns, Tennis Court, and Carriage Drive.

"The Kitchen Garden is about an Acre in extent, has a good Greenhouse with Heating Apparatus, and is well stocked with Choice Fruit Trees.

"The Estate contains 15.023 Acres."

The purchaser was Mr George Leon who, despite often being absent on business in London, was almost immediately elected chairman of the Parish Council. He became involved in an fierce dispute with the Rector within the Council, and this may have contributed to his departure from Plymtree after only four years.

The 'troubles' in Ireland led to Mr A. H. Lee-Norman

bringing his family and servants (including five Irish girls – all of whom married Plymtree men) to Hayne House in 1921 to escape the depredations of the IRA against the Anglo-Irish. It was during his occupancy that Hayne House became known as 'The Manor'.

During the Second World War, the house was home to Major and Mrs G. H. M. Willoughby, and they continued the long tradition of making the grounds available for fêtes and other fund-raising events.

Gen. Sir Edmond Schreiber, former Governor-General of Malta, and his wife bought Hayne in May 1946. They were welcomed to the village by a special peal of bells, and the General is still remembered as a fearsome chairman of the Parish Hall Committee. For part of their stay there the house was divided in two, with Sir Rolph and Lady Dudley-Williams in the other half from 1954-74.

A Mr Fenton then purchased the house, and let it out cheaply to anyone who would keep the huge gardens in trim. One of these house-guests was the 'naked yachtswoman', Rosie Swales – whose presence (with a ladyfriend) was felt at the time to be a great scandal.

A most unpleasant fellow was one of their successors. He used every legal method to ensure that his poor wife would have no rights to his money, and a High Court action she pursued to do so after he left her was rejected, with great reluctance, by the judges.

The present owners of Plymtree Manor are Peter Wylie, proprietor of 'Peter Wylie Fine Wines', and his energetic wife, Sheila: not pretenders to 'squire-hood', they have added greatly to village life by their efforts.

Hayne Farm As this property was rated with Hayne House, both being owned by the Harward family from earliest times, it has not been possible to ascertain the tenants before 1836. James Dowell was there at that time, and remained so until 1850, when William Prouse added this land to that which he farmed for the Harwards at Clyst William. By 1866 William Parris had taken over, and he continued as tenant until 1899, when his widow, Mary Ann Parris, continued in possession. Frank Parris was the farmer for all 'Hayne lands' in 1918.

Mr A. H. Lee-Norman, owner of Hayne in the 1920s and '30s was a horse-racing man who converted Hayne Farm into a racing stud: new stables were built, and 8-foot gates erected. His greatest success was to train a horse which won the Grand National.

John and Miriam Chisnell occupied the farm house for a number of years, but since John's death Miriam has lived there alone.

Hayne Cottages With its delightful thatched roof, this is one of the most attractive houses in Plymtree, and its origins have been the subject of some speculation. It is unusual in being the only old house in the parish constructed of ashlar stone (i.e. stone squared-off by a mason), while all the others are built of irregular stone 'rubble' and cob. The stone drip-mouldings above the windows are another indication of its quality, and

the huge pots on its two chimneys are a further sign of antiquity.

Robin Stanes, local historian and honorary Research Fellow at Exeter University, who lives at Payhembury, has suggested that this modest building could have been the predecessor of Hayne House (Plymtree Manor) as the home of the Harward family when they moved to the parish in the time of Henry VIII.

It is now two houses, the original single 'L'-shaped one having been divided at some time by its owners to provide homes for their agricultural labourers.

By 1841 they were part of the Fordmore estate. The families of Thomas Pearcey and Samuel Hockings lived there, and ten years later Joseph Clarke and his namesake John had their families at Hayne Lane Cottages. In 1881, the cottages not only provided shelter for William and Mary Stiling and their five children but also for their three lodgers.

Early this century the cottages were briefly occupied by a succession of agricultural labourers and their families, but from 1922 John and Beatrice Baker took over one of them; they brought up their family there and remained in the cottage until their deaths, in 1965 and 1973 respectively. Their son, Reg, still lives in their cottage.

Herne (or Hearn) Farm This is another property with a name which has been a 'moveable feast' over the years, appearing in the records variously as Hearn, Hurn and Hern, with or without an 'e' at the end.

John Wright of Clyst William Barton was the ratepayer for Herne from 1618 until 1650, when Mary Wright's name appears. After the Civil War, Thomas Skinner (of Tyes farm) became the owner, followed in 1694 by Bernard Skinner. Christopher Sandford bought Herne in about 1707, some of his family's tenant farmers being John Seward (1715), Thomas Baker (1736), John Copp (1752) and Henry Pyle (1761).

In about 1779 William Middleton purchased Herne Farm, and he and his son Edward farmed it themselves until 1825. The Tithe Apportionment of 1842 identified the almost 88 acres of land of Herne, which by then was owned by Bethel Walrond and occupied by William Pearcey.

The 1851 census showed James Disney as the farmer 'of 100 acres' at Herne, assisted by two living-in labourers (aged 18 and 11): some of this land was obviously outside Plymtree, as he paid Poor Rates only on 87¾

acres. He was followed by James Strong, and then James Loader, and by 1869 the tenants of Mr Walrond were Aaron Broom Pearcey and his wife Mary Ann.

In the early 1890s Aaron Pearcey purchased Herne from the Walrond family, and continued farming there.

A newspaper advertisement appeared in June 1901: 'Herne Farm - valuable freehold farm, comprising 110 acres of grateful [sic] pasture, meadow, orchard and arable land, centrally-placed farmhouse, with ample farm buildings, also dairy house, with good outbuildings, well-watered, extensive road frontages. Price on application.' And in 1918 Herne Farm, 'of about 83 acres', was again offered for sale at auction. Despite these 'sales', Herne remained in the hands of the Pearcey family, and Aaron's son Robert was still farming 60 acres there between 1918 and 1924. Until at least 1936 Ambrose and Gladys Shere were the occupants of Herne Farm.

Today, much of the land has been sold, but Charles and Janthea Newman raise sheep and run a small-holding at Hearn Farm, which they purchased from Mrs 'Doll' Tidball.

Knights Cottage This ancient and lovely house was originally two cottages, known as 'Higher' and 'Lower' Knights Cottages, which became one only after the Second World War. Sadly, since cottages only began to appear in the records in 1836 (when they became rateable), we cannot now prove who were either the owners or occupants before then. It seems fairly certain that the Knight family, which was established in Plymtree from at least 1592, gave their name to the cottage(s): apart from becoming the hereditary Sextons of the parish, they regularly provided (paid) shelter for distressed paupers, and people under arrest, in their home in the 18th

century. In 1780 John Knight paid 6s. land tax for his own cottage, which may have been this building.

What is certain is that in 1836 Edward Quick was the owner: one cottage was occupied by John Richards, a widowed gardener, and his children, while the family of Mark Hartnoll, a baker, was in the other. In 1851 the property was purchased by Rev. Daniel Veysie (son of a former Rector of Plymtree) but Mark Hartnoll was still there, while Henry Westlake, an agricultural labourer, shared the other with his family.

The cottages were sold by Anne Veysie in 1883, for £110, to George Loosemore, a retired butcher, but they were still rented out: Henry Westlake was still there with John Southin and his family, who had recently replaced the large family of John Scribbins, a 'domestic coachman' for Lt. Col. William Veysie (a retired Indian

Army officer who had lived next door at Beech Cottage until his death in 1883).

Tom and Mary Cross lived at Lower Knights' Cottage from 1894 until 1906, when they moved the short distance to Redgate Cottages.

By 1934 George Deam was living in Lower Knights' and H. Burnell in Higher Knights'. Emma Loosemore decided she wanted the higher cottage, but George Deam had been given a life-licence by her late husband, William Loosemore, for his good work for him at Hooklands Farm: it cost her £50 to get George Deam to agree to go. She eventually sold both cottages to Richard E. Davey in 1949 for £1,100, and it was he who combined the cottages into one house.

Knights Cottage has been the home of Col. Michael Cobb and his wife, Elizabeth, since 1969.

Motts Lane Cottage There were two detached, neighbouring cottages of this name when they were first listed, in the Tithe Apportion-ment of 1842, being attached to Woodbeare House Farm – so attached in fact that only rarely were the occu-pants named in the records.

The apportionment named the occupants as William Lemon and William Downey, and the next time anyone was named was the census of 1851, which showed Robert and Mary Brewer and their young son, and Thomas and Ann Stiling with two lodgers, living in the cottages. The families listed in the 1881 census as being at 'Motslane Cottage' were Edward and Lucy Pollard and their three children, and Charles and Elizabeth Trickey (he a 'pauper', she a charwoman). The Pollards were replaced by John Vales in 1882, and he was still there in 1896, when John Pope replaced the Trickeys. Both cottages were empty in 1900.

James Widgery and his family occu-pied one cottage from at least 1908 until 1928, but it is not known when the other cottage vanished – probably being burnt down, as was the fate of so many old village buildings. A Captain Smith was resident in 1948, and Motts Cottage has for some years been the home of Elizabeth Smyth.

Normans Green

The earliest written records which have survived are those of court actions to decide the ownership of land, known as Possessory Assizes, and one of these dated 1244 refers to John Norman, who almost certainly gave his name to his land in this part of the parish. Situated around the crossing of roads (south/north from Hayne House and Fordmore to Kentisbeare and Cullompton; west/east from Greenend, the Exeter road and Plymtree village to Colaton, Dulford, Kerswell and Broadhembury) it must always have been an important part of the parish. The Tithe Map of 1842 shows that the road was very wide on the west side of the junction, extending over all of what is now the front garden of Normans Green House.

Normans Green Cottage This slate-roofed home was originally two-thirds of an extension to Normans Green

House, built on to its western end, and at a slight angle to it, probably in the late 18th century. It was not rated separately in the 19th century, so presumably it was occupied by employees of the Dowell family until the whole property was sold in 1891 to the Congregational Church, when it was perhaps used as accommodation for visitors.

Until 1951 the Congregational Church used the house as a village Reading Room, though it was mainly patronised by 'Chapel folk'.

John and Sue Caller and their family now live in the cottage, from where John runs his business of creating high-quality joinery and refurbishing the woodwork in historic houses.

Normans Green House Edward Salter left this ancient cob and thatch house, with outbuildings, a garden, orchard and a field called Furzepark, in all covering about three acres, to his spinster daughter, Mellor. In 1642 it was occupied by Mellor's brother-in-law, John Baker, and her sister, Joan. When John's daughter Christian became betrothed to Roger Fortescue, Mellor leased the property to her brother, Robert Salter senior, and to Thomas Baker, to hold it in trust for Christian and, after the deaths of Christian and her father, the lease was to pass to Roger Fortescue for 99 years, at an annual rent of 12 pence, paid to Mellor Salter's estate.

By her will made just before her death in 1650, Mellor gave the house and land to Robert Salter junior (Robert senior's son), and he held it under the former trust until 1661, when he sold it to Roger Fortescue for £8. Roger and Christian and their family lived in the house until his death in 1668 and hers in 1674.

William Trump owned and occupied the house in 1780: and the Dowell family had it from the beginning of the Rating of Buildings in 1832.

In 1891 the house at Normans Green formerly occupied by the late Mrs Mary Dowell, by then called Normans Green House, was for sale; a Chapel meeting agreed to buy it, if possible, to create a manse for their minister. The house was bought in August 1891 for £155, plus an additional £32 for a portion of the orchard, and further alterations and repairs were carried out later. A trap-house and stable were built for the convenience of those coming from a distance to attend chapel. When a new manse was built around the corner in Fordmore lane in 1951 the property was sold.

This ancient house not only provides a home for Bill and Paula Tingle and their family, but also serves a 21st-century purpose, since Bill runs the 'PC Workshop' from it, doing all kinds of wonderful things with computers.

Norman House (Cooks Farm)
Cooks Farm seems always to have been a small-holding, in the Plymtree tradition, encompassing (at least in the 19th century) up to 18 acres, including the land known as Cross Park.

In 1668 Robert Cook died, and his widow, Mary, continued to farm his tenement at Normans Green until about 1686, when the Ford family bought the land for the Fordmore estate. Around 1771, John Squire became the owner of Cooks Farm, and the records show that William Trump was the tenant there between at least 1794 and 1823, when he took on parish apprentices 'for John Squire's estate, Cooks'.

John Squire was the owner-occupant in 1836, and he also farmed about 15 acres of land known as 'Normans' (where the Little Normans council houses now stand) belonging to the Fordmore estate. Ten years later William Bickley, previously tenant of Clyst William Barton, purchased Cooks Farm and began farming there. By 1851 William Bickley had rented the farm to Henry Dowell while he took over as miller at Danes Mill: he kept on buying land, however, and four years later the 18 acres of Honours tenement was added to his holding at Cooks Farm.

Since Henry Dowell owned Normans Green House, he didn't need Cooks farmhouse, so William Bickley and his family lived there when he moved from Danes Mill. William Bickley was living in the house in 1881, when the census recorded him as being 73 and a widower, living with his unmarried housekeeper (aged 29), her daughter, and his son and daughter, aged 5 and 1. The house was also shared by the family of James Causley, who was farming Cooks and Honours for him. Causley continued to run the farm after his employer died until the trustees let it to William's son, Herman.

By 1918, Thomas Henry Peters was farming 'Normans Green Farm', which consisted of 36 acres: 30 years later the Tucker family was there.

'Norman House' is currently occupied by Judith and Rebecca Cuncliffe.

Fingle and Fox's Cottages Standing next to Norman House, these cottages were undoubtedly built by the owners of a farm (either Cooks or Sanguishayes) to house their workmen. Neither cottage appears in the Poor Rate lists as a separate dwelling until 1866, when William Bickley was listed as one 'occupant', the other being Henry James. Henry and Mary James, their six children, and a lodger were still living in one of these cottages (called 'Normans Green Cottages' in the census return) in April 1881, and the family remained there for another five years, being replaced by Simon Vinnicombe. Henry Ireland moved into the other cottage from Redgate later in 1881, and when he moved out in the 1890s, Willy James (son of Henry) took over his cottage. Lou James's family was still living there after the First World War, with the Lovering family as their neighbours, in what were still called 1 & 2 'Normans Green Cottages'.

Fingle Cottage is now owned by John and Dorothy Stabb, while Fox's Cottage is home to Lorna, Emma and Debbie Todd.

'The Old Forge' This house was built on 1½ acres of land by Richard Farwell, about the time he married Sarah Salter in Plymtree Church in 1653: they baptised three sons and a daughter here, and two of the sons married village girls, but the whole family vanish from the records in 1691. In 1693, 'Farwell's Cottage' was owned by George Ford of Plymtree, gent, and leased to a Richard Goddard for 99 years. William Harris, a yeoman of Talaton, bought the cottage in 1701 and, when he died, his son John inherited it. In 1753, John Harris mortgaged the property for five years for £310; he failed to raise the money at the end of the term, however, and had to sell the cottage for what he could get.

That turned out to be £70, paid by William Trump, a blacksmith of Plymtree. He opened a forge in buildings he put up on the south-west side of the cottage. In 1799, William Trump junior succeeded his father and carried on the business.

The Trump family did well, and by the time of the Tithe Apportionment in 1842, William Trump owned 34 acres of land in the parish, as well as Perhams Cottages and the cottage, smith's shop and orchard at Farwell's. This, however, was let to John Sanders, who ran the blacksmithing business.

The Sanders family also prospered, purchasing further land at Normans Green. By 1877 Mrs Sanders ran the village Post Office from the front room of what is now 'Old Forge' cottage, and when in 1897 the Post Office granted a Telegraph Office licence, she had to learn the Morse code in order to send and receive telegrams.

John Sanders junior described himself in 1890 as 'blacksmith, ironmonger, shopkeeper, timber merchant, corn factor, and postmaster', and in 1903 he was offering 'Sanders' Patent One-Way Plough – 'recognised by the leading Agriculturalists to be the best Plough of the day' – Price £5-10s.'

His son, George, specialised in steam engines, and gradually expanded the agricultural machinery business across the road on the site which is now Sandersfield. In 1911 he began offering to undertake threshing work for farmers, using his steam threshing machinery. After the First World War, John Sanders moved to Park House, and the old cottage was sold; over the next 70 years it passed through the hands of many owners, each one of which allegedly sold it at a profit.

Noel and Liz Gallagher are the present owners; when Noel extended the cottage in 1997, he found that the western wall had been built within the original, internally-limewashed front and rear walls – the original end wall must have had to be rebuilt many years ago.

'Orchard House' This pretty house of thatch, stone and cob probably dates from the early eighteenth century.

By 1842 it was the dairy house for Fordmore Farm, to which the cottage belonged and which was occupied by the family of Thomas Chorley, a farm labourer. Ten years later the dairy was run by William Smith, and John Denning was there in 1866.

John Vinnicombe took over the cottage and dairy by 1869, and the 1881 census records show that the dairy had expanded, with the families of two dairymen, John Vinnicombe senior and Lewis Melhuish, living in the house, as well as no less than seven members of the family of a retired farmer, Thomas Brice.

James Grant was the dairyman from before 1886, and Frederick Daniels, who had farmed Middle Woodbeer for many years, moved to less strenuous work as a dairyman at the property by 1896.

At the end of the century a William Aplin was there, but by 1900 he had moved out. After the First World War, Ernest Wheaton lived in the house, rather than sharing Fordmore with the rest of his family.

Orchard House was, until 1996, the home of the Member of Parliament for Exeter, Sir John Hannam, who made his one-acre garden available for charitable, fund-raising events on many occasions. The present occupant and owner is Mrs Joss Allfrey.

Pencepool Cottages From at least 1835 John Dimond (of Little Clyst William) owned three cottages, built in the 17th century and occupied by Robert Cook, William Hockey and John Davey, on a site of 615 square yards, south of Pencepool Farmhouse and bounded by a stream. In 1846 he sold the property to William Hole, who added a fourth cottage at the higher end of the site and yet another was built by, or for, Elizabeth Young, though she soon sold it to John Richards for his own use. Three of these five cottages were on 'large' plots of 210 square yards, the other two on small plots of 91 square yards each. Because the stream which crossed the road at the bottom of the slope was liable to flood, the ground floors of those nearest it were set high, their front doors being reached by steps.

The cottage nearest the ford burned down in March 1850. At the time of the census a year later the remaining four cottages were home to 23 people, comprising the families of Edward Baker, Thomas Clarke, William Farnell, James Knight and Thomas Pearce, while the fifth cottage was still being rebuilt. At some time around 1860 William Hole created a sixth cottage by adding what is now No. 6 at the rear of that at the higher end of the terrace. It seems that the cottages had a high turnover of tenants, as agricultural labourers tended to move around a great deal, only two families (the Pratts and the Farnells) becoming 'fixtures' in the terrace.

In 1908, the Honiton Rural District Council received complaints about the state of the ford across the road below Pencepool Cottages. The 'toilet facilities' for the cottages consisted of boards mounted above the stream behind the cottages, and a certain amount of detritus inevitably ended up on the road. The Council decided to build a culvert to carry the stream under the roadway at Pencepool. As the rector noted, 'This will be a great improvement, and do away with what was an unpleasant eyesore in the centre of Plymtree, very evil smelling in the hot summer months, when little

but drainage flowed across the road. The Council has accepted a tender from Mr E. Harris of Clyst Hydon to build the culvert at a cost of £50, provided half of this is found by voluntary subscription'. Various parish entertainments raised the necessary £25.

The resulting 'bridge' over the stream is so small that most people do not realise it is there, and the small size of the culvert certainly increases the danger of flooding during periods of heavy rain - as residents were reminded on 7th August 1997.

In 1881 these six cottages were home to the Burge, Farnell, Harrad, James, Salter and Veysie families – a total of 26 people.

Between the wars, Miss Hole sold the cottages to George Sanders, but they are all now separately owned. The residents include Mrs Barbara Batten and, until recently, the late Ted and Kathy Widgery, – all born in Plymtree, and whose invaluable knowledge of the recent history of the village has been most helpful.

Pencepool Farm, Pens Pool Cottage and Pencepool Cottages.

Pencepool Farm

The first thing one notices about this fascinating range of buildings is the front wall and gate, built of hard, local sandstone in the late 16th century. Behind the wall is the house, the basis of which was built of cob on stone rubble footings in the early 16th century: it is listed Grade II. The oldest part was originally built as a single, L-shaped hall (possibly having a chamber at the northern end, created by a partition to cut off the short leg of the L) with a central fire for cooking and heat. Later that changed to a '3-room with cross-passage' plan, when a fireplace and chimney were built, and a plank and muntin screen kept out the draft from the main door.

The north end of the building caught fire in the early 1600s, but the rebuilding changed little, and it was not until the next century that a ceiling was put in to allow first-floor chambers to be constructed. These were reached by a winding staircase from the kitchen, which was created at the same time in the southern end of the house: a dairy block was also built out from it, which retains its original oak-mullioned windows.

It is clear that part of the cob front wall fell out at some time in the last century, as it was replaced with a single-thickness wall of 'modern' bricks.

The barn nearest to the house may have been built as early as the 15th century (making it as old as the church tower), while the upper barn was actually built as two, end to end, with separate threshing floors, probably in the late 1800s. It is in this barn that excellent cider has been pressed over the past 200 years.

The Subsidy Roll (list of taxpayers to the king) of 1332 includes John atte Penn (he took his name from his land at Penn's Pool) who paid 8d. tax on his moveable property. But it is not until 1627 that the name Penspool appears in the parish records, Robert Salter then paying a rate of 2s.-6d. 'towards the repayring of ye Church' for his estate there. 'Painspool' was still in the Salter family in 1725, and Mary Salter paid poor rates for it over the next few years. It was probably sold in about 1735 to the Harward family of Hayne House, since Mrs Christian Harward was the Poor Rate payer in that year: the family retained ownership of the farm for the next 150 years, with various tenants actually farming the land.

Henry Bryant was the farmer there at least between 1737 and 1763, taking responsibility for various parish apprentices, as well as standing in for the Harwards as an overseer, though the rates were paid by Joseph Brutton in 1750, and by Richard Cullum between 1753 and 1774. From 1787 William Brice was the farmer, followed by his son, William, his grandson, John, and his great-grandson, Thomas – who was listed in *White's Devonshire Directory* of 1879 as 'Farmer & cider-maker, of Pencepool Farm'.

The national census of 1841 listed the household as containing William Brice, aged 68, his three sons and three daughters (all unmarried), plus four male and two female 'agricultural servants'. Ten years later John was running the farm – comprising 104 acres of land – with the help of four labourers and three boys.

When Thomas Henry Baxter (of Greenend) was running the Greenend estate in about 1881 (Pencepool was unoccupied on census night, 3rd April) he installed George Symons as his farmer, then William Trickey in 1886 and W. John Norrish some years later.

In 1917 the whole of the estate was sold, and Pencepool was bought by its tenant, Frederick Hussey: he was active in the parish, being Clerk to the Parish Council for 50 years. His son, Frederick John, and grandson, Robin, carried on farming there (and making very high-quality cider), both personally and through their tenant, Edwin Martin and his son Francis, who carried on the tradition.

In the 1980s the farm was sold to Herbert Persey, owner of Fordmore: a small portion was sold off as land for self-build housing – a plan which failed due to the recession – and the Pencepool Orchard estate was eventually built there.

The present occupants are Simon and Henrietta Hare and their children, who have done much to restore the fine old house, and have plans for it to be thatched once again. They are also sympathetically-converting the ancient barns beside the road into living accommodation.

Pens Pool Cottage This cottage was built in about 1580 as a hall-house, but like many other such houses was gradually divided up into chambers. William Hayman was the occupant in 1781, by which time it was part of the Fordmore estate. When the Tithe Apportionment was made in 1842 it was occupied by the two families of William Clark, a mason, and John Lake, a labourer, and stood in just under an acre of gardens.

Later the same year, Edmund Middleton took over William Clark's tenancy and established a cooperage at the property. His customers were the many local farmers who made cider, and needed barrels in which to store their picked apples, and then their precious brew. The Bristol and Exeter Railway had recently opened, providing a quick means of transporting the Devon cider to London and elsewhere further afield, and this trade no doubt increased demand for his barrels. In 1851, Middleton and Lake were rated separately, the former occupying $3/4$ acre and the latter the other $1/4$. Edmund's son, Henry Middleton, followed in his father's footsteps, and by 1875 the family paid the rates on all the land. *White's Devonshire Directory* for 1878 listed Edmund Middleton as Plymtree's only cooper.

Edmund the elder died in 1899, and Henry carried on and trained his son, Jack, in the art of coopering. 'Cooper Jack' is remembered for delivering his barrels in a small pony-cart. The business was closed between the two world wars, but parts of the garden beside the stream remain impossible to cultivate, due to the many barrel-hoops and other materials discarded by the coopers there in days gone by.

Subsequent owner-occupants have been Mr Garnett (the originator of 'Garotta' soil conditioner), Miss Molton-Browning (a descendant of Robert Browning) and a Mrs Rutter. Glyn and Barbara Benfield have lived at Pens Pool Cottage with their family since early 1967.

Perhams Green The name of this property has caused village record-keepers great problems throughout the centuries: it is recorded variously as 'Perrams', 'Perriams', 'Perrys', 'Pirims', 'Pearms', 'Perms', 'Permans', 'Pernhams' and 'Parhems' Green, and sometimes even the way it appears today!

The land was the home of the Veryard family, many of whom were doctors, from at least the 1590s. 'Ellis' was the favoured Christian name for the eldest son in each generation. An Ellis Veryard was churchwarden in 1613, and another in 1634. Four members of the family, Ellis, Robert senior and junior, and William, signed the Protestation Oath in 1642. After the Civil War – in 1661 – an Ellis Veryard, physician, was paid 10s. by the Quarter Sessions for examining former royalist soldiers from five East-Devon hundreds who were claiming pensions for the injuries they had suffered.

The present house at Perhams Green was built at some time in the middle of the 17th century; that it was built as a large house is shown by the fact that Ellis Veryard paid for five hearths when these were taxed in 1674.

It is clear from the rates paid that there was considerable land attached to the property, but it seems likely that it was 'farmed' (i.e. leased) to small farmers, or perhaps worked by other members of the family.

In the early 18th century the best-known Ellis Veryard (a great traveller and author) was of the third generation of physicians in Plymtree and was often paid by the overseers for treating the Plymtree poor. When he died in 1714, his work was continued by the next Dr Ellis Veryard, whose daughter, Grace, continued to live at Perhams Green for 40 years after his death in 1734.

William Trump then purchased the property, though it seems he did not live in the house, as a Mary Mawlick was the occupant in 1780. 'Perhams Green estate, a comfortable residence for a genteel family', comprising a house, barn, stable, outbuildings, and 16 acres of orchard, arable and pasture land, was advertised in the *Exeter Flying Post* in January 1841. Those interested in leasing the property were invited to contact the then tenant, Mrs Seaman.

The property was once again worked from 1842, with John Shiles as the farmer. There were then $16^3/4$ acres of land, but by the next year that had increased to 43 acres, and John had a labourer to assist him. In the 1860s Thomas Walters bought the house and 32 acres, but let them to Henry Dowell: he in turn sub-let the house. The next owners were the Bastin brothers, from 1875, but Henry Dowell remained the head-tenant. In 1881 the land attached to the farm had not increased, but the then tenant, Richard Sanders, rented other land, and farmed a total of 125 acres, assisted only by 16-year-old David Vinnicombe, his agricultural labourer. Richard was still farming there at the turn of the century, being succeeded by Henry and Willie James.

In 1948, Mr Ballman was living at the Farm, and the present owners are Pam and Dennis Cooper-Jones.

Perhams Green Cottage

Now a single house, this property was originally built - probably in the early 18th century - as two cottages for farm workers.

By 1842, William Trump owned the cottages as part of Perhams Green Farm, the occupants being Simon and John Vinnicombe and their families, including their father (John) and younger brother (Robert), making a total of 12 people. John junior was still there ten years later, but the other cottage was occupied by James Trickey and his family: Simon was still an agricultural labourer, but had moved his family into Plymtree village.

The Bastin brothers obtained the cottages when they purchased the farm in 1875. In 1881 another Simon Vinnicombe (son of John) lived in one cottage with his wife and children, while in the other were William Melhuish and his family.

Five years later Henry Causley occupied one cottage, while the other was empty: the position was unchanged ten years on, but shortly thereafter the Willis family had moved into the empty half.

Until 1998 the cottage was the home of Dr Russell Shove, a much-loved general practitioner, who had moved to the area in the 1930s.

The Post Office-Stores

James Fouracres was a hardworking shoemaker and, from at least 1843, he paid poor rates on four cottages, one containing his shop – a fifth on the same site was owned by Melony Woollcott. The five cottages were tiny; they and a small garden were fitted into an area of only 363 square yards, the whole being the site of our present stores, and the drives alongside. Apart from an entry to Mayors Alley (now the Blacksmiths Arms garden), the frontage of the cottages must have filled most of the 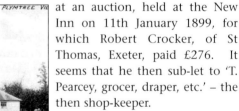 space between the east wall of the ancient Church House and where the side of the inn now is.

James Fouracres and Melony Woollcott's son, William, sold their properties to different buyers in about 1852: Miss Mary Ann Veysie opened a grocer's shop in one of the cottages, and she was still there in 1878. In 1865, Alfred Harvey bought all five cottages from Joseph Quick, bootmaker, who continued to live in one. James Vinnicombe junior, 'shoemaker', lived in another and both were described in the census return of 1881 as the 'Village Boot Shop'. The same source shows that the five cottages housed a total of 23 souls.

In 1887 Mr Harvey sold the properties to Mrs Eliza Ware, and Lewis Ware was the owner on 10th June 1895 when fire raged through the cottages and the medieval Church House next door (see 'Fires'). Lewis Ware built on the site 'a very substantial detached house, of brick, stone and slate' and sold a long lease of the property at an auction, held at the New Inn on 11th January 1899, for which Robert Crocker, of St Thomas, Exeter, paid £276. It seems that he then sub-let to 'T. Pearcey, grocer, draper, etc.' – the then shop-keeper.

At the beginning of 1909 William W. Morgan arrived in Plymtree with his wife, Annie, and set up as 'Grocer, Draper and General Goods Supplier'. William at once joined in the life of the village, becoming Parish Clerk, but tragically Annie died within a year of their arrival, and William followed her in 1913, neither having reached 50 years of age.

The shop did not include a Post Office at this time, that being run by the Sanders family at Normans Green, in what is now 'Old Forge Cottage'.

In recent years, with competition from town supermarkets to contend with, the shop has seen a large turnover of owners. Jeremy and Judy Bloomfield took on the challenge in 1996, and by careful stocking and innovative marketing, as well as dedicated hard work, have kept both the shop and Post Office running as the vital village facilities they have always been.

The Rectory The first Rectory, known as the Parsonage House, was a medieval hall-house (possibly 14th century), built of stone and cob, and thatched, standing on the site of the present Greenend House opposite the church: there is a view that it was originally built as the manor house of Plymtree, and most early manor houses were indeed built close to their parish church. Technically a 'coupled-hele house', its framework consisted of the trunks of oak trees butted up on end. The original hall was 43 feet by 16, with two huge fireplaces and an oak muntin screen to the entrance lobby at one end. Over this was an oak-floored sleeping chamber.

In Tudor times the big hall was partitioned off into an entrance hall and three rooms; the sleeping chamber was also made into three rooms – the inner for the maids, the middle for the rector and his wife, and the outer for the men – the only entrance being through the outer to the middle, and from there to the inner. Later on, an annexe about 8 feet wide was built along the outside wall, with a staircase replacing the original ladder, to provide a landing giving separate access to each of the sleeping rooms via entrances pierced through the original outside wall. When hearths were taxed in 1674, the assessors noted that the Rectory had five.

The house stood in grounds of nearly two acres, surrounded by shrubs and trees, and with a large kitchen garden at the rear.

The Rectory went with it when the advowson of Plymtree (the right to appoint rectors) was purchased in 1737 from the then rector for £880. The buyers were the Provost and Scholars of Oriel College, Oxford, who needed a means of providing livings and accommodation for its married fellows.

The original house (*top*) was extended in the 18th century, by a wing built at a right-angle to the original, and the end result was a building containing nearly twenty living rooms, two halls, four staircases and lengthy passages. The whole was 'improved' in Victorian times by the addition of fancy barge boards at the eaves (though the roof remained thatched, not slated).

An 'old tithe barn on the site' was mentioned by the rector in an article in the *Parish Magazine* in 1907, though where this was, and of what construction, is not known. Luckily Oriel College kept the ancient Rectory fully insured for, on 10th August 1911, it was consumed by fire (*bottom*). The building was replaced the following year by a red brick one (*centre*) on higher and, as the Rector noted, drier ground, and Oriel College marked its patronage with its coat of arms being placed over the fireplace in the study.

From the 1920s through to the '50s Bill Bray kept his forge in a fenced-off part of the grounds, near where Greenend House now stands. For a time, he also ran a threshing-machine business.

In the 1970s the Church Commissioners sold the Rectory house to the Coplestone family, and prior to offering the gardens for sale sought planning permission for a whole estate of houses there: the villagers had for some time wanted to buy the large, flat area of the Rectory grounds (now part of the garden of Greenend House) for use as a village recreation field, and many were outraged by the plan. Eventually the Parish Council bowed to the inevitable, and agreed to five houses being built.

John and Heather Bewick now occupy the Old Rectory which, with its still-large garden, has plenty of room for their children to roam.

Redgate tenement and cottages

The land comprising what was known as 'Reed Gate' or 'Red Gate' tenement (and occasionally as Potter's 'Town Tenement') of something over an acre, extended along the north of the churchyard, together with a strip of land along the east side of the road towards Pencepool. It was owned and occupied from at least 1723 by William Potter. Houses were built on the tenement as need or profit demanded. However, since Rose Cottage, Carriers Cottage, Redgate Cottages and Old Bakery were known variously in the records as 'Redgate' or 'Village' or 'Town', (and the latter two names were also applied to the cottages on the site of the present Post Office-Stores), tracing which cottages were built when and by whom, and who then occupied them, has proved somewhat difficult.

Rose Cottage

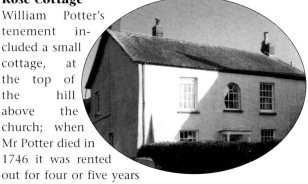

William Potter's tenement included a small cottage, at the top of the hill above the church; when Mr Potter died in 1746 it was rented out for four or five years before the whole tenement was purchased by Grace Bishop. It may well have been she who built the present lovely house, by extending the original cottage southwards; a 21-inch-thick wall survives across the centre of the house, pierced through for the first-floor landing

A Mr Scading was the owner from around 1780, with George Bennett as his tenant, though from 1795 until 1808 only George Bennett's name appeared in the rate lists, so perhaps he had purchased it. William Brice became the ratepayer from 1816. In 1836 the owner and occupant was William Brice senior, who farmed Pencepool Farm for the Rev. Charles Harward of Hayne House. His son, John Brice, succeeded him at the farm and was the owner of the house from William's death in about 1843, but William's widow, Elizabeth, remained there until she died three years later.

Thereafter it became the home of Henry and Jane Brice, the latter running a 'Ladies School' there, which continued as such after the opening of Plymtree Mixed Elementary School in February 1873. The house was owned by Thomas Brice and his sister-in-law Mary.

George Loosemore bought the house and land (which had been an orchard throughout the century) in 1882. In 1900 Eli James was living in the house, then owned by William Loosemore (though strangely Eli owned the land, which William harvested) and thereafter the house came into the ownership of Edward Coe, who sold it between the wars to Arthur Sanders. After he died, in May 1950, it was sold to Elsie Hussey for the princely sum of £2000, including the adjoining Carriers Cottage.

Mrs Diana Cook, a renowned watercolour artist, has owned Rose Cottage for the past 25 years and, despite not being in the first flush of youth, still keeps the huge garden and orchard under perfect control.

Redgate Cottages

The terrace of four dwellings now known as Redgate Cottages was the second development of the tenement, being built at right-angles to Rose Cottage in the 18th century, probably by George Bennett as a speculative development to provide homes for rent to village tradesmen and labourers. Given that the western end overlaps the front of Rose Cottage, it may be that the terrace was built before that house was re-modelled. In 1843, William Brice's tenants in three of the cottages were Samuel Bearn (the future landlord of the New Inn), John Davey and Elias White. The fourth cottage was empty, and since it remained so until 1870, it was probably used as a store-house or workshop. By 1851 John Brice was the owner: the New Inn was open, and Edward Quick, a blacksmith, and his two carpenter sons, had taken over Samuel Bearn's tenancy, but the Davey family (John and Mary Ann, their young son, and John's father William) and Elias White, his wife Mary and two of their adult sons still lived there.

By 1866, Henry Salter had replaced Elias White, but Edward Quick and the Daveys were still in situ. The fourth cottage became a home again in 1870, with John Scribbins as the tenant, while Elias White's widow, Mary, had moved back into her old house.

John Davey died in 1872, but Mary Ann was still living (and working as a laundress) in the same house in 1881, the other residents being Henry Salter, Henry and Harriet Ireland and their son John (the men were tailors), Charles Knight (the carpenter to the Greenend Estate as well as being church sexton and captain of bellringers) and his family, and Henry Rice (a carpenter) and his family, whose home was known as 'Step Cottage'. The same year the Brice family sold the terrace to M. S. Payne, and the Irelands moved to Normans Green, being replaced by Aaron East and his family.

By the end of the century Sarah Payne owned Redgate, renting to Charles Knight, Henry Rice, John Scribbins (the rector's coachman) and Robert Bishop. Thomas Bray, a blacksmith, moved in in 1901, and when Charles Knight died in 1906, Tom Cross moved in, his family remaining there until 1967.

It is alleged that, when Henry Rice was found out to have been running an illegal still in his back garden, the outraged villagers literally chased him out of the village, banging pots and pans and making an horrendous noise! The present residents are Richard Walton, Mike Bagan, Ian and Wendy Wilson, and Guy and Lou Maddocks.

Carriers Cottage William Veysie junior 'and another' moved from Colliers Court to this 'new house' which he built in 1843 beside Rose Cottage. The census of 1851 shows that William was a master carpenter, employing two men, one of whom lived-in with him, his wife Mary Ann, and four of his children.

Thirty yards down the road was a saw-pit which he undoubtedly kept in use, probably created by the Brice brothers who were then timber dealers at Pencepool Farm – the site is now a mini-car-park for occupants of the 'town' terrace. In the mid-1860s he sold the house to the Brice brothers, moving down the road to what is now Old Bakery Cottage (perhaps to be nearer the saw-pit).

The Old Bakery
In 1842 this small 'new house' on a large site was owned by Charlotte Seaman and rented by William Scovern, an 'ag. lab.', and his family. By 1850 William's school-teacher daughter Louisa ran a 'school' in the house, teaching the two Farrant sisters from Clyst Hydon.

In the mid-1860s William Veysie purchased the cottage from Thomas Hussey, and moved his carpentry business there. During the next decade another carpenter and joiner, Thomas Harrad, entered into an agreement with William Veysie which resulted in another cottage being built beside the original one, each man owning that occupied by the other.

In about 1880 William Veysie died, and Thomas Harrad not only purchased his own house, but sold William's to Alfred Harvey (who also owned a small cottage on the site of our present Post Office); this was then occupied by William Salter. In the 1890s Benjamin

right to left: end of Rose cottage, Carriers Cottage, Richards Cottage, Horseshoe Cottage, Stones Cottage and The Old Bakery

For the next 20 years Rose and Carriers Cottages remained in the ownership of the Brice family, but George Loosemore then purchased them, and lived in Rose Cottage, while Carriers was unoccupied. During the Second World War the cottage was used as the store for emergency food supplies for the parish.

By 1950 the cottage was a workshop, still part of Rose Cottage, and sold as such by Arthur Sanders' executors. It had a side door into, and now includes two rooms above, the carriage entrance to Rose Cottage, so at some time it may well have accommodated the village carrier.

In addition to the usual well, there is, for unknown reasons, a separate water-storage tank below ground outside the back door.

Cook became the owner of both cottages, though William Salter remained his tenant, letting the property out to various under-tenants, into the present century.

The cottage nearest Pencepool became the shop of W. A. Jarvis, 'Family Bread & Biscuit Maker', his bake-house being converted from the carpenters' workshop at the rear.

Jarvis's successors as bakers and confectioners were, for two years from 1905, J. Woodley, and then Frederick W. Minifie, who made bread only for a short time, converting the bakery into a general grocery shop. It remained as such until Mrs Minifie closed it in 1953.

From about 1900 the cottage used as the bakery was known as the Bakehouse, and that next door was called Bakehouse Cot.

The two cottages were made into one in the 1970s, and 'Old Bakery Cottage' is now the home of Rick and Karen Tillett and their family.

Other Cottages

The remaining cottages were built during the 20th century to fill in the gap between Carriers Cottage and Bakery Cottage. Until the 1960s they had virtually no gardens at the rear, having a tall wall a few feet from their back doors, all the land behind being the property of Bakery Cottage. The wall was then demolished and their gardens extended.

Richards Cottage During the Second World War Frank Burge and his family lived here.

It was also sold in 1950 by Mr Sanders' executors, at which time Mrs Burge was the 'sitting tenant', so the freehold only raised a disappointing £55 in the hectic property market of the day.

Stores Cottage and Horseshoe Cottage In the 1960s, Mr Gilbert Disney created the two cottages from the original 'Stores Cottage', adding front and rear walls to the open ground floor of the larger part (now 'Horseshoe Cottage') to end postal confusion – the two homes originally having been 'Nos. 1 and 2 Stores Cottage'.

Sanguishayes Farm The records show that in 1238 a William Sangwin held land in Plymtree; he undoubtedly gave his name to the farm that became Sanguishayes.

Until the beginning of the 18th century, however, the name of the farm varies in the records: it clearly gave the churchwardens and overseers great difficulty, and the different spellings throw little light on the name's pronunciation. What can one make of 'Sanguisrs', 'Sanghees' or 'Sangullsees'? – although 'Sanguishes' in 1626 is reasonably close to the present name.

By that time it had become part of the Ford family's Fordmoor estate, represented at various times by Roger Ford, Mrs Marjerie Ford, another Roger Ford, his widow Jane, then George Ford and his widow Ann. Some of the tenants' names survive in records of apprentice indentures: one Ager Gilbert was there in 1638, Henry Wright in 1650 and Henry Cookney in 1673.

It was Ann Ford who, in 1703, sold the farm to William Harris, and it was then owned by generations of William Harrises. One of these Williams incurred the ire of the county gentry in 1775 by not cracking down on the activities of local poachers, and was forced to insert the following advertisement in the *Exeter Flying Post* newspaper on 16th February:

'William Harris of Plymtree, having been prosecuted by the Association of Gentlemen of the County, for encouraging Night Hunters and the Killing of Game, apologises for his actions, and promises not to re-offend.'

Eventually a John Harris succeeded in 1815, but John died in 1821, at the age of 50, and his wife Mary the following year, aged only 43. The farm was then let for some years to James Dowell, senior, but from 1834 John Harris's son, also John, re-established the line at the 50-acre farm. He let 'Sanguis Hayes' to William Crook from 1845, then to Samuel Bazley from 1865, and John Cook from 1875. A John Harris was still the owner in 1900 when John James was his tenant.

Harry Leatt was farming 60 acres here in 1918. After the Second World War, Sanguishayes was taken over by Percy and Amy Lock and is now being run by their son, Alan, his wife, Jean, and their sons. The old cob, stone and thatched farmhouse has changed, now having a slate roof, and it is hard to spot, being hidden by essential outbuildings.

Stockland Head Farm Stockland Head was always a small tenement, typical of many in Plymtree, though including some poor, marshy land on the bank of the River Tale: one of the fields was named 'Frog's Parlour', indicating its boggy nature, while another was 'Starve Acre'.

From at least 1836 the 21-acre farm was owned by Samuel Upcott, and occupied by Samuel Granger: The latter continued as the tenant when Mr Upcott died, in about 1870, but in Spring 1875 a puzzling advertisement appeared in the *Exeter Flying Post* newspaper: 'To let for 7 years: 'Woodbear' otherwise 'Stockland Head' Farm. House, gardens, farm buildings, and about 140 acres.' Thomas Hussey had farmed the neighbouring Lower Woodbeare farm for the previous ten years, and the two farms together comprised 'about 140 acres': however, the two farms remained in separate ownership, with Mrs Upcott retaining Stockland Head, though as an absentee landlord she relied on the Harward trustees at Hayne House to look after her asset.

In the early 1890s John Pearcey became the owner of Stockland Head, but after he died it was offered for sale, on 7th September 1898, the particulars in the newspaper being, 'The small compact freehold farm of Stockland Head, comprising a convenient farmhouse, with suitable outbuildings and about 22 acres of land (numbered 42 to 53 on the Tithe Map), 15 acres or thereabout being meadow and pasture of excellent quality, and the remainder well-cultivated tillage, the whole lying within a ring-fence on the east side of and adjoining the road leading from Kentisbeare to Honiton. Each pasture field is well supplied with water.'

The farm was then in the occupation of Charles Pearcey, as yearly tenant, and was purchased by Aaron Broom Pearcey of Herne farm for £102. (A second lot, a watered meadow of just two roods called Baker's Meadow, in Broadhembury, fetched three times as much, giving an indication of the poor quality of the land, despite the glowing description in the advertisement.).

During the First World War, Arthur Pearcey, son of Charles, was farming the land at Stockland Head, plus another 28 acres in Broadhembury.

The Pearcey family continued to live at the farm until some time after the end of the Second World War, and they were followed by Arthur Sanders and his family.

In November 1998 the property, including 28 acres of land 'divided into eight main enclosures, with a former orchard area, pasture, woodland, a pond and some rough marshy ground', was put up for auction: the guide price of £175,000 to £225,000 demonstrated the escalation in land and property prices over the previous 100 years. Whatever the property reached, Stockland Head is now home to Linda and Ian Liddell.

Tyes Farm The original part of this stone and cob house, beside Greenend Lane, was probably built in the 1540s by Richard and John Tye as a 'hall house' (i.e. a single room, with a large fire at one end, and with sleeping areas separated off by wooden screens). Shortly thereafter, though, they built bed chambers above part of the hall, warmed by the chimney stack, and reached by a ladder beside the fireplace. The building would originally have continued southwards to form a shippen for the cattle and their feed. A couple of generations of Tyes farmed the land before 'good marriages' allowed them to move on.

By 1650 the farm was known as the Town Tenement, (being the nearest farm to the village or 'town') and it was owned for the next 80 years by Thomas Skinner and his son Robert. The next owner was the Rev. Thomas Troyte, and then his son William, though part of the farmland remained owned by the Skinner family until 1795. In 1771, William Pratt, of Greenend, purchased Tyes: his whole estate was bought by the Blake family in 1774, and they kept it until 1869, when it was sold to Thomas Baxter. The farmers during this period were William Holway (1780-94), William Morse (1794) and John Salter (1836-66). Richard Patch was farming Tyes in 1881.

Late in the 1700s, the house had been extended northwards to provide extra accommodation for the farmer's extensive family as well as his staff of labourers

Tyes (formerly Clarkes) Cottages
The ancient Clarkes Cottage belonged to William Blake, and formed part of the Greenend and Tyes estate when it first appeared in the rates list in 1844, Joseph Stokes being the occupant.

In 1851 Clarkes Cottage burned down, and John Ireland and his family (who had only recently been displaced from the cottage which formed the basis of the 'New Inn') were made homeless. William Blake had a pair of cottages built on the site to provide accommodation for his farm workers: their style is exactly similar to Greenend Cottages, and it seems likely that the same builder was used.

The new cottages were still known as Clarkes; one was let to James Knight (the parish sexton), and the other to William Salter. By 1866 the occupants were Richard Knight and William Auton, and three years

and apprentices, and this part now makes up 'Tyes End'. For example, John and Elizabeth Salter shared the house in 1841 with four of their adult children, and two male and one female 'agricultural servants'.

Tyes was one of three farms offered on lease by Thomas Henry Baxter of Greenend in 1901: 'TYES FARM, containing about 89$\frac{1}{2}$ acres (34 acres of arable, the remainder excellent grass land), with comfortable farmhouse and convenient outbuildings, now in the Tenancy of Mr Robert Lear, whose term expires at Lady-day 1902. There is also a capital Cottage on this farm.' Robert Lear stayed on, and he became the owner of Tyes Farm in 1917, paying £3200 for the freehold when the Baxter family sold their Plymtree Estate. He lived at Tyes and worked the land until he died in 1942, being succeeded by his son, Gordon, who continued to live and farm there until the farm was sold to Brigadier Acland (for £9,300) in 1947.

During 1959 the Brigadier exchanged Tyes for a farm owned by Lewis Clarke at Buckerell, and the Clarke family became important members of the community. Despite the fact that Mrs Pru Clarke has moved away to Cullompton, the presence of her son Tony and of her many treasured friends in Plymtree have ensured that she returns regularly to the village.

Tony and Anne Eames now occupy the older part of the building, while 'Tyes End' is the home of Peter and Julie Field.

later James Baker and Francis Langsford were there. Francis Wyatt's family replaced James Baker after 1875, but Francis Langsford stayed on until he was succeeded by Charles Langsford (a shepherd) by late 1882, when Charles Salter was in the other cottage.

In 1886 Samuel Summers moved into the second cottage, and he was still in occupancy at the turn of the century. The other cottage had meanwhile been home to William Stiling junior, and then to Walter John Salter.

Richard and Mary Pratt lived at No. 2 Clarkes Cottages in 1911.

I have yet to discover when the cottages were re-named 'Tyes Cottages', which are now owned by their occupants, being Steve Pettitt and Warren Killen and their families.

Weaver Farms

The churchwardens' accounts for 1618 (being the earliest year for which such lists survive), show that the rector, Rev. Thomas Payne, owned nearly half of the land at Weaver, plus Mutters tenement. From about 1630, Rev. Thomas Trosse was the owner of Mutters, while the rector continued to own the largest part of Weaver. His successor, Rev. Nicholas Monk, paid rates on the land in 1650. By at least 1678 Mr Thomas Trosse had taken over this large parcel of land at Weaver. The rest was in the possession of John Tilley (who also owned Clyst William and Danes Mill), Henry Wright and Henry May – the names of these last two having appeared in the church accounts since 1638.

In 1734 Trosse's land passed to Elizabeth Forde of Fordmore, but the following year a Mr Pearce (or Pierce) took over the whole land-holding; when he died in 1738, his widow continued as proprietor. A Mr Taylor became the owner in 1755, and we know from records of parish apprentices that John Vaulter was the farmer responsible for all of this large area of land in 1760. John Pidgeon purchased Taylor's land in 1767 but sold a sixth of it to Thomas Blake (of Greenend) in 1774, and over half of the remainder of his land was sold off, in 1779, to Richard Hall Clark of Middle Woodbeer and William Trump of Perhams Green.

John Tilley's family held his part of Weaver until 1721, when the Butter family succeeded. In 1735 John Humphries was the ratepayer, though he was prosecuted for putting in false accounts while acting as overseer, so he sold his land two years later to Mrs Mary Richards. She appeared in the rate books until 1774, when she was replaced by John Were for four years, until in 1778 Richard Hall Clark bought the land.

Henry Wright was named as owner of his land at Weaver until 1739, when John Wright's name appears, followed by Philip Wright 20 years later. John Venn became the owner of Henry May's holding in 1686, and it stayed in the ownership of his family for the next 65 years. When his name vanished from the records in 1751, it was replaced by that of William Channon. The story of each of these farms now continues separately.

Lower Weaver (Weaver House) Farm Weaver House Farm was purchased from John Pidgeon by William Brice in about 1785. William's son Henry took over shortly after he married Elizabeth Shiles in 1792, and William retired to Redgate. After Henry died in 1835, his sister Elizabeth continued as owner, the 47 acres of land being farmed for her by William Cook junior. John Trump then purchased the farm, and for a few years William junior took over the additional $16\frac{1}{2}$ acres of Lanes tenement, previously farmed by his father at Middle Weaver.

In about 1850, Robert and Sarah Pearcey came from Dunkeswell with their young family (aged 13, 9 and 7) to run the farm for Mr Trump. But in the 1860s Trump sold off half the land and moved into the house himself for a time, before briefly installing Henry Chown as farmer, and then selling the property to a Mr Frederic Kent. Kent employed John Lommon to run the 36-acre tenement for nearly 20 years from the 1870s until his

death in 1889, when John's daughter, Elizabeth, took over – she was still the tenant in 1900.

Kenneth and Doris Jones have occupied the farm for the past few years.

Lower Weaver Farm Richard Hall Clark retained this farm in his ownership (as well as keeping Middle Woodbeer), letting it out to tenants from 1778 until 1822, when he seems to have died; as an absentee landlord he was not buried in Plymtree. Mrs Mary Clark then took over until 1828, and she continued to let the farm to Ann Pratt. Pratts had farmed the land since at least 1753, and Ann was the widow of William Pratt, who had died in 1820, at the age of 53, after which Ann employed John Salter to run the farm for her.

Elisha Berry became Mrs Clark's tenant in 1839, and he farmed the 52 acres for the Clark family until 1850,

when Henry Baker brought his family from Uffculme to succeed him; Henry used two of his young sons and employed a labourer to help him run Lower Weaver. Henry died in the early 1860s, and his widow, Elizabeth, continued to run the farm for ten years. The farmhouse was rebuilt at some point in the 1800s.

William Cook became the farmer in the early 1870s, and he continued to lease the farm from Richard Hall Clark into the present century.

During the First World War T. J. Lock was in occupation, and the Lang family have worked the farm since the last war.

Middle Weaver Farm   Like its close neighbour, Lower Weaver (the Long House), this graceful Devon long-house was reached by a private road which cut off the large bend in Weaver Lane.

In 1778 Philip Wright sold his land to Festus Philips, a maltster, who unfortunately became bankrupt. In 1788, his estate was advertised for sale to meet his debts. It comprised '76 acres, including good orchards and a nursery: also a leased farm house and 40 acres, including 5 acres of orchards & 11 acres of wheat'. Only a little of the land was sold, and another advertisement appeared the following year: 'Sale of all the remaining part of Festus Phillips' freehold Estate at Lower Weaver:- Dwelling house, outhouses, malt-house, 60 acres of meadow, orchard & pasture, including a nursery of 1000 apple trees'. The purchaser was John Woolland, who leased the farm to James Baker at £87-12s. per annum.

It was farmed in 1842 by William Cook senior, the owner then being Thomas Buller Woolland. William was in his late 50s, and was assisted by his wife, three of his grown children, and three child servants (two girls, aged 12 and 15, and a 13-year-old boy), to farm nearly 46 acres of land there, plus 13$\frac{1}{2}$ acres at Weaver Woods (owned by the overseers of Cullompton) and Lanes tenement (owned by John Trump) amounting to

another 16$\frac{1}{2}$ acres. When Trump purchased Weaver House Farm in 1845, that and his land at Lanes tenement was transferred to the care of William's son, William junior, while William senior continued to work Middle Weaver.

By 1855 the farm was being run by another son, John Cook, who gradually took over the farming of other tenements (including Sanguishayes between 1876 and the late 1880s), until his death at the age of 72 in 1891 when his nephew, Benjamin Cook, began to farm the original 46 acres of land.

The farm was offered for sale on 15th July 1898, being described as 'with comfortable double-fronted dwelling-house with grass plots in front, prolific garden at side and rear, yards and convenient accessible buildings, good water conveniences, stream intersecting the land and court, and rich closes of watered meadow, pasture and well-stocked orchard, and fertile arable land, extending to 58a. 2r. 19p., all in a high state of cultivation.'

It was then in the possession of James Pratt, and at the auction (at the Half Moon Hotel in Exeter) it was sold to Mr C. Hitt, of Langford, for £2,600.

During the First World War the arable land being farmed by Mr E. Potbury at Middle Weaver amounted to 47 acres. The house has for some years been the home of Richard and Dianne Clatworthy.

Lower Weaver Farm ('The Long House', Weaver)
One of three farms known as 'Lower Weaver', this lovely, Grade II listed Devon long-house was built in the early 17th century of plastered cob on stone rubble footings, with a thatched roof and oak-framed mullion windows. It is now reached by a private lane off Weaver Lane, but originally it faced the other way, with a driveway (shared with Middle Weaver Farmhouse) cutting off a bend in Weaver Lane. That this is so is shown by a

two-storey porch sited at the present, and original oak, back door (*below*).

The house was built on a plan of three rooms with a through passage, the rooms on the ground floor being a large hall-parlour on one side of the passage, and a kitchen and dairy or buttery on the other. The parlour wall of the cross-passage is of solid stone, incorporating a large inglenook fireplace, while on the 'kitchen' side it is an original, oak plank-and-muntin screen. There is a

less elaborate fireplace in the kitchen, originally with a side bread-oven, on the outer wall.

Upstairs (there are two separate staircases), the master chamber is above the parlour, and it, too, has an inglenook fireplace, built into the same chimney. There are a number of other chambers, now formed into three bedrooms and a guest room, which in days gone by would have been filled by the farmer's large family and his live-in farm servants.

William Channon's successor was his son, Edward, from 1752, and the next absentee owner from at least 1793 was William Collard, being succeeded by his widow in 1816. In 1842 when the Tithe Apportionment survey was undertaken, it was owned by Rev. Charles Gribble (who seems to have purchased it in about 1825), and occupied by William Lawrence, his young wife Elizabeth, and three servants, who together farmed 56 acres. Two decades later they were still there, tenants of

Mr Gribble's widow, but ten years on another young farmer, John Hine, moved in. However, William Lawrence obviously liked the farm, because he bought it when Mrs Gribble died, and John Hine continued to farm there, with his growing family, until about 1885. Then James Pratt became the farmer of this Lower Weaver Farm – still of 56 acres – but by now owned by a Mr Hitt, and he was still there in 1900. His successors were Albert Coles, then the Kynaston family, Chris Pratt being the last farmer-owner.

Until 1997 Peter and Gill Cox lived in this lovely house, the outbuildings being used by Gill for her Lipitzaner horses.

Mike Crane and Siddy Langley now own the property, where Siddy works from home creating her beautiful blown-glass creations in some of the outbuildings, while others are home to their collection of exotic fowel – and some llamas!

Woodbeer Farms and the Manor of Woodbeer

At the time of the Norman Conquest, Woodbeer was a Saxon manor (its name is derived from the Saxon 'wide-bera', meaning wide or broad wood). It was held by Winemar, and the Domesday record shows that his lands had been given by the Conqueror to Goscelm, a Norman knight, and rented to another Norman called Godfrey. Some of the hedges on the present farm have been assessed as dating from Saxon times.

The manor was held by William the Chamberlain of London in 1166, but by the early 13th century the lord of Woodbeer was Geoffrey de Albemarle, and by 1250, his son, Sir Reynold de Albemarle, had succeeded, with William de Woodbeare as the resident steward. (In 1285, according to the records of the Devonshire Association, 'John de Kilrinton held the township of Wydibere for one (knight's) fee of Richard de Lomene, who held the same of Joan de Camparville (or Champernoun)' – though it is possible this 'Wydibere' was not the same as our Woodbeer.). In 1296 the occupant of the manor was William de Wodebere, followed by Robert, Richard and Julian de Wodebere.

Woodbeer Court This house is almost certainly the oldest in the parish, the basis of the present one having been built in the 13th or 14th century as a large, open hall with a thatched barrel-roof and a cross-passage splitting off two-thirds of the building for living quarters: there would have been a fire for cooking and heating in the centre, the smoke from which made its way through the thatch; some of the roof timbers are still smoke-blackened. The other third of the hall would have been used as a food store, a butchery, a laundry and for making cheese and beer. Gradually, walls and floors were built up within the hall to create 'parlours' and 'chambers' as privacy became important. By the mid-15th century a stone-built chimney was added, and later work included the addition of a separate kitchen (now the Dairy Cottage) and more fireplaces and chimneys. In Queen Elizabeth's time glazed windows replaced wooden-shuttered 'window holes'.

The old histories say that 'the Dauney family owned Woodbeer from 1346. In the time of Henry IV's reign

(1399-1413), the estate was divided among the co-heiresses of John Dauney, so that Woodbeer Court came into the Ford family'. Documents surviving in the Public Record Office show that other families also owned the estate. Charles Copleston owned it in 1643, but he owed an amount of money to Thomas Stukley on the security of Woodbeer Court, and to pay it off he sold the freehold to one Jaspar Horsey. Since the repayment date had not arrived, however, he sat on the money; Horsey then sold the freehold to Stukley, who promptly arrived with William Cruse [Cruwys] and John Frenston, 'persons of yll fame & name', and threw Copleston out without more ado.

In the 16th century, there were two Ford daughters, one of whom married a Tye, and the other a Stewkley (Stukley). Their children, Edward Tye and Anne Stewkley, were married at Plymtree in 1579. The only child of this marriage was named Dorothy, baptised 25th June 1581.

She appears to have married young, about the year 1598, to John Land (of Tiverton, born about 1575), by whom she had ten children in Plymtree, including twins named John and Robert, baptised in 1602. John moved to Silverton, while his brother Robert stayed on at Woodbeer Court, married, and also had sons named Robert and John. He died when John was only eight, and John's mother remarried, to Thomas Salter. Young John Land left to seek his fortune in London, where he grew rich as a goldsmith and, by his will, ordered that some of his personal silver be sold to provide a legacy for the poor of Plymtree, as well as a plate, pulpit cloth and cushion for Plymtree church: the cushion is still in use in the church, bearing his initials and the date of his death, IL – 1697.

By 1703 John and William Jope had obtained the manor of Woodbeer, possibly by one or other of them marrying one of Robert Land's daughters (he had no sons), and the Jope family remained as owners until 1774 when William Southcote Young took over. William had a map of his estate made, on vellum and in colour, which remains at the house. Richard Polwhele, writing in about 1793, described Woodbeer Court thus: 'The mansion house is built of cob, and thatched; the walls being about four feet thick. It is surrounded with gardens and orchards and high walls, and has a dreary aspect, resembling those mansions of old said to be haunted with ghosts and spectres.'

The last of the Young family, Thomas Ley Young, died at Woodbeer Court in 1864, and their property was bought by Samuel Ford. When he died (c.1885) Amelia

Collings became the owner of the Woodbeer estates. None of the above-named actually farmed the 250 acres of land they owned: indeed, few would have actually lived in the old buildings. In 1851 the farmer was Henry Shiles, aged 77, helped by his 23-year-old grandson, John. They had three Plymtree-born agricultural labourers: Henry Lane (21), George Richards (15) and Francis Farnell (only 11), while their young house servants (also from Plymtree) were Eliza Lane (16) and Harriott Vinacombe (14).

The 1881 household consisted of Henry Halse, the farmer (54), and his wife Sarah (41), both from Ottery St Mary, and their one-year-old daughter, Emma. None of their four servants came from Plymtree; even their indentured apprentice (i.e. a poor child of his parish) was from Broadhembury. Thomas Hussey was the farmer in 1897, and James Cligg (a Chapel man) at the turn of the century.

During the First World War the 216 acres were being worked by W. S. Squire. Mr and Mrs Mason farmed there after the last war, and Mrs Mason researched much of the history of the farmstead: they discovered what appears to have been a large pond near the house, used for keeping fish to eat.

Chris and Dinah Pratt now live and farm at Woodbeer Court: during the 1990s they had a number of redundant outbuildings converted into comfortable homes, collectively known as Woodbeer Gardens.

Middle Woodbeer Farm The early records relating to this farm are confusing, though they do demonstrate how small tenements were amalgamated to make larger ones. Some of those which eventually made up Middle Woodbeer were Pound's, Salter's, Buckley's, Yeo's, and Weeks's, each named after one of its owners. From the 1730s, Joan Weeks paid rates on her 'Home tenement', sometimes called 'Woodbeer', while each of the others was owned

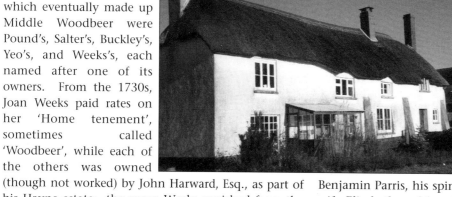

(though not worked) by John Harward, Esq., as part of his Hayne estate: the name Weeks vanished from the records from Joan's death in 1766. In 1781 Richard Coles was the occupant of Pounds, but the following year Nicholas Coles took on a parish apprentice 'for Mr Harward's estate of Salters, Pounds & Buckleys'. In the same year, William Brice was shown as the occupant of

Buckley's, but shortly thereafter he was recorded as occupying 'Buckleys and Woodbear', with Thomzin Rodgers at Pounds and Salters. In 1806 Thomas Parris took an apprentice for 'Salters, Pounds, &c.'

The Tithe Apportionment of 1842 listed 'Pounds, Salters & Weeks' farm as being of $140\frac{1}{2}$ acres, owned by Charles Harward, Esq. and occupied by Benjamin Parris. The census taken the previous year listed the occupants of 'Middle Woodbeare' as Benjamin Parris, his spinster daughter Eliza, his second wife Elizabeth and her three children, and three 'agricultural male servants'. Ten years later the farm had grown to 162 acres: Benjamin and his family were still there, but a house servant now helped his wife. The farmer in 1866 was Peregrine Knight, and in 1869 Samuel Ford took over.

Nine years later the farmer was young Frederic Daniels, with his wife Harriet and their two small children, and also his elderly father. Strangely, the three farm servants included a young man named William Parris (from Broadhembury). He stayed on when the 140-acre farm was sold by the Harward Trustees to Thomas Baxter in 1881. At the end of the century James F. Cligg was responsible not only for Middle Woodbeer but also the 33 acres of Chown's Pool and the 60 of Little Clyst William.

The farm measured 137 acres when it was sold by the Baxter family in 1917, the tenant then being Arthur Sanders. The sale particulars described the farmhouse as being 'a comfortable building of cob and stone, roofed with thatch, and containing 5 bedrooms, sitting room, front and back kitchens, dairy, pump house and earth closet'.

One of the ancient internal staircases has a 'burglar step' which, being much taller than the other steps, was designed to trip up anyone trying to creep upstairs in the dark!

After the Second World War, Brice Vellacott took over the farm, which is now run by Bill and June Vellacott who, as well as more 'normal' farming, produce wheat straw for thatching and exotic vegetables for the restaurant trade.

Lower Woodbeare Farm The first owner of Lower Woodbeare traceable in the records was Edward Webber, who was there in 1618: he was followed by his son and grandson, both named Abraham, until in 1678 Roger Ford (of Fordmore) took over 'Webbers tenement' – as well as that formerly owned by Emanuel Hall – and his widow Thomasine Ford succeeded him. Henceforth both 'Webbers' and 'Halls' appear in the records in the same ownership.

In 1706 John Were bought the property, and his family owned the farm for three-quarters of the century: one was the Rev. William Were, who let Lower Woodbeare to a fellow-cleric, Rev. Philip Chave, in the 1730s.

By 1778 the property had passed to Richard Hall Clarke, and it remained in the possession of the Clarke family for the next 130 years.

The farmer in 1841 was Richard Persey, who lived there with his wife Elizabeth and their children, and three young farm servants. Ten years later James Hussey worked the land with his three grown-up sons and a daughter, helped by one labourer, while his wife Elizabeth ran the home with two resident house servants.

By 1881 the tenant was George Price, but he, his wife Maria and their four children shared the house with Thomas and Eliza Hussey and their eight children. Thomas was the son of James Hussey, the previous tenant, and while George Price farmed 126 acres, Thomas was responsible for another 21 acres on the farm.

In 1910 the farm, once again of 126 acres, was sold by John Were Clarke of Halberton, to George Pine the then tenant, but the following year it was further diminished in size when 30$\frac{1}{2}$ acres were sold on to Eli James of Rose Cottage.

Lower Woodbeare has for some years past been farmed by the Pratt family, and while Richard now lives at Lower Woodbeare, he farms the land jointly with his brother Chris of Woodbeer Court.

Woodbeare House Farm From about 1707 several generations of Richard Whites paid poor rates on three tenements; Woodbeer, Yews and Sackerlands, totalling some 48$\frac{1}{2}$ acres: from later records it seems, however, that each of these tenements was worked by a different small farmer.

Gregory Webber became the owner in 1796 and, from Gregory's death in 1824 until 1842, Mrs Mary Webber was the owner of the land, described as 'Part Woodbere'. The Tithe Apportionment of the latter year shows that Mary lived at the property now known as 'Woodbeare House Farm', and that she kept 12$\frac{1}{2}$ acres of orchards for herself, while renting a similar area to Mr James Hussey and 23$\frac{1}{2}$ acres to Mr Thomas Lane, each of the three portions being described as a 'farm'. Thereafter Charles Romley occupied the whole of the property, which had by that time been purchased by Matthew Hutchingson, and was named 'Woodbeer Cottage Farm': four acres of land were added, taking the total acreage to 52$\frac{1}{2}$. The two cottages at Motts Lane also formed part of the farm.

The farmers were John Wood in 1845, Thomas Mayne in 1847, and Hutchingson himself in 1848. Mrs Amelia Davis, a French-born widow, took over the farm for Mr Hutchingson in 1851, living in the house with her two unmarried daughters and her son and grandson.

By the mid-1860s Thomas Walters was the owner, with John Sanders as his tenant-farmer: ten years later the Bastin brothers had purchased the farm, plus the 11 acres of Pidgeons tenement, John Sanders still being in occupation.

The census of 1881 showed that John Sanders (senior) was aged 68, and his wife Jane 54; they were helped by Sarah Salter, a general servant aged 20, and William Vinnicombe, a 14-year-old parish apprentice.

John Sanders died in March 1896, and Henry Bastin added the land to that farmed for him at Perhams Green by Richard Sanders, John's son. Richard was still working this large farm of more than 101 acres at the end of the First World War.

In 1948 the occupants were the Vicary family. Woodbeare House Farm is now the home of Philip and Doreen Tucker, and is the base for a large agricultural contracting business.

Other farms at Woodbeer

Chowns Pool We do not know who gave his name to Chownes tenement, the earliest reference being in 1613 when Thomasine Chowne, widow of Michael, paid church rates on some land. She died in about 1637, and her son Michael took over her land, together with White's tenement. He and his brother Robert each paid rates on separate farms, but by 1678 Robert Land owned Michael's property as part of Woodbeer Court Farm. (Robert Chowne's land was also called Chownes, but when Philip Yeo purchased it in 1679 it became known as Yeo's tenement.). In 1707 Chowne's was absorbed into Charles Harward's Hayne estate, with John Godfrey as the farmer, but it became a separate holding again in 1732.

The purchaser of Chowns Pool, as it was henceforth known, was Charles Chichester Esq., of the well-known North Devon family, and his name appeared as the ratepayer for the next 62 years. From apprenticeship records we know the tenant farmers at various times during his ownership: Henry Bluet and his wife Mary in 1741; Henry Hatchwell in 1763; Thomas Crago in 1776; and Charles Reynolds (an Exeter weaver) in 1786. In April 1796 an advertisement appeared in the *Exeter Flying Post*: 'Freehold of Chowns Pool Farm for sale. Small Farmhouse and outhouses, with 32 acres of arable, meadow, pasture & orchards. Let for the next 4 years to Thomas Crago, at £14 per Annum.'

In 1798, John Shiles, who for some time had farmed a small tenement called Sock as well as farming Woodbeer Court for Elizabeth Young, and had regularly served in various parish offices, became the ratepayer for Chowns

Pool and was still recorded as such in 1835 when he died, to be succeeded at both farms by his younger brother Henry.

The Tithe Apportionment of 1842 showed that Henry Shiles' own farm consisted of $32\frac{1}{2}$ acres, but the $202\frac{1}{2}$ acres of Woodbeer Court must have taken up most of his time.

By the 1860s Robert Prouse was farming Chowns Pool for John Shiles, plus the 11 acres of Raymonds for Mrs Young, and he was succeeded in 1868 by William Prouse, who also ran the huge Clyst William Barton farm. Ownership passed to Thomas Baxter in 1880, and William Prouse's son Philip became the tenant of Chowns Pool by 1886. By the end of the century the farm formed part of Middle Woodbeer.

The present house at Chown's Pool is Edwardian, though the surrounding cob barns probably date back at least to Charles Chichester's time.

The present owners are Michael and Gillian Jarvis.

Sewards Farm Seawards Meadow – possibly named after John Seaward, who married in the parish in 1698, and was for many years the farmer at Herne – was part of Middle Woodbeer farm in 1842.

Richard Sanders used the name when he built the farmhouse in the 1930s, creating a farm by retaining the fields on the northern side of the road east of Motts Lane when Middle Woodbeer Farm was sold.

Until his death, Colin West lived at the farm with his wife Sara and it is now home to Neil and Sally Woofenden and their family.

Subscribers

Mr G. Amawson, Tiverton, Devon
Mr & Mrs R. A. Andersen, Plymtree, Devon
David J. A. Arbery, Cullompton, Devon
Carolyn Auton, Cullompton, Devon
Mike Bagan, Plymtree, Devon
Mr R. Baker, Plymtree, Devon
Alan & Janet Barnett, Plymtree, Devon
David E. Barrow, Plymtree, Devon
Mrs B. Batten, Plymtree, Devon
Mr Philip & Mrs Sandie Bearne, Plymtree, Devon
Mr Tom Bearne, Kingsteignton, Devon
B. & G. Benfield, Plymtree, Devon
Barbara K. Bentham (née Simmons), Whitland, Pembrokeshire
Graham, Nicki, Mathew & Megan Bere, Plymtree, Devon
John & Brenda Berrington, Plymtree, Devon
Miss E. J. Betteridge, Cullompton, Devon
Howard & Sally Betts, Fairlawns, Plymtree, Devon
John Bewick, The Old Rectory, Plymtree, Devon
Mrs Eveline Bidgood, Tiverton, Devon
Mr J. Blackmore, Plymtree, Devon
Ken Blackmore, formerly of Plymtree, Devon
The Blatchford family, Plymtree, Devon
The Bloomfield family, Plymtree Post Office, Plymtree, Devon
C. H. Bolton, Kilmington, Axminster, Devon
David & Jean Brent, Plymtree, Devon
Avril C. Brown, Diss, Norfolk
David & Ann Bryant, Cullompton, Devon
K. J. Burrow, Bucks Cross, Bideford, Devon
Mr & Mrs J. Caller, Plymtree, Devon
Mr Gordon Campbell (Chief of Campbell Clan), New Zealand
J. J. Carden, Clyst Hydon, Cullompton, Devon
Kelvin & Sylvia Carter, formerly of Plymtree, Devon
Mr Ron & Mrs Teresa Chambers, Plymtree, Devon
Sally J. A. Chapman, Pinhoe, Exeter, Devon
B. Chattey, Langford, Cullompton, Devon
Malcolm E. Churchill, Honiton, Devon
Tony & Julie Clarke, Plymtree, Devon
R. Clarke, Plymtree, Devon
Miss B.A. Clift, Dulford, Cullompton, Devon
Colonel & Mrs Michael Cobb, Plymtree, Devon
The Coldrey family, Plymtree, Devon
Sally & John Connett, Plymtree, Devon
Chris & Andy Cook, Plymtree, Devon
Diana H. Cook, Plymtree, Devon
Ann & Malcolm Coombes, Plymtree, Devon
Dennis Cooper-Jones, Plymtree, Devon
John & Caroline Corringham, Clyst William Barton, Plymtree, Devon
W.C. Cousens, Axminster, Devon
Paul & Chris Crisford, Plymtree, Devon
Roy Daniel, Caravans, Clyst William, Devon

Mavis Darby (née Gard), Farnborough, Orpington, Kent
Richard & Ebeltje Davey, Plymtree, Devon
Dr S.V. Davis, Cullompton, Devon
The Draper family, Plymtree, Devon
Tony & Anne Eames, Plymtree, Devon
Jon Eames
Jason Eames
Hugh, Maureen, Kevin, Philip & Martin Edwards, Plymtree, Devon
Mr R.K. Edwards, Cullompton, Devon
Charlie & Thelma Essry, Plymtree, Devon
David & Mavis Estcourt, Plymtree, Devon
Mrs Pat Fay (Headteacher), Plymtree C. of E. Primary School, Devon
Christopher & Clare Fayers, Plymtree, Devon
Peter G.S. Field, Plymtree, Devon
Andrew Fordham, Tottenham, London
Chris & Pamela Fordham, Hong Kong
Mr E. & Mrs F. Fowles, Tonbridge, Kent
Bryan Franklin, Cullompton, Devon
Graham & Jenny Frankpitt, Cullompton, Devon
Francis Franks, Cullompton, Devon
George French & family, Dulford, Cullompton, Devon
Gavin J. Frost, Cullompton, Devon
Isla Ann Gale, Plymtree, Devon
Neil & Venda Gale, Plymtree, Devon
David F. Gaskell, Plymtree, Devon
M. Gibbins, Plymtree, Devon
Gerald E. Glanville, Broadhembury, Honiton, Devon
Mrs G. Gollop, Tiverton, Devon
Terry Grandfield, Mutterton, Cullompton, Devon
Fred & Pauline Grant, Plymtree, Devon
Rueben John Gratton, Riseley, Bedfordshire
Richard Graham Gratton, Rushden, Northants
Lorna Gwinnett, Eveleigh, Dorking, Surrey
Tony Hamilton-White, Melbourne, Victoria, Australia
Jane Hamilton-White, Brisbane, Queensland, Australia
Pat & Brian Hancock, Plymtree, Devon
Simon & Henrietta Hare, Plymtree, Devon
Clifford J. Harrad, Harpenden, Herts.
Kirsty Harris, Kentisbeare, Cullompton, Devon
Geoff, Jo & Julia Harris, Plymtree, Devon
Adrian & Annabelle Harvey, Plymtree, Devon
Stuart Hewson, Plymtree, Devon
The Higgs Family, Plymtree, Devon
Mrs W. M. Hill, Winsome Hill, Broadhembury, Devon
Mrs Winsom Hill (née Churchill), Plymtree, Devon
Mrs D. J. Hilton, Cullompton, Devon
M. J. & R. V. Hines, Langford, Devon
Leslie S. & Shirley T. Hitch, Plymtree, Devon
Helen Hitt, Langford, Cullompton, Devon
Mr K. P. & Mrs J. L. Hollis, Poole, Dorset

Mr J. K. & Mrs C. J. Hollis, Plymtree, Devon
M. Holman, Parkend, Glos.
Kirk & Sara Holway, Plymtree, Devon
Betty Eveleigh Hooper, Chippenham, Wiltshire
Martin Hopper, Cullompton, Devon
Philip Horsfield, Priest Hutton, Lancs.
Phil & Sue Hossack, Cullompton, Devon
John & Wendy Hussey, Plymtree, Devon
Kate Anne Hussey, Plymtree, Devon
Leisha A. Hussey, Hemyock, Devon
Jenny Ireland, Plymtree, Devon
Nick & Lizzie Jarrold, Plymtree, Devon
Mark & Mandy Jolly, Plymtree, Devon
Hester Joy (née Blackmore), Hennock, Newton Abbot, Devon
Kay Kearsey (née Lear), Lower Bockhampton, Dorchester, Dorset
Mrs Joyce Killen, North London
The Killen family, Plymtree, Devon
The King family, Plymtree, Devon
Mary Lang, Plymtree, Devon
Siddy Langley, Lower Weaver, Plymtree, Devon
Jim & Kathy Leaney, Plymtree, Devon
Mary F. Leaphard, Plymtree, Devon
D.C. & Mrs M. Lewis, Honiton, Devon
Alan & Jean Lock, Sanguishayes Farm, Plymtree, Devon
Pamela D. Lord, Plymtree, Devon
Mrs P. S. Lotz, Langford, Cullompton, Devon
Joan Mackintosh, Plymtree, Devon
Bryan & Anne Mackley, Bingley
Mrs I. P. Marshall, Cullompton, Devon
F. E. Martin, Honiton, Devon
Mason family, Plymtree, Devon
Mrs Lucy Maynard, formerly of Plymtree, Devon
John R. Merriam, The Blacksmith's Arms, Plymtree, Devon
Denise A. Mitchell, Plymtree, Devon
R.E. & M.A. Needham, Plymtree, Devon
Heather Noad, Plymtree, Devon
Irene Oliver, Plymtree, Devon
Margaret Palfrey, Plymtree, Devon
C. J. Palfrey, Cullompton, Devon
Mrs J.M. Parker, Topsham, Exeter, Devon
Michael & Virginia Pearson, Plymtree, Devon
Alan & Kathy Pearson, Plymtree, Devon
Mr & Mrs H.E. Persey, Plymtree, Devon
Mrs Mary Persey, Plymtree, Devon
Mrs A. Pinn, Plymtree, Devon
Jane Piper, Plymtree, Devon
Miss Doreen Pope, Cullompton, Devon
Mrs M.C. Porter, Tockington, Bristol
Christopher J. Pratt, Woodbeer Court, Plymtree, Devon
Dinah Pratt, Woodbeer Court, Plymtree, Devon
Richard H. Pratt, Plymtree, Devon

Mr & Mrs R.E. Puddicombe, Plymtree, Devon
Mick & Helen Purves, Plymtree, Devon
Michael & Louise Pyle, Broadhembury, Devon
Mr C.P. Reed, Kentisbeare, Cullompton, Devon
Will Roberts, Plymtree, Devon
Sam & James Robertson, Plymtree, Devon
R. & G.W. Robinson, Plymtree, Devon
Emily S. Robson, Plymtree, Devon
Mr & Mrs A. Rosser, Plymtree, Devon
Mr & Mrs John R. Rounsevell, Cullompton, Devon
Jean Rowson (née Grandfield), Tiverton, Devon
Roy & Beattie Sanders, Cullompton, Devon
Peter Frank Sanders, Normans Green, Devon
Mary Anne Seeley, London N16
Richard & Susan Shelbourne, Plymtree, Devon
R.P. Shere, Plymtree, Devon
Reta (Glanville-Gigg) Smith, Seattle, Washington, USA
Brian Smith, Plymtree, Devon
Glenn (Glanville-Gigg) Smith, Klamath Falls, Oregon, USA
Penny & Rob Smith, Plymtree, Devon
Elizabeth Smyth, Plymtree, Devon
John Somers, Lower Tale, Payhembury, Devon
Mr & Mrs P. R. Stevens, Plymtree, Devon
David & Catherine Tancock, Plymtree, Devon
Nigel & Jane Tancock, Whimple, Exeter, Devon
Mr & Mrs F. J. Tancock, Plymtree, Devon
Jonathan Tancock & Rosaleen, Glasgow, Scotland
David Teague, Coventry
Mrs S. Tidball, Clyst William, Plymtree, Devon
Mrs Gwendoline Tidball, Clyst William, Plymtree, Devon
Michael J. Tidball, Clyst William, Plymtree, Devon
Ada Tidball, Plymtree, Devon
Tillett family, Plymtree, Devon
D.W. & P. Tingle, Normans Green, Plymtree, Devon
Mrs Lorna K. Todd, Fox's Cottage, Plymtree, Devon
Mrs Molly Tronlin, Plymtree, Devon
Thomas & Kathy Vellacott, Plymtree, Devon
Bill & June Vellacott, Plymtree, Devon
Anthony Clement Venn, Marlow, Bucks.
Joy Walters, Hemyock, Devon
Gareth Wheller, Plymtree, Devon
Gordon & Christine White, Plymtree, Devon
Trevor & Margaret Whitmore, Plymtree, Devon
Pat & Anne Williams, Plymtree, Devon
Bill & Doreen Williams, Greatham, Hants.
Margaret Willington, Plymtree, Devon
Ian & Wendy Wilson, Plymtree, Devon
Bernard & Isabella Wisdom, Middle Clyst William, Plymtree, Devon
Mark & Sarah Witcombe, Plymtree, Devon
The Wylie family, Plymtree Manor, Plymtree, Devon

And the end of all our exploring
Will be to arrive where we started
And know the place for the first time.

(T.S. Eliot - 'Little Gidding')

Also available in the Community History Series:

The Book of Bampton Caroline Seward
The Book of Cornwood and Lutton, Photographs and Reminiscences compiled by the People of the Parish
The Ellacombe Book Sydney R. Langmead
The Book of Lamerton, A Photographic History Ann Cole and Friends
Lanner – A Cornish Mining Parish Sharron Schwartz and Roger Parker
The Book of Manaton
The Book of Meavy
The Book of North Newton J.C. Robins and K.C. Robins
The Book of Porlock Dennis Corner
Postbridge –The Heart of Dartmoor Reg Bellamy
The Book of Stithians, The Changing Face of a Cornish Parish Stithians Parish History Group
The Book of Torbay, A Century of Celebration Frank Pearce
The Book of Trusham Alick Cameron
Widecombe–in–the–Moor Stephen Woods
Woodbury, The Twentieth Century Revisited, compiled by Roger Stokes

Further information:
If you would like to order a book or find out more about having your parish featured in this series, please contact The Editor, Community History Series, Halsgrove House, Lower Moor Way, Tiverton Business Park, Tiverton, Devon, EX16 6SS, tel: 01884 243242 or visit us at http://www.halsgrove.com
If you are interested in a particular photograph in this volume, it may be possible to supply you with a copy of the image.

Ernie Glanville by the pump which served Moor Cottages.